BEYOND MEMORY

▢ ▢ ▢ ▢ ▢

BEYOND MEMORY

*An Anthology of Contemporary
Arab American Creative Nonfiction*

EDITED BY
PAULINE KALDAS
AND KHALED MATTAWA

The University of Arkansas Press
Fayetteville
2020

For Our Daughters

CONTENTS

INTRODUCTION

The desire to make ourselves visible on our own terms drives the creation of this anthology of Arab American creative nonfiction. Within these pages, we have brought together the varied voices of those who live in the Arab diaspora. These voices originate in Syria, Palestine, Egypt, Libya, and Lebanon, encompassing North Africa and the Middle East. They stretch across the ocean to the United States to reveal the effect of traversing these geographies.

Many of these authors are well-established writers while others are just beginning their writing careers. There are stories of those who move between homeland and the United States; for those who immigrated, a return to homeland is a return to a remembered place, and for the second generation it is a return to a place instilled through the memories of others. It is also a return to another self, revealing the ways we continue to carry our homelands and the ways we live beyond our own time and place. Together, the stories included in this anthology explore what it means to move back and forth across the political and cultural landscapes of the Arab diaspora and how that movement has been ever more complicated.

As we are all-too-well aware, recent conflicts in the Middle East have made it difficult to stay in touch with the various homelands from which our authors hail. Mobility and interconnection between life here and life there has served as the circulatory system of the Arab American community, allowing it to renew its dual vision of celebration and interrogation of both America and the homeland. Not being able to return, not being able to witness and to adjust the global perspective to events, as Mohja Kahf informs us, renders one nearly voiceless when one most needs to tell her people's story, and helpless when the story is being told by less sensitive—and in many cases opportunistic—voices. The story nonetheless is told, is gathered in fragments, and quilted together against the tide of forgetfulness and erasure.

The difficulty of returning home is compounded by the difficulty of staying put in America. Even prior to 9/11 and the Patriot Act, Arab Americans had been singled out as suspected terrorists. Hayan Charara, in his essay here included, discusses the well-documented persecution of people of Arab descent, which has upset hundreds of thousands of people's lives and created in the community a deep psychic wound that threatens both its internal solidarity and its greater integration into the wider American culture. The blanket of suspicion that has covered the Arab and Muslim American communities has created a gap in dialogue that is impossible to bridge. It's as if other Americans have no sense of the extent of America's extremely violent engagement in the Middle East. Most confounding is the disconnect between American hegemonic global politics and American racial politics, particularly the racism and Islamophobia directed at Arab and Muslim Americans. Even as our military expands its operations in the Arab lands, the majority of Americans see themselves as victims and are utterly unconcerned about the atrocities caused by our government there. Arab American writers have become anti-imperialist by virtue of the violence committed by their government against their kin abroad. Standing against demagoguery has taught Arab American writers to exhibit a high degree of resilience and has also made them articulate definers of citizenship and belonging.

Although particular to their authors' experiences, Arab American life stories have become emblematic of what it means to have one's identity misconstrued in America and to have to fight to assert one's humanity. For the last half century or so, Arab Americans have been pushed to the margins of society, have had their names and images distorted, their beliefs misrepresented, and their histories denied. Arab American writers, as these essays demonstrate, are well aware that telling their stories has becomes an act of speaking truth to resist and empower others. Yet, as the essays by Layla Azmi Goushey, Rabih Alameddine, Steven Salaita, and Mathew Shenoda argue, the opportunities to speak one's truth are filtered through many layers of cooptation and exploitation; when one refuses to be coopted and insists on rendering their experience as they understand it, the opportunities to speak can be lost, and the retributions can be devastating. Arab American writers share their stories of struggle and sacrifice as cautionary tales and to strip away illusions regarding the cultural politics of our country.

While the external challenges posed to the Arab American community are a daunting task in themselves, Arab American writers have also undertaken the task of critiquing their community to live up to the standards it has been seeking and advocating. We noted in *Dinarzad's Children*, our anthology of Arab American fiction, that a strong feminist critique has been at the core of Arab American writing. This remains so in the creative nonfiction pieces assembled here. Patriarchy, particularly Arab American patriarchy, is indeed named as a powerful negative force within our community that induces intolerance and fractures all potential forms of solidarity. The internal critique, as can be seen in the essays by Susan Muaddi Darraj, Kamelya Omayma Youssef, and Safia Elhillo, has also taken on an intersectional approach, addressing racism, homophobia, and anti-intellectualism, as well as misogyny.

Through their critique of the wider American culture, particularly its increasingly fraught tendencies toward racism and intolerance, and the internal critique of their own community, Arab American writers are creating openings for a vision of a different America, and indeed a different world. One way of envisioning an alternative future is to alter our vision of the past. Joseph Geha's and George Abraham's memoir essays interrogate the monolithic story of American assimilation, especially Arab American assimilation, revealing a diversity of American experiences in order to challenge the monolithic and oversimplified narratives of Americanization repeated in our culture. Furthermore, these visitations of the past in part retell the history of the Middle East. Hadil Ghoneim's remembrance of her family's now unimaginable mobility—traveling unimpeded from the Persian Gulf to the Eastern Mediterranean—remind us of a more hopeful time, before America turned the region into an ever-widening theatre of war.

Traumatized by America's most recent history, Arab Americans are well suited to imagine a different future for their nation. Indeed, many Arab American writers have found their voices by attending to the wounds of their elders, victims of colonialism, occupation, and imperialist adventurism. They are aware that memories never disappear but circle back as dreams and hauntings. While Palestine remains the bleeding wound that inspires much meditation among Arab American writers, as it does in the Arab world, the anguish experienced defies all impulse for solipsism and insularity. If anything, Arab American writers are aware of the privileges they have, and as their writings here express, their experiences of racism, suspicion, and persecution have transformed into a deep sensitivity for the travails of struggling populations around the world. To read an Arab American text as evidenced in these essays is to witness selves broadening their horizons—expanding their, and our, potential for empathy and solidarity. Naturally, such outward opening will manifest itself in the broadness of the question raised, as well as the impulse to experiment with the form of the essay itself, compelling it to accommodate explorations that stem from and go beyond one's experiences and memories.

With this anthology, we add to the work of *Dinarzad's Children: An Anthology of Contemporary Arab American Fiction* and *Inclined to Speak: An Anthology of Contemporary Arab American Poetry*. These two anthologies have made significant contributions to Arab American literature, making visible the literary and cultural community of Arabs in the United States. *Beyond Memory: An Anthology of Contemporary Arab American Creative Nonfiction* enhances what has already been accomplished by these anthologies. The true stories in this anthology provide a deeper look into the lives of Arab Americans within the context of identity, culture, language, politics, and history. Together, these anthologies create a complete set of Arab American writing in all three genres, offering readers a full perspective into Arab American literature.

BEYOND MEMORY

1

◻ ◻ ◻ ◻ ◻

ELMAZ ABINADER

Pain Management

I.

The wrist broke—the fracture circled my forearm like an etched gold bangle. It did not separate hand from arm, the bones did not jut out— the render was nearly symmetrical. The distal radius banged against a surface at the gym, and in time, sent me to the emergency room, my arm swaddled in ice bags and towels.

There was a procedure:

Insurance forms, weight, height, blood pressure, heart rate, temperature.

A nurse typed into a screen and asked, "What is your pain level?"

I bit my bottom lip, held my arm rigidly, careful not to let it drop.

"Ten being unbearable," she advised.

I knew my pain, the throbbing and pressure. The wrist had doubled in size. Since this was the first time I'd ever broken a bone, rating the pain seemed abstract. I breathed deep. Not wanting to seem too intolerant or be mistaken for one of those people hoping for a good drug, I downplayed this new sensation, "Eight point five."

She typed.

Questions about movement, flexibility, fingers, fists, and thumbs. The incident: I climbed onto the wooden side of a BOSU at the Y, holding fifteen pound weights in each hand, unaware that the surface was slick with oil. My feet gave way, I slid backwards, arms akimbo, dropping weights, forming wings that did not lift me, that instead slapped me against the apparatus and then the floor of the aerobics studio.

I jumped up and continued to teach my body-sculpting class. Blood filled the wrist, ballooning it enormous. Someone brought ice. Bracing the bag against my forearm, I continued to teach and ignored the pain, which should have been possible, I thought. But here, it insisted, progressed: six, seven point two, seven point six. At eight, I excused myself. "I am going to the emergency room," I announced.

The nurse's narrative would include the circumstances of the fall, the time from the incident to the arrival in ER, but would not register my deflection, my insistence on continuing—some shadowy bravery, or denial, or ego.

When the doctor arrived, he didn't begin by looking at the wrist, but instead read the computer screen. "What is your level of pain, ten being intolerable?," he first asked.

Numbers are trusty indicators. They measure: an inch is an inch because the ruler can prove this distance. We are relieved from judging, guessing, abstractions. In the case of pain, the numbers mark a place where a plan can begin to form. At the four level, the doctor might say *we'll get you something for that*. When the pain is a seven, X-rays are ordered, slings assembled, casts fitted to the arm.

II.

Writers believe in narratives—connecting the reader to a character, a voice, developing experiences so vividly, we are there: in the city tenement, on the highway, at the farmhouse. We trust words, pick them precisely and combine them in ways that arouse the senses, deepen recognition, illuminate the moment. The experience of reading a story or a poem that moves into the body is nourishing and enlightening.

Rhetoricians trust narrative as one of the ways of making argument. Include a story that illustrates your point, you can attack head and heart. Fundraisers show us the tragedy of a family who lost everything in a flood, the photo albums, Sparky the pet dog, a favorite book, a grandmother's painting. Health care advocates describe a child's family struggling with her medical bills, allowing her sweet voice to be heard, her bravery to be illustrated. Under the surface of each of these devices is the suggestion *this could be you*.

Stories can bring us to tears or to fury or even to delight, all things being equal. These days, we capture their plots and characters in so many ways: dash cam recordings, news clips, phone videos. I keep thinking, these are such precise storytellers: the cop pulling the women from the car and handcuffing her, the team of officers crushing the man selling cigarettes, the footage of children and parents having a few minutes to visit each other across the border, a clip of Israelis tearing down a Palestinian school as the term starts.

My news feed, my Facebook page are filled with vivid narratives that move me. A young Palestinian girl is dead, shot by soldiers, I shudder at the sight of her tiny body splattered with her blood, which makes her dress a constellation. Three thousand Rohingya are slaughtered, a surviving mother curls around her tiny infant's body. A schoolboy is hung by a noose in New Hampshire, nearly killed. The welts in his neck silhouette the texture of a rope.

Ironically, the availability of the images, the stories told in pictures and video, the details that pour into each of our senses, has not provided a greater compassion or recognition. Oftentimes, a story arouses a counter narrative, a sneer, or a fleeting sympathy. What is happening? Why can't the pictures of Native Americans protesting in the freezing cold result in despair so deep, we will do anything to save them?

Lots of reasons—political, cultural, and social. I know. But I am also concerned about viewers and readers understanding the level of pain. Maybe we've become inured to the images of grief, tragedy, murder, and injustice. Or relinquished our social consciousness around pain being universally unfair and unwanted.

III.

What is your level of pain, ten being unbearable? What if, in fact, we looked at each story in terms of physical and emotional impact, using numbers, instead of words, ten being intolerable?

Could we rate the pain in each story with a number? Could we trust victims to reliably apply a number that could lead to a plan?

What is your level of pain? Ten being unfathomable?

What is your level of outrage, ten being unspeakable?

What is your level of humiliation, ten being breathing the tar of the road to refuge?

What is your level of disenfranchisement, ten being loss of your country?

What is you level of anger, ten being firestorm?

What is your level of loss, ten being muted and wandering?

What is your level of disorientation, ten being unwanted foreigner?

IV.

Sixteen years ago, when the Twin Towers in New York City were bombed, federal and local governments seriously considered proposals on requiring Arabs and Arab Americans to have identification cards. My mother, who was hard of hearing, slightly bent over, and shaking from Parkinson's, listened to these possibilities, her television blaring to the middle of the parking lot. She had been in the country sixty-five years. At eighty-eight years old, my mother had sent six children through school and higher education, run a business, lost babies and her mother, and survived heart problems and several fracturing falls. But the prospect of filing for an ID card broke her. In a pain haze, lying on the couch, she turned her face to me and said, *I didn't come to this country to lose my freedom.*

Often a defender of the government, a respecter of authority, my mother rarely butted heads with the powers that be. Here she was, one year from her passing, feeling the loss of a lifetime. *Mother, what is your pain level, ten being erased?*

This was greater to her, at the moment, than the death of two children, or the passing of her sister and mother, of her loss of her home in Lebanon. Her face broke to pieces.

Mother, your level of pain when:

You left your country as a child?

You were separated from your mother?

When your father died before you got married?

When your children disappointed you?

When you were rejected by the society around you?

When your business failed?

Mother, what was your level of pain when you couldn't dance, or sing, or listen to music, ten being inconsolable?

V.

Does it help to have what feels like an objective rating? Would we then know how to react?

What is your level of pain when your country is occupied?

What is your level of pain when the dictatorship murders entire towns?

What is your level of pain when you are suddenly a refugee?

What is your level of pain when it's your son showing up in the video of a police shooting? Or dying on Rikers Island?

What is your level of pain when your dreams are legislated and then withdrawn?

What is your pain?

VI.

I am constantly reaching for the better language to surround the stories that illustrate our inability to feel compassion or our loss of the importance of human rights. They elude me, or maybe, I've used up the supply. The combinations of words do not go on into infinity like the arrangement of numbers.

If we follow the example of the fine doctor, ratings may connect the dots from pain to prescription. Give a prognosis, perform surgery, embrace it to stability, exercise it gently, then vigorously.

We can make up charts. If a person, or family, tribe, culture, society, or citizenship is having a pain rated at five, we have a discussion in the United Nations and pass a resolution. At eight, we put the opposing parties into negotiations, and at ten, we operate—remove the tumor, fix the break, replace the limb, assist the heart, rewire the brain, engorge the implant, radiate the area.

It's four months after the fall—my wrist is healed. Monday I was cleared to go back to full performance of my duties as a fitness instructor.

Memory of pain: six. Level of pain: zero.

◻ ◻ ◻ ◻ ◻

2

GEORGE ABRAHAM

in which you do not ask
the state of israel to commit suicide

The officers, speaking harsh fragments of Hebrew, run your boots back and forth several times through the security scanner. After carefully inspecting the zipper, they decide to place your shoes in a metal tray and slide them to you. You are given a red badge to wear with your name printed in bold font. They keep your passport at the front desk. You are instructed not to ask questions.

You proceed to a waiting area, while the officers inspect your classmates, two-by-two, in five- to fifteen-minute intervals. Slowly, the waiting room begins to fill with familiar faces; your American classmates, marked with blue badges and blue passports in their hands.

A sign reading *Israeli Ministry of Foreign Affairs: security cameras in use* prompts your friend to joke about the room being bugged. It is important to mention that she is also wearing a red badge. Both the humor and exhaustion in her statement are familiar. Or maybe she reminds you of home.

Eventually, you are ushered out of the cramped waiting room and into a large lecture hall. A dark-skinned woman stands at the podium. You see her last name flash across the screen and are relieved by the familiar space it occupies in your mouth.

The woman introduces herself as an Iraqi Jew who is now a political law advisor to the Israeli state. She begins explaining her job and the difficult legal nuances of counterterrorism; how international law forbids targeting civilian infrastructure in combat. Hence, the terrorists tend to use international law to their advantage. Hence, war places unfair pressure on Israel to operate on the higher moral ground.

The distinction between this woman and a terrorist is a matter of semantics; she has a terrorist name, speaks the terrorist's language, even grew up living among terrorists. And now, she is the one dropping the bombs on the terrorists, on behalf of a state that views her as the acceptable kind of terrorist.

The woman is only the first of several speakers, the rest of whom are white. The speeches begin to blur, as the politicians recite similar, rehearsed arguments, none of which are unfamiliar to you. Your haze breaks when the last speaker, a white-haired man, starts answering questions from the audience and says, "1948 happened. 1967 happened. And we won. This is war, I mean, history tells us things like this just happen."

The words escape him without the slightest hint of remorse. His stare, gray and rigid as stone; the kind of cold only a politician can know. You lock eyes with the Palestinian woman to whom he responded.

"So what you're saying is, my mother, who was born in Haifa, cannot return to her home, but any random American Jew can?" The exhaustion in her voice is familiar to you.

"Listen," the man sighs and removes his glasses. "I don't know your mother, but I assume she can find a home in another Arab country; that's how war works. If we were to accommodate every refugee who claims this land, that would be a logistical improbability. That would, in essence, be asking the state of Israel to commit suicide. I hope this answers your question."

You want to say you are surprised by all of this, but in truth you are just numb. Or maybe the language escapes you.

An hour later, you are ushered out of the building by a woman who is introduced to you as an intern. You attempt to make small talk with her, only to receive half smiles and nods. The security guard up front hands back your passport in a small metal tray. "She doesn't speak your language," the guard explains.

ı|ı|ı

"What you have to understand about 1948 is they not only destroyed our village; they destroyed our lives." Yacoub's voice crackling through the bus mic's static almost resembles your grandfather's. The way he'd pause and let "*ya'ani*" bridge the countries in his sentences: "Ya'ani, this was my home. My childhood. My paradise."

The bus shifts left to exit, Hebrew signs painting the side of the road, as you approach what remains of Lifta: mountainside speckled with stone remnants, structures half-standing, swallowed by the overgrowth.

Your moments in Lifta begin to blur: first, the descent, steep, as if the land itself is beckoning your return. Then, the runoff—you see a white man bathing in the desolate remains of a spring. Another Israeli man is reading a newspaper. He sits on a boulder as if he didn't know a house once stood there.

"This is the house where I grew up; that used to be the bakery downhill," Yacoub points onward as the rest of the class lags behind. In the distance, a building gapes like God smashed his fist down on its frame in a tantrum.

As you near the hill's bottom, Yacoub points to the opposing hillside: "that hill—ya'ani—is where my father and his fathers were buried. The waste . . . ya'ani . . . sewage from Jerusalem runs down the hillside and erased his grave marker." You ask yourself, how many times has the state of Israel asked Palestinians to marvel at their own land's suicide?

You reach the bottom. In the distance, there is a playground with a newly renovated park, speckles of white children running around. "The government started building a, a . . . ya'ani, a new Israeli quarter at the base of our village. This is our land, but they want to pave over it. We are fighting them, ya'ani, in the courts . . . but the construction has already begun."

You ask again: how many times has the state of Israel forced Palestinians to abandon their own; to have their very conception of home paved over and forgotten?

It is important to mention that, on your way to the bus, Yacoub points out a hybrid tree species that produces both almonds and berries. It is the result of decades of competition between an invasive species, and a fruit gene indigenous to the region; two lineages, intertwined into a finite body, refusing erasure. Science says that there are two likely outcomes to such speciation: either one species will conquer the other, or another entirely new species will emerge over generations. Yacoub calls it a genetic anomaly. A miracle of God.

ı|ı|ı

Six months later, you are back on your American college campus. The gaze of a hundred eyes fixed on you and the equations displayed in light behind you; both are a language of their own. A vial filled with Lifta's soil hangs on a strand around your neck. You feel it against your chest as you speak to the audience in their own language of proof and theorem.

You reference an equation from a paper in your hand, and as you glance down, notice TECHNION UNIVERSITY OF ISRAEL dominating the top of the page.

"Their argument was a logical fallacy, so in a sense, the paper authors cheated. They're Israeli, so I suppose it makes sense."

You don't know why the words slip out of your mouth. And, for a second, time ceases to exist, and you are not a mere college student defending his thesis, but instead a Palestinian college student defending his thesis to a wall of petrified, white faces. Maybe it being Israeli independence day weighed heavy on you. Or maybe every day is Israeli independence day, and your ancestors slipped out of your throat. Maybe it was the soil, hanging from your neck like a key might. It is often the case that Palestinians who fled during the Nakba still have the keys to their homes, even if their homes are no longer standing. In either case, there is always a mourning; there is always the lack of home placing a weight around your neck, a bullet in each word that escapes you.

A well-intentioned white professor pulls you aside after your presentation and lectures you on professionalism. You want to tell him your history; how Technion's existence is at the expense of your ancestor's land and lives; how this same university makes an open-air laboratory of Gaza and calls the people there the necessary expense.

How, despite all of this, you are expected to sit docile, as your own academic institution funds the crumble and rupture of a land you called home. As if this same academic institution didn't turn their back when the Birthright campaign and other friends of Israel threatened to put the Arab students on a watchlist. As if this same institution didn't try to swallow you into the night's mouth, tempting a moonlit suicide attempt from you, or that copy of you who craved most an escape that night. Were you to die, would they write you into a boy on a godless ledge, and speak not of the demons you fled, or the gravity forming a hollow country in your heart? Or would they say you were just abandoning your body; would they say, *this is war, I mean, depression. Things like this just happen?* Would they remember, first, the history and not the body it haunted?

But you are not the self you survived, nor are you the version of yourself who takes in words of the white professor, who you remind yourself, is well-intentioned. You are, instead, the copy of yourself you found at the entrance to the Aida refugee camp, six months prior, taking a selfie in front of a life-size statue of a key. While you are off being the literal Palestinian diasporic stereotype, your white classmates give candies to children walking in the streets, and ask to take selfies with them. The children hold up 2 fingers next to their saviors in the photographs. #PeaceInTheMiddleEast. 128 likes on Instagram.

Inside the camp, a youth program director tells you about the role of art in the lives of the Palestinian refugee communities. "We began to notice our children were born into such desperate conditions that they dreamt of no other reality than becoming martyrs," the director says, "It was our goal to teach our children that they could live for Palestine; that they didn't have to die for their country."

And at this point, all past, present, and future selves of you converge, as you ask again how many times the state of Israel brought Palestinians to the brink of suicide; how the state instilled a learned helplessness in you; how the state molded you into the monster they always feared you to be, the monster you always feared in yourself. What of the self can exist outside a political rhetoric which, at best, will write you into something nonexistent?

ı|ı|ı

As they are written, Israeli zone laws give the state legal control over the hilltops, aquifers, and other natural land resources in the West Bank. This is how the state writes Palestinian ethnic cleansing into "abandonment," hence "legal," hence "digestible" in some sense of the word.

For instance, Palestinian homes are not connected to Israel's central water system. Forty-gallon tubs of water are sold to Palestinian families at ten times the price Israelis pay. As you drive through the land, you can immediately discern which houses are Palestinian and which are Israeli – the Palestinian houses bearing the mark and weight of black water tanks, like lamb blood on a front door. The partition of water has always been the difference between holy and crucified.

You arrive at your destination: a cramped UN office, responsible for monitoring the environmental situation in Gaza. A man tells you how Israeli scientists monitor and control the net sum of water and caloric content of food entering Gaza. This is how the state legalizes experimentation on Palestinian bodies; they ensure that just enough food is distributed to keep people alive, in case anyone accuses them of starving you out. In case you want to engineer an escape with your own hands—when locked on 3 sides by wall, the only place you can turn to is a sea who betrayed you. The story is too familiar now. The unholy betrayal of fluid is how history makes an open-air prison of home, of country; call it, sink or swim; or, Unidentified UN Report stating, "the Gaza strip will be environmentally uninhabitable by 2020."

In the case you would try to escape and abandon your own, history says you will become the next unidentified Palestinian thing to disappear into an Israeli jail. The newspaper headlines talk of Israelis holding barbeques outside of prisons housing Palestinians on a hunger strike. In case you forget the way they not only stole your land, but dance on it too.

ıIıIı

There is a small village in the central West Bank named Nabi Salih. Due to the village's location, Israeli zone control regulations make state-sponsored housing demolitions legal on this land: another suicide placed on your people's shoulders by the state.

In the case that the stubbornness clings to you and you refuse your home's literal destruction, your home becomes a riot. This is how the state will beat you until your bones cannot heal themselves. In both resistance and compliance, you are still asked to make a massacre of home.

For the past few years, the residents of Nabi Salih have been protesting home demolitions every Friday. A month before your arrival, you shared a viral video of a Palestinian teenager named Ahed Tamimi, who would often organize and attend such protests. You called her a hero. The recent history says, she was taken from her home in the middle of the night, her parents beaten half to death, and is currently being prosecuted in an Israeli prison with her mother.

As it is written, the history says you invited the soldiers and their tear gas into your living room. The history goes, children are often shot or injured in tear gas canister explosions. As it is written, the history says this is still your fault; says, your children suffered at the expense of your stubbornness.

The woman invites you into her rebuilt house and explains all of this to you, because you are not her; there is nothing connecting you but your stubborn blood, diluted, and the hyphenated American identity you uninherited. Because you are not her, or Ahed Tamimi, or any other Palestinian taken in the night, you can write this testimony, and although it will never become History, it is a history nonetheless. Were you to disappear, there would at least be a body and country to mourn. There is no metaphor for this learned helplessness because the people of Palestine are always prisoner, here, in their own home.

ıIıIı

After taking in both the histories and its erasures forced upon you, this want and love for the land your ancestor's made nostalgia of, you end your journey in Jaffa—a town on the Mediterranean sea coast. You strip to your bare skin and walk into the sea for the first and perhaps the last time. You close your eyes and there is only quiet. A solemn quiet, but not a lonely one; these waters that no longer belong to you, cradling your body in all its unfamiliar, and all the history running through you: the ghost of your grandfather's smile, his laughter waning like sunset; the ghost of your grandmother's baptism and her Jerusalem; the weight of all your family and all their ghosts that could not exist here.

When all is done, you will go back to your country. You will retreat to western diplomacy and it will fail you. Again. You haven't a language in which this trauma is both digestible and reconcilable.

Suppose, instead, you began this by demanding the return of your rightful home and land, at the expense of the Israeli state. In that case, you would be asking for the destruction of the state that stole that home and forced death upon you, but the reality is this narrative is never mentioned because this narrative has no language digestible to western diplomacy, hence no space to call its own. Your demands for the dissolution of the Israeli state are always labeled "a suicide," despite the fact that you are not advocating for bloodshed, despite all the suicides the Israeli state has forced upon Palestinians. This would be the predictable ending, the ending your oppressor expects.

So, out of necessity in this logical framework, you do not ask the state of Israel to commit suicide because you cannot ask the state of Israel to commit suicide. By choosing this path, your words become the ivory paving over Lifta, the tear gas canisters making a hollow echo of Nabi Salih, the steel-tipped soldiers' boots that first kicked your own grandparents out of their house. This would mean ignoring history at your own expense; would mean writing yourself into something nonexistent.

In any case, you haven't a home to call your own, nor do you exist in a reality in which you can reclaim the home you deserve. Hence, you are told to rebuild, like your parents have rebuilt, survive like your ancestors have survived. And even that is its own type of amnesia: rebuild home long enough to see your oppressor in its walls and eventually your own veins. Or escape. In any case, your oppressor has successfully engineered a reality in which you cannot see yourself existing.

Hence you arrive at a contradiction: you exist, hence you survived, but without a language to name that survival history. Hence, any attempt to give existing language to that history would be to give your oppressor agency over your history, hence write yourself out of History. To ask the oppressor to stop killing your people would be to ask the impossible; would be to beg wine out of a water that has failed you. Your ancestors have tried, time and time again. And failed.

You are stuck between the present reality and a utopia where you have a land to call home, or at least, one where your homes converge into one body. So you are trapped, by necessity, in this unsolvable binary between what is owed and what is realistic; between what is deserved and what is expected.

Proof that an equation is unsolvable in a given logical framework is of infinite value, compared to a solution damned to contradiction. Peace cannot be achieved through dialogue when one side has two guns at their temple: one held up by the oppressor, the other held by the oppressed.

In any case, the blood is always on your hands.

In any case, the blood is always your own.

▢ ▢ ▢ ▢ ▢

3

NABEEL ABRAHAM

On the Road with Bob

Peddling in the Early Sixties

The blue and white 1959 Ford Galaxy had been cruising on the Ohio Turnpike for less than thirty minutes when Bob unexpectedly pulled off at a service area. As the car slowed to a stop, Bob clutched his abdomen moaning in Arabic "Ahh . . . ach, it's burning."

"What's burning?" I asked, restraining my alarm.

"It's my stomach. The heartburn is killing me, *wa'lek*," he murmured through a painful grimace.

Bob was in the habit of calling his sons by the impolite *wa'lek* (*boy* in Arabic). It was his way of maintaining a respectful distance from me and my four brothers. In a subconscious twist, we acknowledged the emotional gap separating us from our father by referring to him as *Bob* (short for *baba* or *daddy* in Arabic).

The rush of traffic seemed distant against the sound of Bob's breathing. Traces of white chalk from the antacid tablets he was chewing accented the corners of his mouth. How would we get back if he became too ill to drive? I thought about the Oriental rugs and the boxes of Irish and Portuguese linens packed snugly into the car. In place of the back seat, an old blanket disguised several expensive rugs. If we had to leave the car behind, thieves would surely break in and take the goods.

These worries emboldened me to make a barely audible offer: "I can try to drive if you can't manage." Before I could reassure him that a thirteen-year-old boy could handle the wheel of a car, he cut me off with *tik* followed by a slight nod of the head that Palestinians make when they want to say no with a minimum of effort.

"You're just a kid," he said, still gripping his abdomen. A long silence fell over the car. Then, without warning, Bob turned the ignition key, put the car into drive, and wheeled back onto the turnpike. This was my first trip out of Detroit since Bob had moved the family from Erie, Pennsylvania, in 1955, some eight years before. This was also my first and last peddling trip. Going on al-Bay'aa was a way of life for people from Bob's native Beit Hanina, a small Arab village lying just north of Jerusalem on the road to Ramallah. Peddling often took precedence over school for the adolescents and young men from Beit Hanina. That's why Mother declared peddling unsuitable for her sons. It wasn't so much that she objected to our working and earning spending money. On the contrary, she encouraged us to deliver newspapers, mow lawns, shovel snow off sidewalks, and even sell Christmas cards and boxed candies on consignment door-to-door. What Mother feared about peddling was the social milieu—the potential for gambling, sex, and other delinquencies. Going on al-Bay'aa with the boys from Beit Hanina was, in Mother's opinion, to fall in with the wrong crowd.

My brothers and I never aspired to be peddlers. We were too pro-education; and anyway going door-to-door peddling tapestries, towels, watches, and trinkets held absolutely no appeal for us. Peddling was what our cousins from Beit Hanina did, and we weren't interested in emulating them. The episodic sales of Christmas cards and boxed candies, which we sold in the neighborhood one year, were viewed as a quick way to earn money with which to buy Christmas presents and clothes of our own choosing. Curiously, when Bob learned of our neighborhood peddling forays, he didn't appear pleased, telling mother his children weren't in need of the money. But since he was away so much of the time and had relegated our upbringing to Mother, his opinion in this matter, as in many others, held little sway.

I had fought to get on this peddling trip with Bob, not from any desire to learn the ropes, but out of an unremitting curiosity about my father's work, the places he visited, and the people he met. And, anyway school was out, and I wasn't interested in spending another frustrating summer confined to the streets of southwest Detroit. After a year or so of idle promises, Bob had in a weak moment agreed to let me come along for the ride. Then in a moment of anger at Mother, then at me, he tried to wriggle out of it. Ironically, Mother had lobbied on my behalf. She had her own reasons for wanting me on the trip and the ever-suspicious Bob knew it. My presence would serve as a constraint on him, principally on his meanderings to the gambling tables in the back-alley coffee houses he frequented. As I would discover, it was a tough assignment.

The belief in our house was that Bob's relatives thought Mother a bit too uppity and unconventional. She had cut them off from Bob's largess, which they had grown accustomed to ever since his brother's death in a factory fire several decades earlier. She saw her role as protector of her family and didn't care much what they thought. She was aided by her class attitude—she was from an upper-class Jerusalemite family; they were country people. Adhering to deeply-rooted Palestinian social cleavages, she wasn't reluctant to let them know that city people were better than country people.

My family was unconventional in other ways as well. Bob was twenty-five years older than Mother. Yet he became angry when strangers mistook him for our "grandfather" and Mother for his daughter. He was fifty-four years old when I was born and sixty-one when my fourth and youngest brother arrived. Bob immigrated before World War I, which placed him among the early Arabic-speaking immigrants to the United States, and certainly among the pioneers from Beit Hanina.

Peddling was in his blood. When a fellow peddler from Beit Hanina, Abdel-Hamid Shouman, invited him to return to Palestine and be his partner in a banking venture, Father responded by asking, "What do you know of banking?" Shouman went on to found the Arab Bank, one of the largest banks in the Middle East. Bob loved to boast that he had passed through every state of the Union with the exception of Alaska and Hawaii. He was also the consummate salesman. I learned late in life to wonder about some of his boasts, yet he taught me to be leery of free offers and other sales gimmicks.

Bob had long made the transition from peddling to store ownership. He liked to say that he had to pay protection money to the mob during Prohibition to protect his Madison Avenue store in Manhattan. He also owned stores in Charlotte, North Carolina, where I was born; Erie, Pennsylvania, where three of my brothers were born; and Detroit, Michigan, where the youngest was born. He owned other stores in and around New York City, Yonkers, and White Plains. When a store went bust or he decided to move on, peddling was his fallback position. After he closed his Detroit store, thanks in part to the unpaid bills his relatives had piled up, he officially retired and returned to peddling in Pennsylvania, New York, and North Carolina. He loved to say that he never worried about money; even during the Great Depression he made money. When money ran out, he would take to the road. Although he was socially conservative, when it came to money he was an inveterate gambler; money flowed through his fingers like water, with little thought to tomorrow.

Tall, slender, and dressed in expensive gray business suits with matching gray fedoras, Bob cut the figure of a high class peddler. He remained a New Yorker until the end, in the way he comported himself, in his preference for suits tailored in New York, in his slight New York accent. He took pride in the fact he sold new and antique Oriental rugs and fine linens to America's wealthy classes. His Palestinian country-men, in contrast, never shook off their old-country ways and habits. They sold sundry dry goods, inexpensive scarves, linens, watches, and throw rugs decorated with garish prints, which they peddled door-to-door in working-class neighborhoods. We lived in such a neighborhood, and one day a Palestinian peddler from Ramallah unwittingly knocked on our door, throw rug slung over his arm. Insistent on showing me his wares, he moved on only after I explained it would be futile to peddle to a peddler's family. As recently as the early 1990's, some boys from Beit Hanina could be found peddling cue sticks in Detroit's bars and pool halls.

ı|ı|ı

Bob drove straight through Ohio, reaching Union City, Pennsylvania, where we took a room in an old hotel, at nightfall. The next day, we traveled in an arc through Titusville, Oil City, and Meadville, before cir-cling back to Union City and onward to our destination, Erie. We drove with the aid of a tattered map. In the span of a day, Bob made a handful of stops to call on established customers. To my disappointment, I was ordered to stay in the car, missing the chance to see the inside of the old stately houses and meet their owners. Occasionally, a customer would invite him in and he would disappear for a half-hour or so. He would reappear suddenly, and without saying a word drive off to the house of another customer. On one stop, the elderly matron who answered the door noticed me sitting alone in the car and instructed Bob to fetch me so she could offer me a cold drink. On the way in Bob instructed me to keep my mouth shut. Happy to be invited in, I eagerly nodded in agree-ment. Inside, I listened as the matron waxed on about how much she loved the Oriental rug Bob had sold her on a previous trip. He, in turn, discoursed on the Persian rug's design and workmanship, while lament-ing the migration of the rug weavers to Iran's oil industry. She wondered if he could find her a similar carpet for another room, which they went off to see, leaving me behind to sip my drink and admire the spacious living room and its antique furnishings. Bob assured her he would look for a rug the size and type she wanted the next time he was in New York City, where the wholesalers were located.

I had come along on the trip hoping to be of some assistance to Bob but it was becoming painfully obvious to me that Bob preferred to work alone. He took great care to cultivate his relationships with his valued customers and wasn't going to let a parvenu like me muck things up for him. There is an old family chestnut that indicates the depth of Bob's desire to please his customers. The story involves an incident during my brother Nazeeh's trip with Bob the following year. Ever since Nazeeh was a toddler, Bob loved to kid him about his lips, which he referred to using the colloquial Palestinian term *jalagheem*. On one stop, the lady of the house remarked to Bob, "Oh, what a handsome boy you have, Mr. Abraham!" As they entered the house, Bob whispered to Nazeeh in Arabic, "tuck in your jalagheem boy, the lady thinks you're good looking."

ı|ı|ı

As we drove down the scenic two-lane roads of northwestern Pennsylvania, its undulating hills a relief from the monotony of Michigan's flatness, I halfheartedly hoped Bob would tell me something about the places we were passing through. He wasn't accommodating. When he wasn't in his usual state of reticence, he would burst out singing a few lines from the old Palestinian folk song "Ala del'ouna." Just as often, he would launch into a diatribe against Mother. "Your mother . . . ," he would begin, "accuses me of frittering away my earnings. Do you see me spending on anything but food and gas?," he would ask plaintively.

Bob once startled me during one diatribe by asking rhetorically, "Are we spending any money on women?" Before I could grasp what he had in mind, he volunteered an answer: "You're too young and I'm too old for women." I nodded in agreement at the glibness of his observation, even though I felt like protesting the part about my being too young.

During a quiet stretch of the two-lane road, a lime green station wagon carrying six nuns suddenly appeared and then disappeared as it headed around a bend going in the other direction. The image of the car and its passengers in their black habits was still fresh in my mind when Bob jolted me by saying, "Hey, boy, make like this . . . like this." Unable to follow what he was saying, I tried to catch a glimpse of his eyes but he was watching the road.

"Look here, make like this," he repeated. This time I caught sight of his eyes glancing downward momentarily, where I noticed something rather queer. With his right hand Bob made a tickling motion near the crotch of his pants.

"What's that for?" I asked with a mixture of disgust and curiosity.

"Nuns bring bad luck. You should always scratch your balls when you see a nun," he explained.

His advice ran counter to everything I had been taught in school about respecting other creeds.

"Oh, I don't believe that," I said, looking away in embarrassment. "And, anyway, it's not nice to make fun of other religions," I added.

"It's bad luck, I'm telling you," he persisted. Convincing myself that it was better to placate him then to put up with his jabs at my indignation, I feigned a quick tickle. The drone of the car's engine filled the space between us again as I ruminated quietly over the wisdom of coming along on the trip.

Erie

When we reached Erie, Bob headed straight for his regular haunt, the Richmond Hotel. The luster of its grandeur long faded, the Richmond offered Bob easy rates. He and I would share a double bed in a cramped room lit by a wall lamp at the foot of the bed. There was a sink and a mirror under the lamp, but the toilet and shower were located at the end of a dark, musty corridor. I didn't allow the state of the hotel to quell my excitement at being back in Erie, the town where my parents settled when I was an infant and the place we left when I was five years old. We dropped our bags off and left as quickly as we had arrived.

Bob drove by his old store on French Street and past the park that we used to stroll in. He parked the car and we walked to the large marble fountain in the park. We shared a box of popcorn and reminisced about the evenings the family watched the fountain's multicolor light display. From there we paid a visit to the Akabe'ya family, one of two families from Beit Hanina residing in Erie. I had a vague recollection of them from childhood. They gave us an enthusiastic welcome, insisting we stay for dinner. The head of the household, Abu Mahmoud, was wearing a pair of overalls, which made him seem like an Arab version of the TV character "Mr. Green Jeans." Abu Mahmoud ran a dry goods store in the Italian part of town. He sold tapestries, towels, and linens on consignment to peddlers from Beit Hanina who drifted through Erie.

I was surprised to hear him say he had recently gone to the movies to see *Lawrence of Arabia*.

"This is the first time the Arabs appear in the cinema; it's an accurate story," he said excitedly. His wife added that Abu Mahmoud was so taken by the film that he sat through the credits—every last one. Everyone laughed because it was obvious even to me that Abu Mahmoud was barely conversant in English. Later that week Bob and I caught sight of him in a movie theater as the lights came on at the end of *Lawrence*. Abu Mahmoud was seated several rows in front of us engrossed in the film's credits, just as we were. As we stood up to leave, Bob and I felt taller than usual.

The Richmond served as a kind of base camp for us during the two weeks we spent in Erie. After breakfast, Bob would place some calls on the hotel pay phone, and then decide the day's itinerary. Often this included a foray to one of the small towns in the vicinity of Erie. We usually returned by late afternoon or evening. The rest of the day was spent whiling away the hours in an Italian American coffeehouse where Bob would play game after game of pinochle or gin rummy. The coffeehouse was noticeably cleaner and airier than the Arabic coffeehouses my father frequented back in Detroit. Still, I preferred to see the sights than remain confined to a place were a bunch of men sat around gambling, smoking, and bantering in foul language. One night I convinced Bob to let me go to the movies alone. Most of the time, however, I was stuck in the coffeehouse sipping soft drinks and watching my father play cards, as I looked for ways to nudge him into leaving. Once, a denizen of the coffeehouse took pity on me as midnight approached and prodded Bob to take me back to the hotel. Without looking up from the game, Bob mumbled, as he always did when prodded to leave, "We'll go when I finish this hand." If I were lucky, "this hand" would stretch only another hour or so.

Forever etched in my mind is Bob's image seated behind a card table. He is dressed in a gray suit, white shirt, and tie. Deep in concentration, he is holding his cards guardedly in his left hand, while alternatively tugging and flicking the corners of the cards with his right hand. A Chesterfield King hangs precariously from his lower lip, its gray ash snaking delicately upward. Unlike the movies, Bob and the other gamblers never leave money on the table. The year before he died, after leaving a card game in Erie, Bob was mugged. He had won big that night. He wouldn't say exactly how much, but it was over a thousand dollars. The mugger struck him on the forehead with the butt of a gun. Mother said that he got his comeuppance.

Dining Out

Back in Erie after a day on the road, Bob suggested that we dine on salami and cheese sandwiches. I had Bob's yen for salami ever since he introduced Best's Kosher Salami to our kitchen table as far back as I could remember. Dusk stretched over the town as we headed to a Jewish delicatessen he knew. He pulled up next to a building with a Star of David painted on the storefront. The place appeared closed. But seeing a light in back, Bob knocked anyway. A man wearing a soiled apron appeared behind a partially opened door. Bob convinced him to sell us some salami, bread, and cheese even though the deli man insisted he was already closed for the night. As the man took his place behind the counter, Bob peered through the glass case on the other side. I stood just inside the door, marveling at the strange shapes and colors among the shadows of the cramped, dimly lit store. Bob turned and told me to wait in the car.

What seemed like an eternity passed. Hunger gripped me. I began to wonder if something terrible had happened inside the store. I was still deliberating about going back to the store when Bob appeared. As he slid behind the wheel, I noticed he was empty handed. "Let's go somewhere else," he murmured.

"What happened?" I asked with gnawing hunger. Bob explained that the deli owner was willing to sell him the salami but wouldn't slice it.

"Why not?" I asked somewhat astonished.

"It's after sundown on the Jewish Sabbath," Bob said.

"But today is Friday; isn't the Jewish day on Saturday?" I stammered, still confused. Bob appeared frustrated and in no mood to talk. It was only in adulthood that I discovered that Jews and Middle Easterners calculate the beginning of a new day from sundown the previous day.

"So, why did you take so long?" I asked, hoping he wouldn't become upset with my persistent questioning.

"The deli man told me he had some sliced chicken in the basement. I agreed out of desperation. But he took so long to come back I began to grow suspicious," Bob explained.

"Suspicious?"

Bob hesitated momentarily before elaborating, "Who knows what he brought back? Maybe it was cat meat."

"Cat meat? How could that be?" No one would knowingly sell cat meat, I thought to myself. That is too far-fetched. A grin suddenly came over Bob's face.

"How about a steak dinner at the Richmond Hotel?" he asked. I eagerly accepted.

Seated behind a table draped in white linen, I fingered the assortment of forks, knives and spoons arrayed before me, contemplating my good fortune. Here I was on my *first* trip out of Detroit and I had already tasted shrimp (beer-battered) and eaten a genuine spaghetti dinner, both at the Aurora Restaurant in the Italian section of town. And now another first—dining on a New York strip steak in a fancy hotel restaurant. Bob startled me by vigorously rubbing the flatware with his napkin, instructing me to do likewise.

"Aren't they clean?" I asked.

He responded with a *tik* and nod of the head, adding in Arabic, "You can never be sure."

As I rubbed the flatware on my side of the table, Bob pointed out the soup spoon and the salad fork. When the waitress arrived, he ordered a strip steak dinner for himself and a children's steak dinner for me. Fortunately for my sake the waitress convinced him that the children's portion would be insufficient for a boy my age. In the end, I got the full steak dinner along with the uneasy feeling that perhaps Bob couldn't afford it.

Hoping to convince Bob that my presence on the trip was helping further my education, I marveled at the large crystal chandelier hanging from the ceiling and the images of the linen-draped tables reflected in the full-length mirrors along the wall. Saying nothing, Bob pulled an envelope from his suit jacket and handed it to me along with the pen he borrowed from the waitress. In a hushed tone he asked me write his name on the back of the envelope. Confused, I asked for clarification. He repeated his instructions. Thinking he might be interested in seeing how I might spell his name, I printed it in block letters.

After briefly scrutinizing what I had written, he said, "Is this how you *sign* my name?"

Incredulous, I asked, "You want me to *sign your* name?" He nodded in the affirmative. I tried not to imitate his signature, even though I knew how, fearing he might accuse me of having forged his signature on some other document. I handed him the envelope, which he held up to the light and scrutinized intensely. He then asked for the pen. Placing the envelope on the table, he slowly copied the signature, comparing his with mine. He did this twice before the waitress returned, at which point he tucked the envelope back into his jacket and returned the pen.

Puzzled, I asked what was going on. Bob said he wanted to refine his signature. I felt sad, for at age thirteen I had more years of schooling behind me than he had at age 67. "After a lifetime in business, you certainly know how to sign your name," I reassured him. "And, even though you haven't had much education, you read American and Arabic newspapers. That's more than what most people can do." I pointed out that he was probably the only person in our entire neighborhood who read the *New York Times*. In a final, and self-deprecating, attempt, to make him feel better, I reminded him that he was a whiz with numbers and would chuckle when I had to pull out pencil and paper to multiply double-digit numbers. "Look Bob, the fact that you can do the calculations in your head tells me you're smarter than most people," I concluded. Bob listened stone-faced.

Long after he died, Mother revealed that Bob had learned to read and write during a stint in prison. This chapter in his life occurred long before he married Mother, probably when he lived in New York City. Mother told the following story about it, which she had heard from Bob himself. My father had a policy to help new immigrants from Beit Hanina when they first arrived in the country. One day a man from the village arrived at his doorstep with a stranger in tow. The man asked Bob to reimburse the stranger for helping him. Bob was later arrested and tried for smuggling an alien into the country. He served a four-year sentence behind bars, losing his business in the process. Curiously, he never spoke of the incident or his time behind bars.

Lake Chautauqua

One morning Bob returned from his round of phone calls to say we were going to New York. I cloaked my excitement lest Bob think I was turning the Bay'aa trip into a kid's vacation. I desperately wanted to set foot in New York City, America's premier city and the town Bob had spent much of his life in. Bob, however, had a different New York in mind—Lake Chautauqua, New York—a short drive from Erie.

The air around Lake Chautauqua contrasted favorably with the smoke-filled coffee house and the musty hotel back in Erie. Bob was hoping to break his no-win streak at Chautauqua. His mood had picked up and he was back to rolling the syllables of town names around his tongue. "La-ka-wa-na," he would toss back and forth like a cat playing with his food. On the way to Erie his syllabic toy word had been "Astabula."

Bob parked in front of a sprawling ranch house tucked away in a corner of the countryside around Lake Chautauqua. As usual, I sat in the car as Bob made his call. After exchanging a few pleasantries, he returned and instructed me to help him pull a rug out of the car. At last, I thought, I would be able to justify my keep. We wrestled a big Kerman into the living room of the house. By morning's end, two more Orientals would be unrolled in succession, one laid on top of the other. Each time, Bob busied himself laying the rug just so—a tug here, a flap of a corner there, until it harmonized with its surroundings.

He then reestablished eye contact with the couple, zeroing in on the wife, who, he knew from experience, would have to like the rug if the hoped-for sale was to materialize. Bob discussed each rug's design, while attempting to educate the couple, who were relatively young, on the investment value of the rugs. The couple's attractive daughter entered the room briefly. I looked in her direction, hoping not to arouse any suspicion on the part of her parents. Bob would never forgive me, I thought, if he lost a sale because of my flirtatious glances. My eyes shifted back to Bob and the couple.

The couple seemed unsure of themselves. Three new Kermans, not costly antiques, lay before them. Questions and answers went back and forth, Bob expounding on the merits of Orientals over wall-to-wall carpet. Watching him work convinced me that peddling Oriental rugs was not in my blood. The idea of entering people's homes to sell them something they weren't certain they needed or wanted didn't sit well with me. Too many unknowns, too many possibilities for rejection, too nerve wracking. It was too much like gambling.

In the end, the pretty daughter disappeared, and so too did the possibility of a sale. One by one, we rolled up the rugs and carried them back to the car. Bob's assessment: the couple was too young to appreciate Oriental rugs and too taken in by the fashion of the day—wall-to-wall carpeting. He also thought the couple had found the price too steep. The fifteen hundred dollars he was asking for one of the rugs was equivalent to a fifth of the average annual income at the time.

Detroit

My brothers jumped with excitement when they saw Bob and me entering the house. We were like warriors returning from a battlefield. Mother gave me a big kiss, and my brothers wanted to know what it was like going out on al-Bay'aa. I told them about the shrimp at the Aurora restaurant, the steak at the Richmond, the vineyards on the way to Lake Chautauqua, the rolling hills of Pennsylvania, and whispered about the incident with the nuns. I knew the questions my brothers would ask because I once had them too. I had voyaged to the world of al-Bay'aa, a world that was as much a part of our consciousness as the West is part of the American consciousness.

‖‖

Road's End

Six years after Bob and I returned from al-Bay'aa, we set off on separate journeys: I on my first trip to the Middle East, he on his last al-Bay'aa. The year was 1969. On the eve of my departure, Bob handed me some fatherly advice, "I hear refugee women make good wives," he said.

"Bob, I'm not interested in finding a wife," I replied indignantly with a hint of embarrassment. "I'm going to see the Palestinian Revolution."

It was around Labor Day when my plane landed back at Detroit Metro. On the drive home I regaled my brothers with stories of what I had seen during my summer trip to Lebanon, Jordan, Syria, and Turkey. It was a heady time, filled with foreign lands, revolutionary politics, unfamiliar languages, new customs, and exotic foods.

As the car wheeled into the garage behind Casper Street, it dawned on me that we had been riding in my father's holly green 1966 Ford Galaxy. No one mentioned that Bob was back from al-Bay'aa. "Hey, this is Bob's car. So he's home," I said knowingly.

My brothers' momentary silence was broken by Sameer who responded, "He's not here." Too weary from the trip, I didn't probe as I headed indoors to see my mother and younger brothers. They let me fall asleep without bringing up the subject of Bob's whereabouts.

The next morning Mother broke the news to me in the only way she knew how. "Your father," she said in simple Arabic that I could understand, "died." Years of experience attuned me to the nuances of my mother's voice. Her steady, somber cadence amplified the seriousness of her message. "He died in New York. Sameer and I went there to retrieve his body. We buried him here. Hundreds attended the funeral. Your half-brother Richard was there; and so were all the people from Beit Hanina."

Mother remained impassive as she spoke. I now know that she would have preferred to throw her arms around me, but my family always leaned toward restraint. We grew up never expressing the deepest emotions between parent and child. "I could have sent word to you to come back, but decided against it because I knew how much this trip meant to you," she added. I was too stunned to take umbrage at her decision.

At nineteen, I hardly knew the man we called Bob, for his emotional distance mirrored his frequent physical absence from our lives. He was the quintessential loner. He had married at least three women in his seventy or so years (we never knew his real age), he seemed to prefer the solitary life of the peddler to the sedate life of father and husband. It was in his blood, and he wasn't about to change, even after my four brothers and I came along.

After Mother broke the news I sat in the bathtub and sobbed quietly. That was the extent of mourning for my father. I never really buried Bob, and to this day I haven't mustered up the emotional strength to visit his grave. I dammed a reservoir of emotions that I still refuse to let out for fear of their enormous power. So there they remain—tucked away in my subconscious, safely out of reach.

ılılı

A perforated stomach ulcer felled my father as he played cards in New York City one summer night. The coffeehouse owner called Mother. She and Sameer flew to his bedside at Bellevue Hospital. He survived the initial surgery, but it failed to stop the hemorrhaging. Father was unable to speak through the oxygen mask as he was told that he must undergo a second operation. For the first time, Sameer noticed fear on Father's face.

Barely eighteen years old, Sameer was sent to Erie to pick up Bob's belongings from the Richmond, where as usual he left his things while on a quick buying trip to New York. Sameer drove Father's car, laden with unsold rugs and linens, back to Detroit. Mother waited in New York. Sameer flew back to New York City, and headed straight to Bellevue, where he discerned the news on a nurse's face. Father died on the operating table.

ılılı

Father died the way he had lived: on the road. He was the consummate peddler—a lone wolf who preferred to meet everyone in his life on his terms whether they were customers, family, or fellow gamblers. He preferred to roam unhindered and unencumbered by familial obligations, yet was exceedingly generous to his relatives and covillagers, and he loved and took pride in his six sons. Anomalies were his stock-in-trade. For most of the seventeen years he spent with his first wife, Grace, he lived in New York City, leaving her to raise their son in Scranton, Pennsylvania. Father was an urban cowboy. He rode into town, swaggered into the local coffeehouse and gambled the night away. When he was out of money, he rode away, looking for opportunity on the trail. He was good at his trade, and it rewarded him in untold ways. To his credit, my father never gave a second thought to the road not taken.

◻ ◻ ◻ ◻ ◻

4

RABIH ALAMEDDINE

Comforting Myths

Notes from a purveyor

Before he died, my father reminded me that when I was four and he asked what I wanted to be when I grew up, I said I wanted to be a writer. Of course, what I meant by *writer* then was a writer of Superman comics. In part I was infatuated with the practically invulnerable Man of Steel, his blue eyes and his spit curl. I wanted both to be him and to marry him, to be his Robin, so to speak. But more importantly, I wanted to write his story, the adventures of the man who fought for truth, justice, and the American Way—if only I could figure out what the fuck the American Way was.

How could I tell the story with such glaring holes in my knowledge? I was terribly bothered that I did not know what the American Way was, and became even more so when I began to wonder whether there was such a thing as the Lebanese Way and whether I would recognize it. My parents were Lebanese, but I was born in Jordan, raised in Kuwait. Could my way be Kuwaiti and not Lebanese? Since most of my classmates were Palestinians, I had a Ramallah accent. Did that mean I'd lost my way?

I wanted to tell stories that belonged to me. Superman would be my friend, his world mine. In a single bound, he would leap the tallest buildings, basically my house and my cousins' across the street. My Superman would be more powerful than a locomotive, stronger than my father's red Rambler. I wished to share my story with the world, and it did not occur to me at that age to ask whether the world had any interest.

Who gets to tell stories? Let me answer this quickly: for the most part—and the exceptions are relatively recent—the writers who are allowed to talk are those who prop up the dominant culture, who reflect it with a gilded mirror. But wait: writers have been critical of the dominant culture for quite a while, you may say. Look at James Baldwin, look at Margaret Atwood and *The Handmaid's Tale*. Well, fine, but criticism of the culture is not necessarily a threat to it. When the story is truly threatening, the writer is marginalized, either deemed a political writer or put in a box to be safely celebrated as some sort of minority writer. In his day Baldwin was considered more a black writer than a writer, and so he still is. If he is inching his way into the canon, it is because the culture has shifted. Overt racism is a bad thing now, so a liberal American can read *Another Country* and think, sure, there were a few bad apples back then, but this is not about me or how I live. It is easier now to tell ourselves that Baldwin is not talking about us, that he is criticizing people we no longer are.

When I bring this up in conversation, people stop me in my tracks because, you know, Conrad, *Heart of Darkness* and all that. Didn't he criticize empire?

He didn't. A story about a bickering couple does not threaten the institution of marriage. *Heart of Darkness* might disapprove of colonialism, but it's not an attack on empire itself. The book deals in strict dualities and reinforces the superiority of Western culture and ideas. Africa, its jungle, is what blackens Kurtz's heart, and just in case you start to feel uncomfortable because you find yourself identifying with him, the supposed bad apple—the Lynndie England of nineteenth-century Europe—Marlow, the novel's cordon sanitaire, is there to make you feel better. If that's not enough, it's actually some other shadowy narrator telling you what *he* heard when listening to Marlow's story, so you, imperial citizen, are at least two steps removed from the apple and its African rot. No need for you to feel yourself in jeopardy. Your world might not be perfect, but that other world, that world of the other, is just simply horrid.

In Chinua Achebe's 1977 essay on *Heart of Darkness*, he accuses Conrad of "thoroughgoing" racism and adds:

> That this simple truth is glossed over in criticisms of his work is due to the fact that white racism against Africa is such a normal way of thinking that its manifestations go completely unremarked.

In other words, Conrad not only shares the dominant point of view but makes it stronger. He might prick it with a pin every now and then, but he is by no means threatening the culture. In fact, he is glorifying it. Achebe uses a phrase that I will return to: Conrad is a purveyor of comforting myths.

Where I disagree with Achebe is that, because of the racism in *Heart of Darkness,* he refuses to consider it a masterwork. Like all books, Conrad's novel is limited by his vision, his biases, his worldview. There is no writer with limitless vision, no writer whose worldview is shared by everyone. The problem is not that people read *Heart of Darkness* as a masterpiece—it is one—it's that few read books unsanctioned by empire, and even if you wanted to, there aren't that many available. Today's imperial censorship is usually masked as the publisher's bottom line. "This won't sell" is the widest moat in the castle's defenses.

Heart of Darkness echoes everywhere today. Take the American war novels about Vietnam, Afghanistan, Iraq. They are often considered critical of war, hence you might think of them as dangerous to the institution of war. But most of them deal with the suffering of the American soldiers, the Marines who were forced to massacre a village, the pilots who dropped barrel bombs and came home suffering from PTSD. If anything, this is helpful to the cannibalistic war machine. Such war novels make us feel bad and at the same time allow us to see ourselves as the good guys. We are not all terrible, for we suffer, too.

In one of the most gorgeous passages at the end of *Heart of Darkness,* Conrad describes at length the suffering of a mass murderer's widow, though he glosses over that of the murderer's victims. Conrad did not create the original mold for this kind of writing—from Homer to Shakespeare to Kipling, everyone has done it—but he became the standard because he was so good. We invade your countries, destroy your economies, demolish your infrastructures, murder hundreds of thousands of your citizens, and a decade or so later we write beautifully restrained novels about how killing you made us cry.

Among the many writers who have responded to *Heart of Darkness,* my favorite is Tayeb Salih in *Season of Migration to the North.* This short novel, published in Arabic in 1966 (the first English translation came out in 1969), refers to a number of classic works of Western literature—*Othello, The Tempest*—but primarily it engages with Conrad. Where Conrad wrote of colonialism as a misadventure that forced enlightened man to encounter his opposite in the heart of darkness that is Africa, Salih, who is Sudanese, calls the entire enterprise of empire a "deadly disease" that began "a thousand years ago," a contagion that began with the earliest contact, the Crusades. Conrad's Kurtz is mirrored in Salih's Mustapha Saeed, who leaves his small Sudanese village and moves to his heart of darkness, London. Once enmeshed in the city's web, Saeed decides he will "liberate Africa with his penis." Like Kurtz's time in Africa, Saeed's stay in London results in a trail of dead bodies—his lovers who commit suicide, the wife he murders.

Salih's novel simultaneously emphasizes and breaks down the dualities between self and other, between white and black. Saeed is shown as both the other and the double of the unnamed narrator, a man from the same village. The line demarcating the dualities is not clear-cut. Compared with *Heart of Darkness*, *Season of Migration to the North* is a study in subtlety. Whereas the denizens of Conrad's Africa are "just limbs or rolling eyes" who grunt and snort or are cannibals who want to "eat 'im," Salih's Africans think, act, and speak—an amazing concept. And Salih is more generous than Conrad: he allows the denizens of his heart of darkness to be human as well. Even these imperial interlopers are allowed to talk, if only to act on ridiculously sexist and racist sentiments, as with a woman who says to Saeed, "Ravish me, you African demon. Burn me in the fire of your temple, you black god. Let me twist and turn in your wild and impassioned rites." (There are prejudices and there are prejudices, of course, and suffering under someone else's does not inoculate you from subjecting others to your own. In Salih's book, in other words, sexism "is such a normal way of thinking that its manifestations go completely unremarked.")

The gravitas in Salih's novel is in the return home. Conrad's Kurtz dies, Marlow returns to England a tad traumatized. In *Season of Migration*, both Saeed and the narrator return to Sudan after a stint in London, and they find that they no longer fit where they belong. The narrator says:

> By the standards of the European industrial world, we are poor peasants, but when I embrace my grandfather I experience a sense of richness as though I am a note in the heartbeats of the very universe.

Neither man can be that note any longer; neither can recover the experience of being part of the village. They are caught in countercurrents.

The novel ends with the narrator in the river, not the Thames or the Congo but the Nile, struggling to stay afloat:

> Turning to left and right, I found I was halfway between north and south. I was unable to continue, unable to return. . . . Like a comic actor shouting on a stage, I screamed with all my remaining strength, "Help! Help!"

Think "The horror! The horror!"

Colonialism dislocates you in your own home.

I don't have to tell you that Tayeb Salih is not widely read in our dominant culture; or, to put it in the terms I'm using, he isn't allowed to talk here. He isn't a purveyor of *our* comforting myths. He is, however, read among Arabs, at least among the intelligentsia. The book was published to great acclaim and is now recognized as one of the masterpieces of Arabic literature. So: Is Salih the purveyor of comforting myths in *that* world? His novel might not subscribe to the American Way or the Colonialist Way, but does it subscribe to the Arab or the African Way? One has to wonder if it fits into a dominant Arab culture that blames all its ills on colonialism.

The question is important for me, so let me take it a little further: even though Salih wrote the book in Arabic, he was still a Western-educated man who spent most of his life in London. To the Sudanese, he may be closer than an Englishman, but he isn't exactly one of them, and of course few actual Englishmen would consider him one of their own. He is seen by both sides as the other. Even though his work might sound foreign to most Western readers, his foreignness is the tip of the iceberg, that humongous iceberg of the *other*. Or, if there is such a thing as an otherness scale, then Salih falls at a point along this scale, but not at the far end, and maybe a lot closer than you think.

No matter how bleak things look these days, what with Trump and other racists yelling on the airwaves and committing overt acts of violence, we are living in a time of greater inclusivity than any other. More people are being allowed into the dominant culture, more people are being allowed to talk, maybe not all at the same volume, and there are still not enough voices, but things are quite a bit better than when Salih and Baldwin wrote their novels, and that is reflected in our literature. Every year, novels by women, African Americans, Latinos, queers, by all kinds of *others*, are released alongside the white-male-authored books. We have novels by Somalis, Filipinos, Chinese, Indians, Peruvians, Nepalis, you name it.

World literature is now a genre. And as you might have guessed, I have a problem with this.

Let's take an example: Which Chinese writer gets to talk? Amy Tan was born and raised in California and still lives there, so at times she's a Chinese American writer. Yiyun Li lives in the United States and received her graduate education here, but she was born in China; she's definitely classified as a Chinese writer. They both write in English. Ma Jian lives in London but writes in Chinese. Mo Yan is Chinese and lives in China. He has been accused by the West of not being sufficiently antigovernment, which basically means he does not get to speak for the Chinese. Liu Xiaobo was born and raised and jailed in China, but he was a critic and academic, and who reads that?

It might be fun to play Who Is More Chinese, but that's not the point here. This isn't about good or bad. I love the work of all the writers I mentioned above. What I'm interested in is who gets to talk. Arguably, Tan and Li are the only "Chinese" who are allowed to talk, who are allowed to tell the story in the United States. There might be one or two others. This is still very limiting, not just in terms of how few are permitted to speak but in how the writers are perceived. We're adding another modifier, creating another box—black writer, queer writer, and now the world-literature writer.

On the back cover of one of my novels I am called "one of world literature's most celebrated voices." (I have a voice, I get to talk, though I often have the impression that I'm supposed to do it sotto voce.) If we look at the impressive list of writers who are part of this world literature thing, we see Tan and Li, Aleksandar Hemon representing Bosnia, Junot Díaz representing the Dominican Republic, Chimamanda Ngozi Adichie and Teju Cole representing Nigeria, Hisham Matar for Libya, Daniel Alarcón for Peru, Salman Rushdie for India or is it Pakistan, oh, what the hell, let's give him the entire subcontinent. I get Lebanon.

The thing is that we are all Westerners, if not exclusively American. We have all been indoctrinated with a Western education. We can cite Shakespeare with the best of them.

A number of years ago I was a juror for the Neustadt International Prize for Literature, an award sponsored by the University of Oklahoma and the magazine *World Literature Today*. Since this is an international prize, the jury is always composed of international writers. There were jurors representing Lebanon, Mexico, Egypt, Nepal, Palestine, South Africa, Ukraine, the Philippines, and Italy. Only the Italian actually lived in Italy. The rest of us were primarily Americans, living in the United States, almost all associated with American universities. The Mexican was a Texan, the Egyptian a New Yorker; the Nepali taught at Ohio State. Every interview I did as a juror included questions about peace in the Middle East and whether we can achieve it in my lifetime, what it is like in Beirut, and whether I found the trip to Oklahoma tiring. Norman is a four-hour flight from San Francisco. (And while we're talking about universities: MFA programs are a kind of indoctrination, too. Certain stories, certain types of stories and certain ways of telling stories, are made more valid than others, and this can be dangerous. From the Congo to the Punjab, if you go to Iowa, you will be learning the Iowa Way. You risk becoming a purveyor of comforting myths.)

This is not a discussion of authenticity. I'm not sure I believe in the concept, particularly in literature. Think of Michael Ondaatje's *The English Patient,* a fully imagined novel with four other characters set in other locations. Nabokov did not have to be a pedophile to write *Lolita.* After all, art and artifice are related. What I'm talking about, in my roundabout way, is representation—how those of us who fall outside the dominant culture are allowed to speak as the other, and more importantly, for the other.

This is not to say that we were not, or are not, "world literature." We might be different from what passes for regular American lit, or as I like to call it, common literature. What I'm saying is that there is more other, scarier other, translated other, untranslatable other, the utterly strange other, the other who can't stand you. Those of us allowed to speak are the tip of the iceberg. We are the cute other.

I use the term jokingly, but also deliberately. All of us on that world literature list are basically safe, domesticated, just exotic enough to make our readers feel that they are liberal, not parochial or biased. That is, we are purveyors of comforting myths for a small segment of the dominant culture that would like to see itself as open-minded. I don't mean that as an insult—I love to be read; we all do—but we are serving a purpose that we might not be thinking much about.

In a *New York Times* review, one of my novels was called a "bridge to the Arab soul." I find this phrase discomfiting, mostly because of the words "Arab" and "soul." Is the Arab soul like the American Way? Do Arabs have just one soul, and if so, can someone please tell me how to find it? "Bridge" I understood. You see, my novel was seen not as American but as representing the Arab world. My novel is a bridge to this world of otherness. I get to talk because I am the bridge. No one on the other side of the bridge gets to. And truly, who would want to cross that bridge and touch the heart of darkness, be soiled by that dark other?

We get to talk because we are seen as the nice tour guides. We can hold the hands of readers of the empire as we travel a short distance onto the bridge and get a glimpse of what's across it, maybe even wave at the poor sods on the other side. We make readers feel good about themselves for delving into our books because they believe they are open-minded about the other. We are purveyors of comforting myths.

Now, again, I want to be read. I love holding hands. If there is such a bridge, I'd love to take readers for a stroll along it. I doubt any writer feels differently. What I want is to allow other writers to talk, all kinds of writers, or should I say, more others, more-other others.

The problem today is that this culture we live in is lovely and insidious, able, unlike any that has come before it, to integrate criticism of itself and turn it around faster than Klee's *Angelus Novus* can blink. The culture co-opts others, co-opts their culture, makes us cute and cuddly and lovable, but we never integrate fully.

Every group needs to have an other. I don't know how a society can exist without classifying another as the other. The question for the writers who are getting to talk is where we stand. Inside, outside, in the middle? For so-called world literature writers, it's a troubling question.

You might think this is diversity, but it seems more like homogenization. Sometimes, not always, when I read a novel presented or marketed as foreign, I feel that I'm reading that common thing, a generic novel hidden behind an alluring facade, a comfortable and familiar book with a sprinkling of exoticness. The names of foods are italicized. Instead of visiting Beijing, I end up at its airport with the same bright Prada and Starbucks stores, maybe one dumpling stand in the corner.

And sometimes even that little stand is troublesome. When I wrote a novel about a reclusive woman who bucks society's rules by having a rich inner life filled with books and art, I was surprised by how many readers identified with her, and more so that many considered her a tragic figure because she lived in a country that had no respect for women. You know: we live in an exceptional country, it's only over there where they ostracize women who refuse to conform. (Our world might not be perfect, but that other world, that world of the other is just simply horrid.)

How to get out of this cycle? I don't know. I'm a writer; answers are not my forte. Complaining certainly is. Moreover, as I said above, I'm a writer with a limited view. Like many writers, when I begin a novel, almost all I worry about is making the damn thing work. I move from one sentence to the next, from one section to another, wondering how and whether everything will fit. I try, however, to write in opposition; by that I mean that whenever a consensus is reached about what constitutes good writing, I instinctively wish to oppose it. When I started writing my first novel, a friend suggested I read John Gardner's *The Art of Fiction*, which allegedly explained the principles of good writing. I hated it, not because it was bad advice but because it felt so limiting. Writers are supposed to show, not tell? I wrote a novel where the protagonist does nothing but tell. A short story should lead to an epiphany? Who needs that? When I'm told I should write a certain way, I bristle. I even attempt to write in opposition to my most recent book. If my previous novel was expansive, I begin to write microscopically; if quiet, I write loudly. It is my nature. I don't know whether this childish rebelliousness helps keep my work foreign. Most days, I doubt it. I write a book thinking it is subversive, that it might not be a comforting myth, and if it gets read, if I'm lucky, the dominant culture co-opts it like Goya's Saturn devouring his son.

I might think of myself as living in opposition to empire, or I might insist that I write differently from everyone else, but I recognize that I believe this to make myself feel better. Whenever I read reviews of my work, I notice that I am still the tour guide. "Look at those cute Arabs. See, not all of them are bad. And the homosexuals are nice, too." Which is to say that opposing the dominant culture is like trying to whittle down a mountain by rubbing it with a silk scarf. Yet a writer must. I may not be able to move mountains like Superman, but I have lovely scarves.

◻ ◻ ◻ ◻ ◻

5

HAYAN CHARARA

Going Places

On the morning of September 11, 2001, from the shoreline of the Jersey City neighborhood I lived in, I watched the World Trade Center buildings collapse and engulf the streets below in billowing clouds of debris.

I was scheduled to teach my first class that day as a full-time faculty member at a college in Queens. I'd been living in New York City for seven years, and I had only visited the World Trade Center once, and only the ground floor, to buy discounted tickets to a Broadway show. I never made it to the observatory deck of what was once the world's tallest manmade structure. A few weeks after the start of the semester I admitted this to my students, most of whom were lifelong New Yorkers. To my astonishment, I discovered that barely any of them had been to the now-gone skyscraper either. Or to the Statue of Liberty, or Ellis Island. Only a handful had taken the subway to the Bronx to watch a Yankees game. Even fewer had spent any time in Grand Central Station, except to transfer between trains. I asked if they'd been to the Met, or MoMA, or the Guggenheim, or the American Museum of Natural History. What about the New York Public Library on 42nd Street? Almost every student answered no.

"OK," I said. "Visit a landmark."

I was teaching an introduction to creative writing. In addition to visiting a site, I required they write something related to their visit—a poem, a story, or a scene. One of my students, Mohammed, who was shy and quiet, asked me to suggest a place to go.

"Have you gone up to the Empire State Building?"

He shook his head.

"Go there."

The destruction of the World Trade Center returned to the Empire State Building its status as the city's tallest skyscraper. Mohammed went there, paid the admission fee, and rode the elevator to the 86th floor observatory, which offers visitors three-hundred-sixty-degree panoramic views of Manhattan and the surrounding landscape. On a clear day, a visitor can see for up to eighty miles. After a short while, Mohammed sat down and began collecting his thoughts in a notebook. Within minutes, two men approached him. One talked while the other stood watch.

"What are you doing?"

Mohammed looked up but didn't answer.

"What are you doing?"

"Excuse me?"

The man repeated himself, this time deliberately stopping between each word. "What . . . are . . . you . . . doing?"

"I'm writing."

"What are you writing?"

"Notes."

"Notes?"

The two men looked at each other, and then back at Mohammed.

"What are your *notes* for?"

· ı|ı|ı

Across the country after 9/11, numerous acts of violence were committed against Arabs and Muslims, or against people who merely looked Arab or Muslim. The number of attacks on business owners and employees alone was astounding. I took note of these attacks because my father used to run a grocery store in Detroit.

On September 11, a man in Palos Heights, Illinois, attacked a Moroccan gas station attendant with the blunt end of a machete.

The next day, in Gary, Indiana, a man wearing a ski mask fired a high-powered assault rifle at Hassan Awdah, who survived because he worked behind bulletproof glass.

On the same day, in Long Island, New York, a man with a pellet gun made threats to a gas station attendant who he believed was of Middle Eastern descent.

Nearby in Brooklyn, less than twenty-four hours later, an Arab grocer was threatened with violence by one of his grocery suppliers.

That same day in Salt Lake City, a man tried to set fire to a Pakistani family's business.

Four days later on September 15, in San Gabriel, California, Adel

Karas, 48 years old, of Egyptian descent, was shot and killed. The FBI investigated his murder as a hate crime.

In Mesa, Arizona, Frank Silva Roque gunned down a gas station owner, Balbir Singh Sodhi, because Roque mistook Sodhi for an Arab. After killing him, Roque shot at another man who was Lebanese, and then he fired at the home of an Afghan family.

Also on this day, in Dallas, Waqar Hasan was found shot to death in his grocery store.

Nearly a week after the attacks, on September 17, an Afghan restaurant in Encino, California, was set on fire at 1:40 a.m.

South of San Francisco, in Fremont, an Afghan restaurant was attacked with bottles and rocks.

Further south, on a Los Angeles freeway, someone displayed a sign that read *Kill All Arabs*.

West of Los Angeles, in Oxnard, which is home to two large US Navy bases, four men threw a Sikh grocer to the ground and beat him.

On the 29th, a Yemeni grocer was killed at his convenience store in Reedley, California, after having received a death threat. The grocer's name was Abdo Ali Ahmed.

My student Mohammed noticed, while the two men approached him, that others in the observatory were staring. Soon the two men moved closer. They told him to get up and come with them. When he refused, they flashed badges. They were FBI agents. They found his notetaking suspicious, and they did not immediately believe his college assignment explanation. They interrogated him for a few hours. At our next class meeting, Mohammed told me what had happened. "They might call you," he said, after which he dropped the course and I never saw him again.

ı|ı|ı

A month later the FBI contacted my father, who lived in Dearborn, a suburb of Detroit. Two agents went to his house. The inquiry took place early in the morning. Normally a loud and irate man, my father was nice to them. He welcomed them into his house and asked them if they wanted something to drink. They didn't. They wanted to ask him questions—about me.

"Where does he live?"

"New York."

"Did he contact you on September 11?"

"He called."

"What did he say?"

"He was OK."

"What do you mean?"

"He was OK—nothing happened to him."

"Did he say anything about the attacks?"

"What do *you* mean?"

"Did he say anything about the attacks?"

"No."

"Are you positive?"

"Yes."

The FBI's visit and questions unnerved my father. He was troubled most by what might happen next—to me. I hadn't done anything wrong. He knew that, but he also believed that the FBI could do whatever it wanted. So he gave me advice on how to deal with the agents when they showed up. "Be polite. Offer them coffee. If they stay long, ask them to sit. Don't give them any reason to screw you."

I told him, "Don't worry, I'll be good," but I was indignant at the FBI for suspecting that, because of my ethnicity, I might know more about what took place on 9/11 than the next guy. To let off steam and to let people know what had happened, I shot off an email to friends, family, and colleagues; I explained that being Arab made others believe I had an intimate relationship to treachery and violence. I also sent a letter to the *New York Times* and several other newspapers, and I talked about the incident with my students, my colleagues, and with my fellow poets and writers. The FBI's presumption made me feel negated. No longer a man, or a teacher, or a writer, I had been turned into a suspect, a profile, something less than human.

Eventually, I received a phone call from the Department of Justice. They wanted to know if I would speak with them. I said yes, but only under the following conditions: the agents would have to come to the college where I taught; this way, I could have my colleagues with me as I recorded the conversation. The college president had in fact suggested this. Faculty I hadn't even met volunteered to be at my side.

I never again heard back from the FBI.

ı||ı|ı

A few months later, for the first time since 9/11, I boarded a plane. I was with Rachel, my wife. We were heading to the Midwest to attend two weddings over the same weekend. The itinerary was to fly from New York to Chicago for the first marriage and the next day take a short flight to Detroit for the second. We planned on spending another day in Detroit before heading back to New York.

We purchased our airline tickets at the same time. We requested side-by-side seats. At the airport, we arrived together, and we checked a single piece of luggage. My carry-on was a suit. Rachel brought along knitting materials to keep herself occupied during the flight. Her knitting bag contained a set of sharp metal needles, each more than a foot in length. At the time, security regulations prohibited the carrying-on of such items as nail clippers and small scissors. When she first took up knitting, I used to make wisecracks about using the needles as weapons. "I heard Jesse James once killed a man with knitting needles . . . just for snoring." Given the circumstances, I laid off the jokes. After all, the 9/11 hijackers had overtaken four airplanes using only box cutters.

Somehow, at JFK, at O'Hare, and at DTW, Rachel managed to get the needles, and herself, through security without a hitch. I did not have the same experience. I was pulled aside for a search—*randomly selected*—at every single airport.

ıIıIı

Day after day, he told himself, "I am an American.
I speak American English. I read American poetry.
I was born in Detroit, a city as American as it gets.
I vote. I work. I pay taxes, too many taxes.
I own a car. I make mortgage payments. I am not hungry.
I worry less than the rest of the world. I could stand
to lose five pounds. I eat several types of cuisine
on a regular basis. I flush toilets. I let the faucet drip.
I have central air conditioning. I will never starve
to death or experience famine. I will never die of malaria.
I can say whatever the fuck I please."

The above is an excerpt from a poem of mine titled "Usage." I make no apologies for being an American. I am fully aware of the fact that as an American I am privileged. Because I was born and raised in the United States, I inherited many of the benefits that come with membership in this most prestigious of clubs. But I'm also an Arab man, and as such I am regularly associated with the most negative of traits.

The Arab male is considered by some to be essentially dangerous, uncivilized, barbaric, hostile to Americans and all things American, unreasonable, capable of understanding only through violence and brute force, religiously fundamentalist, possessing little to no regard for human life (especially the lives of innocents), misogynistic, oppressive (to women, to families, to communities, to non-Muslims, and to Muslims), antihuman, anti-Semitic, antimodern, politically militant, uneducated, backwards, militarily weak, illogical, overtly emotional, and intolerant of difference and change (particularly if that change is viewed as progress). Most commonly, Arab men are associated with the sheik, the terrorist, or the religious radical. To make matters worse, for many years public enemy number one was an Arab guy named Osama.

When I lived in Detroit, the perception most people had of Arabs was bad. We were repeatedly called sand niggers and camel jockeys, and we were told to go back to where we came from. We saw ourselves on the news, usually as hijackers or hostage-takers, and strangers worried about what we might do to them. Yet no matter how poorly the media portrayed us then, the lives of every single Arab I knew flew in the face of those depictions. On a daily basis, and several times each day, I encountered Arabs who were not terrorists.

My father was not a terrorist. My mother was not a terrorist. My aunts and uncles were not terrorists. Nor were my cousins or friends. My next-door neighbor, who was Arab and owned a fruit market, was not a terrorist. The Arab students at Fordson High School were not terrorists. The Arabs attending Henry Ford Community College, the University of Michigan, or Wayne State University weren't terrorists either. The cooks and waitstaff at Al-Ameer and Cedarland and La Shish did not turn out to be terrorists. There were no terrorists among the Arab factory workers at Ford and Chrysler and GM. The Arabs I saw at weddings and funerals never blew up planes or buses or themselves. The dancers and singers and musicians at the Arab festivals at Hart Plaza were dancers and singers and musicians, not terrorists.

A lot of people tried hard to tell us otherwise—politicians, journalists, those who positioned themselves as experts on the Middle East, ordinary citizens—but they were all in competition with a formidable opponent: the everyday reality of living in one of the largest Arab communities outside the Arab world. If I had doubts about what it meant to be Arab or wanted to know how Arabs thought or lived or felt, I turned to actual people, not the representations of them. My view was certainly limited, for Arabs in Detroit—and I certainly didn't know them all—obviously did not and could not stand for every other Arab in America. They were, however, a far better example than I found in books or on TV or in the movies or in the news.

ı|ı|ı

When I read about the trial of suspected terrorists in Detroit, or the breaking up of a suspected terrorist cell in Brooklyn, or the arrest of a group of Arabs anywhere in America for plotting a terrorist act, or funding a terrorist organization, you might think my first reaction is suspicion or apprehension. You might think that in hearing about Arabs suspected and interrogated and judged guilty even before a trial, I would conjure up the image of my father, or my uncles, or a neighbor, a friend or cousin, or even the face I see every day in the mirror, and feel indignation. I do, but not always.

When I see the faces of the accused or read their names or hear about them in the news, the first thought I sometimes now have is: *They just might be terrorists.* Now, I don't believe Arabs can never be terrorists. Of course they can. It's the immediate rush to judgment that worries me—to assume right away that possibility, of guilt by association. In the past, if the facts took me to that conclusion, then fine. But I never started out assuming the worst.

They seem different, the Arabs I now see on the news. I know I'm wrong in thinking this. I tell myself to step back a moment, and when I do, after a while, I'm eventually able to reserve judgment and condemnation. Of course, none of this alters the fact that I went there to begin with.

ı|ı|ı

first, please god, let it be a mistake, the pilot's heart failed, the plane's engine died.
then, please god, let it be a nightmare, wake me now.
please god, after the second plane, don't let it be anyone who looks like my brothers.

—SUHEIR HAMMAD, from "First Writing Since"

Unfortunately, the hijackers did look like her brothers—they looked like me.

All nineteen hijackers were Arab, the majority from Saudi Arabia, a few from the United Arab Emirates, one from Egypt, and another Lebanon. They were also young. Except for Muhammed Atta, thirty-three years old, who crashed the first plane into the north face of the North Tower at a speed of roughly five hundred miles per hour, every other hijacker was only in his twenties.

The image of the Arab terrorist was obviously not invented on this most infamous of days. The swarthy Arab, whether portrayed as a hijacker or a suicide bomber or one of many dark, keffiyeh-wearing, gun-toting, American-flag-burning types in a mob, was so engrained in our minds and had for so long been a part of the American imagination that even most intellectual Arabs—poets, scholars, activists—immediately went to that image when it became clear that the crashing of two airliners into the World Trade Center was not an accident. It's hard not to go there. The Arab (especially the Arab Muslim) has been cast as a menace by the Western imagination for nearly fourteen centuries. America came late to the game but caught up quickly, and the dissemination of the "menacing Arab" image is so vast and pervasive, I don't know why I am surprised that even Arabs fall back on the negative stereotypes and presumptions about themselves. If we cannot help but fall into the trap, what chance do men and women who know close to nothing about Arabs have in arriving at something like an uncorrupted image of us?

According to the 2000 census, seventy thousand Arabs live in New York City. That's more than double the number recorded as living in Dearborn during the same period. Yet, for me, Dearborn feels significantly more Arab. A reason for this must be the concentration of so many of them in a relatively small area. I think of my family's house: to the right lives an older Arab woman, and to the left, an Arab family. Across the street and over the back fence, there are more Arab households. In fact, I would have to walk past several blocks of houses before arriving at one in which an Arab does not live. In New York City, I could go days without seeing an Arab. In Texas, where I live now, if not for a handful of friends and a few students at the university where I teach, I could go weeks, even months, without running into an Arab.

When I fly into Detroit, I take I-94 home. I head east. The twelve-ton, eighty-foot-tall Uniroyal tire on the side of the highway still brings a smile to my face. When I pass Telegraph Road, I think of the summers

I worked at Jack Dunworth Memorial Pool, where Dearborn's families—Arab and otherwise—dropped off their kids for hours at a stretch. I continue down the Ford Freeway and pass the exit to the Southfield Freeway, which I took countless times to Fairlane Town Center and where I got into my fair share of trouble as a kid. Across from the shopping center, on Evergreen Road, is Henry Ford Community College, where I taught for a semester and where, for the first time as a teacher, I had Arab students. My family's house, where my sister still lives, is on Dearborn's eastside not far from Hemlock Park, which for a while went by the nickname "Yemlock" because of the Yemeni boys and girls who played there. I go past the house and park and I take Miller Road and keep driving until I reach Warren Avenue. I pull into the parking lot of Al-Ameer Restaurant.

Al-Ameer may not be the best Middle Eastern restaurant in town, but it is still my favorite. I used to eat there two or three times a week. Usually, I sat in a window booth. I liked to see people coming and going, and I was constantly running into friends or acquaintances. The waiters and waitresses knew me—if not by name, then by face or by what I ate. For years, I ordered the same three items off the menu: a shawarma sandwich, a plate of hummus, and a cup of coffee. On one of my visits not long after I'd moved out of Detroit, a former student from HFCC who'd been working at Al-Ameer for some time waited on me. I recognized her immediately, and vice versa.

"Professor," she said, "You want a coffee, right?"

"Yes."

"And a shawarma and hummus."

I smiled and nodded. She turned to walk away, and I stopped her. "I'm sorry, I don't remember your name." She told me, and I greeted her again. "One other thing I don't remember . . ." I hesitated a moment but finally asked, "Did I give you a good grade?"

She thought about it a moment and then returned the smile I had given and walked away.

A short while later, I invited her to sit with me. I had shown up just before the lunch rush, but the restaurant was mostly empty, and I was the only customer seated in her section, so she agreed. We chatted for a while. She was still a student but had transferred to Wayne State University. She was also applying for admission to pharmacy school. She had a daughter, a little girl, about to enter grade school. She was a single mom. I learned more about her in those five minutes than I had in an entire semester.

"What about you," she said. "Where are you now?"

I began telling her about New York but before I got very far a customer showed up and was seated in her section; soon enough the restaurant started filling up. We talked a bit more but only when she came by to refill my coffee—nothing more than chitchat.

In 2004, my father moved back to Lebanon after living in the States for nearly forty years. With him gone, I went to Detroit less and less. Suddenly, I had been away for sixteen years. I still go to Al-Ameer first thing when I visit, and the last time I went, I showed up at dinnertime. The place was packed. I waited close to fifteen minutes before being seated. I asked about my former student—she'd quit a while back, and no one at the restaurant knew what had become of her. I imagined her in a hospital or a pharmacy wearing a lab coat. As for the wait staff, they were entirely new to me. A few of the cooks looked familiar, but I couldn't say for sure if I knew them or if they knew me.

I ordered the usual, and while waiting for my food to come I took a good look around. At nearly every table in the restaurant was a man or a group of men who could have passed for the ones I saw on TV or read about in the papers, those accused of masterminding terrorist plots right under our noses. The thought ran through my mind again: *They just might be terrorists*. Something felt different this time—not for a second did I believe that thought. I realized too that any one of these men I was looking at could have stopped what he was doing and looked up and had exactly the same thought about me—*He just might be a terrorist*—and of course, he would be wrong. For all I knew—for all I know—any of us, any day, could be accused of something sinister. More than ever before, the monumental differences between people and my perceptions of those people were becoming clear to me. Just as meaningful, I also realized, was being *in* a community as opposed to looking at one from the outside. I'd known this my whole life—I relied on it to make my way through the world. I was ashamed for having forgotten. There, in Al-Ameer, I vowed to go back home as often as possible, if only not to forget.

ı|ı|ı

I was living in Detroit during the first attempt to bring down the World Trade Center. On that day, February 26, 1993, I was scheduled for the lunch shift at the Soup Kitchen Saloon, a blues bar now long gone. I showed up to work just as news of the attack was being broadcast on TVs and radios across the country. I walked into the Soup Kitchen Saloon and one of the bartenders, a burly, middle-aged man who liked to joke about everything, stopped me and looked me dead in the eyes. Shaking his head in disgust, he said only, "You people."

I am pretty sure he meant Arabs, but he could have also meant Muslims. It was also possible he assumed these to be one and the same.

If *you people* referred only to Arabs, the facts did not entirely accommodate the reference. Not all the men involved in the 1993 bombing were Arab. Ramzi Yousef and Khaled Shaikh Mohammed, two of the central figures, were of Pakistani descent. If by *you people* the bartender meant to associate me with Muslims, he either knew close to nothing about Islam or he mistook me for the worst kind of Muslim. After all, I worked at a bar, I was dating one of the bartenders, and at the end of my shifts, around 3 a.m., I would pull up a seat at the counter, where he would mix me a drink or pour me a beer. Now and then—sometimes before the start of a shift but more often than not at the end of one—he would offer me a hit from a joint, and several times I took up his offer. I never brought a prayer rug to the saloon. I did not fast during Ramadan, and not once in the time I'd known him had I ever invoked the name of God—not as a Muslim, or as any other kind of believer. Regardless of what he knew about me, on this day he saw me as an Arab and as a Muslim, and in his eyes, put together these were a singular threat. It was also clear that he had arrived at this notion (Arab = Islam = terrorism) long before we had ever met, for he expressed it immediately, less than a minute after hearing about the attack, which was before anyone had claimed responsibility and long before the suspects involved were identified.

He wasn't the only one presuming a link between terrorism and Arabs and Islam, nor was he alone in blurring the distinctions between them. Even supposedly educated persons routinely, and wrongly, used the terms and what they represent interchangeably. This became painfully clear two years later, following the bombing of the Alfred P. Murrah Federal Building in Oklahoma City, not by Arabs or Muslims but at the hands of Timothy McVeigh and Terry Nichols, who were homegrown terrorists. Nearly every journalist and terrorism expert in America took it for granted that behind the worst act of domestic terrorism yet visited upon American soil were men from the Middle East who prayed to Allah. The fact that no Arabs or Muslims were involved did not deter many of these same people from continuing to make sweeping generalizations about the Middle East and Islam. Even after McVeigh and Nichols were arrested, Steven Emerson, a leading authority on terrorism whose documentary film *Jihad in America* aired on public television following the bombing, repeatedly made references to Oklahoma City as a "hotbed of Islamic fundamentalism."

A little over six years later, the sheer scale of the 9/11 attacks seemed to prefigure the extent to which Arabs and Muslims would pay for them. Within months, the United States announced it was going to war in Afghanistan. Soon after, it began making the case for going to war in Iraq. Even the most conservative estimates of the combined death tolls of these two conflicts are staggering. The destruction to the infrastructures of Iraq and Afghanistan, to the land and environment of each country, and to their futures and the future of their people, is equally devastating. Difficult to measure, but deeply felt, is the way the war on terror—of which the wars in Afghanistan and Iraq are a part—affects the lives of Arabs and Muslims in America. One thing is clear: what happens in the war on terror dramatically shapes the way Arabs and Muslims are perceived and treated. As a result of US foreign policy in the Middle East and in the Islamic world, Arabs and Muslims in the United States (many of whom are, of course, Americans) often find themselves having to apologize for crimes they did not commit or having to repeatedly prove loyalties that are never questioned of other Americans.

Over the last few years, a shift seems to have taken place in terms of this byproduct of the war on terror. Americans still worry about Arabs and Muslims, and Arabs and Muslims must still worry about how Americans view them and how their lives will be impacted by those views. But attention has switched over more so to Muslims—Muslims who aren't necessarily Arab. The shift, early on at least, may have had something to do with the fact that since 9/11, a host of incidents involving attacks carried out by people who identify or are identified as Muslim. Two Muslim men, neither of whom was Arab, who each attempted to blow up an airliner over US soil; Richard Reid, the shoe-bomber, a British citizen and convert to Islam, who tried but failed to ignite explosives in his shoes on a December 22nd flight in 2001; the failed attempt, eight years later, by a Nigerian man, Umar Farouk Abdulmutallab, to detonate an explosive on a Detroit-bound flight; the nearly forgotten Jose Padilla, a Latino and a Muslim convert, born in Brooklyn, who most news reports described as having tried to build and detonate what is known as a dirty bomb—a crime for which he was never charged or convicted; the American citizen born in Pakistan who tried to blow up an SUV in Times Square (like the other examples, also a failed attempt). These instances—these Muslims—helped to shift focus.

Of course, these men pale in comparison to the specter of ISIS. With its gruesome tactics, black-clad soldiers, apocalyptic rhetoric (which makes the speeches and declarations of Osama Bin Laden come off as relatively reasonable), and its almost cinematic identity (before ISIS was born, Hollywood had created its predecessors many times), no group or individual can claim to be a greater villain. Those who carried out attacks in the name of ISIS (the so-called ISIS-inspired attackers) upped the ante by bringing the villainy to places like San Bernardino and Orlando—places that, despite their fears (real or imagined), many Americans believed to be safe.

When I travel now, which is more frequently than in the first few years after the September 11th attacks, I experience the shift that is taking place. Which is to say I am hardly searched anymore, or bothered in any way, except for the usual—waiting in long lines and having to keep up with changing regulations about what can and cannot be carried onto a plane. These, however, are inconveniences most everyone endures. Arabs are still profiled. Just ask them. But attention is moving away from Arabs—not entirely, but significantly—and toward Muslims. For a while, this turn paralleled the shift in attention of US foreign policy. While the Reagan-era war on terror focused mainly on the Middle East threat, as did the Bush-era's, the Obama administration's version focused more on Islam. The spotlight turned from the Arab world—again, not entirely, but significantly—and toward Afghanistan, Pakistan, Indonesia, and even Africa. The Arab Spring, with the disintegration of Syria, the rise of ISIS, and the terrorist attacks in European cities, have returned the attention of world leaders, and their militaries, back to the Arab world. But more than ever, perhaps, the Arab world is seen as Muslim—more specifically, as a Muslim threat, even when (as with the refugees pouring in from Syria and elsewhere) they are the primary victims of the actual threat.

For many Americans, Muslims are easier to spot than Arabs. Islam marks Muslims, at least the more traditional among them. The headscarf worn by women, the hijab, serves as a marker, as does the abaya sometimes worn by both men and women. These and other signs—entering a mosque, praying, reading a Qur'an, and so on—are read as signs of an Islam that is understood to be the polar opposite of everything American and Western or modern and civilized. By this logic, Islam is a thing to be feared; it is the ultimate threat. Today, we are more likely to hear about a group of Muslims—rather than a group of Arabs—being asked to get off a plane. In most cases, the removal is prompted by the concerns of a passenger who was made to feel, in some way, uncomfortable by the Muslims on board. Features or traits as inherently non-threatening as a headscarf or a beard have caused people to feel unsafe. In one case a Muslim family was removed from a flight after one of them commented, in English, about the safest place to sit on a plane. The Council on American-Islamic Relations noted in a complaint to the US Department of Transportation, "We believe this disturbing incident would never have occurred had the Muslim passengers removed from the plane not been perceived by other travelers and airline personnel as members of the Islamic faith."

An ABC News story from a few years ago about opposition to the building of a mosque highlighted and brought to national attention the extent to which "Islam" is deemed threatening. The Islamic Center of Murfreesboro, which has had a center in the small Tennessee town since 1997, planned to build a larger facility. At a county commission meeting where over six hundred residents turned out to express their concerns about the new mosque, Allan Jackson, the pastor of World Outreach Church, said, "We have a duty to investigate anyone under the banner of Islam." Of the Muslims living in Murfreesboro, one resident was quoted as saying, "They seem to be against everything I believe in, and so I don't want them necessarily in my neighborhood."

I have no doubt that I experience less discrimination now (especially on airplanes) in large part because there is little about my appearance or manner of dress that labels me a Muslim. I look Arab. That's undeniable. I have the dark hair and dark eyes, and the stereotypical Middle Eastern nose and bushy eyebrows. But more than Arab or Middle Eastern, the markers that the fearful and the reactionary and the ignorant and the bigoted among us are looking for are Muslim. An irony of all this is that for a very long time now, people from all walks of life have worked hard to explain and make clear the distinctions between things Arab and things Muslim—many people are now finally making distinctions, but for all the wrong reasons.

ıiıı

A few hundred Arab Muslims gather, elbow to elbow. The atmosphere is that of a fair. There are signs in the prevailing languages, rows of newspaper boxes, magazine stands, smells of food in the air, smokers arguing politics around ashtray stands, garbled announcements made over loud speakers, flashing lights and sirens, carousels, and, every few minutes, on center stage, an airplane touching down or taking off.

The flight, which originated in Mecca, finally lands and the crowd erupts with cheers. Several of the Arabs and Muslims, young men, join hands and raise them high above their heads and dance in a circle. Later, as the arrivals they've been waiting for begin exiting customs, a chorus of trills fills the terminal.

We're in the Michael Berry terminal of the Detroit Airport. I'm with my parents. We're standing next to a young woman with braided blond hair. She is wearing a Star Wars T-shirt and dark blue jeans. If her hair were just a few shades darker, she'd look like Brooke Shields in the famous Calvin Klein ads. My mother turns to her and asks, "Who are you here for?"

"My boyfriend," she says smiling.

"Ah. Was he on the Hajj?"

"The . . . ?"

"The Hajj."

"I don't think so," she says with a degree of uncertainty and tugs at her hair. "He's on American Airlines."

"Oh, I thought . . ."

But before my mother has a chance to explain or change the subject, the woman looks away, taken by the scene the Muslims are making, which is boisterous, carefree, and jubilant, as if they are celebrating a marriage, not the arrival of a flight. A minute or two later, she turns back around.

"Can I ask you something?"

My mother nods her head.

"These people coming off the plane," she says, and once more she gives the crowd a long hard look and takes a deep breath. "Are they all like famous movie stars or something?"

ılılı

In 1982, a young woman mistakes a mass of Muslims and Arabs for celebrities. This is one of the most vivid memories I have of Detroit in the pre-9/11 world—that of airports and air travel, of the way that some people saw Arabs and Muslims. How much has changed? Today, I simply cannot imagine a few hundred Arabs and Muslims descending on a major US airport without incident. When I travel by airplane, I present myself accordingly. Before leaving for the airport, I shave so not to resemble too much the physical profile of a hijacker. At the airport, I never request last-minute changes to my itinerary so as not to send the wrong message. At security, I smile and make pleasant chitchat but I don't overdo it. I keep my small talk to *Hello* or *Good morning* or *Have a nice day*. I don't want to give anyone any excuse to single me out. I wear shoes without laces so I can pass quickly through security, and I never wear my favorite T-shirt, which has on its front the stylized McDonald's *M*, and just beneath the golden arches, the fast food giant's name spelled out in Arabic. Years ago, my fellow passengers might have found the graphic amusing. Now, it would probably alarm them, so I leave it at home. My goal is to reach my destination on time. The last thing I want to do is encourage security personnel to have an extended conversation with me about who or what I am, or what I am not.

I liked going to the airport once. I met people there—grandparents, aunts and uncles, cousins—for the very first time. My family got dressed up to meet airport arrivals. Sometimes, we drove to the airport early to eat dinner there. The airport was fun. When I was a boy, I thought of the terminal as a kind of playground. I played games with other children—races up and down the escalators, hide-and-seek in the visitor waiting areas, and when no one was paying attention, rides on the baggage carousels. Even as an adult, for a few short years at least, I liked going to the airport. So much so, now and then I would receive phone calls from friends who were stuck in the terminal during a layover, and I would drive out to meet them for a drink at the airport bar.

Not anymore. That chapter of American life is over. Gone with it, I suspect, is the innocence of the young woman who asked my mother about the men and women returning from the Hajj. She expressed not fear but something like exhilaration, even wonder, at being surrounded by so many Arabs and Muslims. She wasn't threatened. She didn't immediately arrive at the worst possible conclusions. She didn't think terrorists or hijackers or villains. She thought movie stars.

◻ ◻ ◻ ◻ ◻

6

SAFIA ELHILLO

at the intersection

american boys who flirt with me often open with the question, *what are you.* if i am feeling cute i say, *an alien. a sagittarius.* simpler times, before the world started to crack along all its invented edges. now i wake up every day more tired, every day at the intersection of what is most hated, most hunted. black. arabophone. muslim. a woman too, so my death might not get a name.

&, you know, american muslim, taking my god for granted. *ya allah, the benevolent, the merciful. hi.* now six, seven prayers a day, just to offer the plea each night: *please let everyone i love still be alive tomorrow.*

please don't forget us. i am here i am here & it hurts.

fourth of july, second to last day of ramadan, end of a week marbled by explosions. holy month i used to think would protect us, would lock all the demons away. our neighbors set off fireworks & don't know what the sound means in the rest of the world. i sit inside & watch the news even though it makes me tired. i watch gray bits of body carried from piles of rubble. died breaking their fast. died drinking mint tea. died buying little gifts for loved ones for eid.

& on eid, still dressed in our bright festival scarves & gold, hands painted with henna, we watch the black man on the news dripping blood. our wound reopens & our holiday clothes turn to mourning garb. my brother is out late at a party & everything in my body tells me that he too is dead. killed for his skin or his god or the language he calls home. killed for his height or the length of his name. everything in my body tells me that we, all of us filling up dark bodies, are all dead. a race with more dead than left alive. a ghost people, haunting the world that killed us.

i hear him return at dawn & only the smell of leftover molokheya heating in the microwave can convince me he still lives in his body.

i spend days & nights & hours at poetry readings where we pick our scabs & name & rename our traumas & most days i am desensitized, immune by habit to the smell of conjured blood. but tonight a poet says a dead black name & the hurt reopens & this time i cannot close it back up. & they all float backwards into the room, every ghost, the ones i knew & the ones i will never meet & the ones i know only by name, the ones whose names we never learned. all the missing dead & all the murdered dead & all the ones assigned a bullet at birth. light pouring from their wounds. this time i cannot make them go away.

   i wake up in the mornings unconvinced that i am still alive. i line up my wet blue hurts & take inventory of the things that mark me to die. bloodied language in my throat. my hunted god. my black hand pressed to my black mouth to keep the tears in.

◌ ◌ ◌ ◌ ◌

7

JOSEPH GEHA

Where I'm From—*Originally*

"You're not from around here, are you."

The man had put it like a statement, but I recognized the question that was being implied. By that time, having lived around here for over a dozen years, I also knew that if I didn't answer as expected, I'd be leaving the door open for the outright questions that were certain to follow: *Where are you from?* and *No, but I mean, where originally?* Asked openly, I ought to add, in a friendly spirit. Even so, I still wasn't used to it. I tried a smile.

"That's right," I said, and volunteered nothing more. I was just asking for trouble, of course.

"So, where are you from?"

I turned and faced the man fully now. "Toledo," I told him. Which I knew perfectly well wasn't at all what he was asking. He looked to be a nice sort, a youngish grandfather. Why was I being so contrary? All he was doing was making small talk. It was a sunny autumn day and here we'd found ourselves two adults among children—my daughters, his grandkids—on line at a county fair carrousel in Iowa. The white crispness of the short-sleeved shirt he had on, along with his hairless arms and clean, pink-tipped fingers made me think he was maybe a dentist. That, and his no nonsense persistent manner.

"Originally?" he said, as if to specify.

I answered "Ohio. Toledo, *Ohio*," pretending to specify too, since there is a Toledo, Iowa not far from here. I was behaving badly. Was it my fear of dentists? My nerves frayed from being with the kids all day? It was not as if this man's curiosity wasn't understandable. After all, I didn't look like I was from around here—here being a part of the country that was more familiar with a pale-skinned, blonde Scandinavian/ Irish/ German mix than with the olive skin and black curly hair common to people from Lebanon.

Nor could he know that I heard that question a lot around here, the last time only a few days before. I'd taken my daughters swimming, and a little blonde girl they'd made friends with at the pool kept glancing at me out of the corner of her eye. I was in a bathing suit, and I'm fairly certain it was the body hair. "Your dad's not from around here, is he," she stated just as I dove under water. Surfacing, I heard, "No, I mean *originally*."

In '71, before the war in Lebanon, I visited Zahleh, the town where I'm from—originally. Although I'd bought my clothes locally, I was easily recognized (from my manner? my gait?) for an Americanized Lebanese. Even so, I still felt I fit in. The people looked as if they all could be members of my family. I could see where my sister got her classic dark beauty. The men looked like my brother, my father, me. I saw hair that grew in the same curly whorled patterns as my own. I remember one small boy in particular, dashing past me with a familiar lopsided, just-got-in-trouble grin that instantly brought to mind my own face as a child shortly after we came to America; me grinning and saluting for the camera on the pavement in front of my father's newly opened grocery on Monroe Street in Toledo.

I felt the same grin forming on my face as the dentist, having helped his smallest grandchild onto a pastel pony, stepped down off the carrousel to join me once more.

"No," he said, taking right up where he'd left off, "no, I mean *originally*." He squinted a pale eye at me as if to underscore his persistence.

"Ah, you mean *originally*. The country of my *origin*, you mean!" I was taking it too far, and I considered relenting. Back in the sixties I used to save bus money by hitchhiking to my classes at Toledo University. I didn't find it strange that on the basis of my looks the driver might begin talking to me in a foreign language (Greek, Yiddish, Italian, Spanish—eventually I learned to identify them all). In Toledo, with its ethnic mix, this wasn't unusual. My parents used to do it, calling out *Ibn Arab intah?* to any olive-complected fellow on the corner or in the car next to us at a stoplight, while my brother and sister and I slid groaning to the backseat floor, out of sight of the stranger's puzzled shrug.

Now the dentist waited, and I could feel my grin widen as his eye unsquinted for my answer.

Which I delivered straight, deadpan: "Norway."

He didn't call me a liar. Instead, he simply nodded his head. This was Iowa—heaven in the movies—and not only are the people nice, they have a hard time believing anyone else is not nice.

But, being an Iowan myself after all these years, I couldn't leave him like this. Besides, Iowa's a small world; what if I needed dental work some day? (I pictured myself in the chair, helpless, and him in his business whites, pliers in hand: "Norway? I'll give you Norway!") So I took it all back, beginning with, "Not really."

What I didn't tell him was that most of my life, child and adult, had been an attempted escape from my Arab roots, and that these innocent questions—from dentists, from my daughters' playmates—were reminders that I hadn't yet blended into the Great American Melting Pot.

ılılı

My family left Lebanon and came to America at the end of World War II, when I was still a toddler; we traveled by ship and underwent processing at Ellis Island. It wasn't until I started first grade that I began to speak English. So I remember feeling different at an early age, and not liking the feeling; I was teased for my accent, for the garlicky smelling food in my lunch box. I remember schoolmates calling me "Dirty Syrian," chasing me and yelling at me to go back where I came from. (They didn't know any better; being kids, they were slow to extend to humans the empathy they lavished on puppies and goldfish.) When they eventually did know better, many of them would become the first friends I ever made. I remember too how American women made a fuss over my thick curls, pausing in department store aisles to pat them fondly with their white-gloved palms. Of course, I was fully aware of how cute those curls were. But I also remember wanting those curls to be blond. Because Americans, real through-and-through Americans, were blond. They had blue eyes. And nobody would ever think to tell a blond-haired, blue-eyed American to go back where he came from.

During the first couple years of school, my accent faded, and I remember helping it along, mouthing Peter Piper and his peck of pickled peppers over and over on the long walks home. (More than a tongue twister for Arabic speakers, since the language has no 'P' sound.) Perversely, this accomplishment seemed to only make me all that much more aware of my parents' heavy accents. Fixing a self-conscious gaze on my mother and father, I was ashamed at the way they haltingly massacred English in front of Americans (who, from my view, were an impatient, finger-drumming lot), but I'd be absolutely *mortified* whenever they backslid into Arabic. They couldn't open their mouths around me, neither in Arabic nor in English. They couldn't win either way, those two.

After school, I wanted to eat only American food. I insisted that my mother make hamburger for dinner; and she—being a good sport—not only gave it a try, she figured to do hamburger one better. And so, what I ended up getting was more like lamb-burger, with garlic and parsley and vinegary onions ground into it. Couldn't she see that I didn't want better than hamburger? What I wanted was not to be different.

My new-found friends weren't much consolation in this; they never seemed to notice the differences so much, or if they did, they invariably took my mother's side. For reasons that are obvious enough to me now but which I couldn't at the time fathom, my mother's cooking was famous among my friends. They loved being asked to stay for supper, even though this meant being served something as strange as lemon chicken stuffed with pine nuts and pilaf and ground cinnamon lamb; sweet greens cooked down in olive oil and garlic, then mashed and rolled into well-salted, paper thin bread; almond butter cookies or baklava for dessert.

ıĺıĺı

I had begun writing fiction while working nights in the stockroom at Sears, Roebuck and Company and attending the University of Toledo on partial scholarship.

Luckily, the first teacher I showed any of it to—Gregory Ziegelmaier, a young playwright who was new to the English faculty—proved to be both kind and generous in his encouragement. From my first course with him, he urged me to begin taking my writing seriously. Sometimes I used to drop by during his office hours just to chat—about writing, usually, or the advantages of one program of study over another. And because he seemed interested, I soon found myself telling him about my family, about my parents having had less than three years of schooling between them, about my father being so superstitious he kept a piece of what he called the True Cross wrapped in a bandage under his armpit, claiming that if he lost it he would lose all his luck, about my mother uttering startled blessings whenever I chuckled over something funny in a book—she never could understood how, outside of demonic possession, anyone staring at an inanimate object could suddenly be moved to laugh out loud. Another time I told him the story of how my father had tricked the steamship officials when my sister came down with typhoid the day before we were scheduled to sail from Beirut, rouging her fever-yellow face and tickling her to alertness as we ascended the gangplank. I told him about how my whole family got stuck on an escalator in our first days here—the stairs in America just wouldn't stay still! And about the childless Jewish couple who adopted our family, about the trip to the art museum (where, we were told, they have pictures on the walls and music) that ended with all of us listening to piped music on the lawn of a gas station that was celebrating a grand opening, its plate glass windows painted with cartoon characters.

My teacher enjoyed these stories, and I had to admit that I liked telling them. So why, he wanted to know, wasn't he seeing any of this in my writing? Taking my writing seriously meant, of course, taking my experience seriously too, including my immigrant heritage.

But what he didn't understand was that to include such material would be to identify myself with exactly what I'd been avoiding all my life. So, while my writing skill improved under his guidance, even my better stories remained imitations in the mode of whatever writer I currently admired.

ılılı

My first teaching job was over seven hundred miles away from home, at a college in Springfield, Missouri. The people there were friendly, welcoming—in fact, they were downright sunny. Strangers trimming hedges chirruped hellos as I bicycled past their tidy yards. The mailboxes all bore standard American names like Anderson, Stone, Douglas, Brady. If I looked hard enough I'd probably find Cleaver, too. Word had it that the wife of Gene Autry—the cowboy hero of my childhood—had once attended school here. The campus itself, like the town, was a sea of freckled good looks. Who'd have thought that this country had such a concentration of blonde-haired adults? (I hadn't yet been to Iowa.)

I'd located the real America, as only television of the fifties could have imagined it, and I was determined to belong.

So why, after a few weeks, did I find myself giving in to the urge to grow back the beard that I'd shaved off months before for my job interview? Sure, beards were common enough then—then being 1968 and the dawning of the Age of Aquarius. But this was also the Deep Midwest, where college men still wore crew cuts and flattops. What was I up to growing a black curly beard? Well, this much was clear: if blending in was my aim, I seemed to be having second thoughts.

In fact, I was having a whole chain reaction of second thoughts, all triggered by the most minor incidents. For example, one day in my first month there I remember standing at a supermarket counter and waiting while the checkout clerk searched for an item on her produce price list. Finally, she indicated the item, a bulb of garlic, and asked me in her soft Missouri twang, "Whatcha call this?"

"You mean garlic?" I asked.

She nodded and thanked me. A small thing, memorable only because at a different grocery less than a week before another clerk had asked me the same question about a bunch of parsley. "This is parsley—right?" she'd said.

I was amazed. How could somebody not know parsley? Swiss chard, I could understand. Endive. Even watercress. But ordinary parsley? And garlic! What sort of pot was I melting into here? Instead of being eager to blend right in, I found myself holding back, realizing that I did want to be different, after all—but on *my* terms.

Meanwhile, during session after session at my writing table, my mind kept straying to images of Monroe Street in morning sunlight, and my brother a small boy on its pavement sweeping wine bottles from the entrance to our father's store; hearing the mutter and coo of pigeons and looking up at the flat tarred roofs for the arrival of the homeless man we called the Pigeonman who used a fishing rod to snag pigeons and sell them to my father for food. I saw the apartment above the store, and myself, dark-eyed and olive-skinned, looking like exactly what I was, an Arab boy in a Gene Autry cowboy hat, peeking from behind the blue velvet armchair at the window, watching my mother serve Turkish coffee to the aunt who wore two pairs of glasses on her nose at once, and the uncle who was so simple that even my brother and sister and I used to look at one another and wink.

Now in Missouri, living far from those streets, and as if freed up by the distance, I found available to me the landscapes of my past—people, situations, places—all that I'd rejected while breathing the actual air of those landscapes.

ı|ı|ı

Fiction, as I tell my students, presents us with the opportunity to walk in someone else's shoes, and picturing the other guy—in this case the Arab American immigrant—as a complex person with human frailties as well as human virtues, defeats the possibility for sentimental simplifying: good or bad, black or white, us or them.

Such a lesson is especially important today, when the politically hot Middle East has turned even hotter, when Arab American businesses are fired upon and torched, and college-educated students in Ames, Iowa chant *Death to all Arabs!* out their dorm windows.

These feelings are understandable; it's difficult not to get carried away at the sight of classmates and neighbors marching off in desert camouflage. And yet, *all Arabs* includes me, includes my daughters; the words alone do damage.

To say that gunmen and arsonists don't know any better may or may not be stating the obvious. But the chanting students? As understandable as their feelings are, and despite their college educations, I must conclude that they too simply don't know any better—just as I had to conclude years ago when I was mocked for speaking with an accent and thinking my thoughts in another language. Those students, smart as they are, need to get out of their own shoes for a while. Reading stories can help them to do that. Most fiction, if it's any good at all, asks that the reader use at least some measure of empathy—that particularly human faculty whereby one can appreciate what an experience must feel like for someone else. The reluctance to feel empathy can express itself in intolerance for the unfamiliar, in self-preoccupation and narcissism. At the very least it hinders maturation; it's children who stomp on anthills, the emotionally stunted who douse cats in gasoline. Empathy, on the other hand, has a maturing effect and leads us into the world.

ııliı

Shortly after my collection of short stories first came out, I was invited to give a reading at a bookstore in St. Paul, Minnesota. I'd never been to the Twin Cities before, and knew no one from there, so I was quite surprised when a total stranger, an older woman from the audience approached me afterward with a familiar "Hello, Mr. *Jeha*," giving my last name its Arabic pronunciation. What really floored me, though, was her adding, "You're one of Elias' boys aren't you, the littler one they called Zuzu?"

I hadn't heard myself called Zuzu—the Arabic diminutive for Yousef—since I was five years old. (Entering first grade, I remember how I'd insisted that even at home I be called Joe, an American nickname.) It was a shock, hearing the first name of my childhood pronounced by a total stranger.

Who, of course, turned out not to be a stranger at all, but a distant cousin who used to visit Toledo regularly years ago, and she remembered my family when we first arrived in America. Her smile, and the sidelong glance that came with it, I recognized from my father's side of the family.

So now, in a city where I knew no one, I found it was, ironically, my turn to be asking the question: "Where did you come from?"

"Here."

"No, I mean originally."

"Originally," she replied. "I was born in St. Paul, a mile from this spot. I've lived here all my life."

Here? Here looked blonder than Iowa and Missouri put together! And the odd thing was, the more we chatted, the more it began to make sense; why couldn't she be one of my people as well as from around here *originally*? Why not, indeed? After all, who said America must be a melting pot into which we drain and disappear? The nineteenth century, that's who. The Great Melting Pot has always been a nineteenth century notion, and I'd just as soon it stayed there, along with the know-nothings and Manifest Destiny. I prefer instead an image I'd come across more and more in recent years—that of the mosaic. The American Mosaic. Common sense tells us that the American immigrant experience resulted not from melting down the uniqueness in each separate one of us, but from arranging those pieces and joining them together toward the design of a larger more complex picture, one that makes use of differences to create richness and power and harmony. The achievement of which is the promise of Ellis Island. And the struggle for which, in the stories I've written, is what America is all about.

◻ ◻ ◻ ◻ ◻

8

HADIL GHONEIM

Baba and the Pontiac

I saw the words *Pontiac Trail* on the green street sign and a chill ran down my spine. I had just moved to Ann Arbor from the East Coast and didn't expect to be reminded of Baba on this quiet road on the north side of town. I drove by the sign a few more times for no other reason than to feel that tingle again and think about Baba, his cars, and the bitterness they caused in our family. When I ventured out to Detroit, I found in its defaced grandness something strangely and deeply familiar. Why did my father, who never set foot in America, suddenly reappear to me between the rust and the dust of the once-booming city that used to be compared to the gold rush towns of the American West?

When he was a little boy, Baba asked his parents to buy him a horse. He told us this story to back up his rejection anytime my brothers or I requested money for a reason he thought ridiculous. The horse certainly was laughable, not only because his father, who was an Arabic teacher, had seven other children, but also because unless you were a mounted policeman, no one was seen riding a horse in the streets of Cairo in the early 1940s. I doubt that he had ever been to the horse races that took place in some of the elite sports clubs back then. Many years later, while we watched an old Western together, Baba told me that Errol Flynn and John Wayne were his childhood heroes. He even made an impression of the latter by squinting his eyes while drawing on a cigarette. I am guessing that the horse wish came from those Westerns.

The boy soon grew out of his Hollywood-induced fantasies and understood the limits of his parents' means. While still studying for his undergraduate law degree, he couldn't stand to be reined in for four years in his family's crowded apartment and make do with a small allowance from his father. He studied for a teaching diploma on the side, and in a year, started to earn his own small salary. It was nice to have a little extra so he could go out and have a good time, but it was not enough to gain him full independence. Until one day he read about job opportunities in Kuwait. Not many Egyptians had ever traveled there, or even heard about that tiny country sitting on the northeastern edge of the Arabian peninsula on the shores of the Persian Gulf. The massive oil reserves discovered there just before the end of WWII generated wealth and a need for all kinds of jobs to build the newly enriched state. Baba immediately joined the oil rush to the eastern frontier of the Arab world, first as a schoolteacher, and then, after finishing his law degree, as a legal expert in the government. He was quickly able to replace his childhood dream of owning a horse with the reality of owning horsepower. He started with a small Mini Austin of about forty horsepower that he drove around Cairo when he got engaged to my mother. By the time they got married in the early 1960s, he had bought himself a mighty 1961 Pontiac Parisienne that packed the power of more than two hundred horses.

That Pontiac was a classic American beauty. A long and wide yellow convertible with sparkling nickel and chrome trim, and gray leather seats with yellow stripes running down the middle. My mother remembers the original paint color of their car as "chickpea yellow," which is a shade easier for me to imagine than "bamboo cream," as General Motors lists it. The only yellow vehicles I ever get to see on the streets now have much less dreamier shades. They are usually cabs, tractors, or school buses. On the Internet, I found an old Canadian TV commercial for the 1961 Pontiac, in which a slick man wearing a suit asks the viewers: "Are you thinking of your holidays? Where would you like to go?" After showcasing every feature of the car—from the twin grill to the six engine—he urges, "Cross Canada with Pontiac."

In 1960s Kuwait, however, there weren't that many places to go or much to do for the young couple who, having grown up in a big city like Cairo, needed a little more stimulation. The nearest and liveliest attractions lay north of Kuwait, in Iraq, where the weather was also cooler. My mother said that they would drive up there some weekends, especially the long ones, like when it was an Eid holiday. By the mid-sixties, they had two boys and enjoyed driving them around to visit the ancient sites in Babylon, Sameraa, and Baghdad. I have an old photo of my mother, in her puffy sixties hairstyle, posing in front of a huge statue of a lion that reminds me of the ram-headed sphinxes in Luxor.

But my family was more interested in the local food in Iraq than in the antiquities of past civilizations, or at least it appears this way, because of how they still recall these culinary memories in detail. My mother said that on every trip they would buy local fresh meats and dairy straight from the farmers and carry it back to Kuwait. I know from my old geography school textbooks that water buffaloes are raised only in a few countries, including Iraq and Egypt, and they produce rich butter and ghee and creamy cheeses. According to my picky brother, the milk of water buffaloes is tastier than cow's milk and not as smelly. That picky one still remembers the date syrup he had in an Iraqi village a long time ago. The black honey made from dates is believed to be the reason why Iraq was called the land of milk and honey. Yet the real highlight of those trips, I'm told, was masgouf, which entailed not only a special dish of delicious grilled fish, but an entire afternoon riverside outing spent in any of the casinos serving it on the banks of the Tigris.

I was told that later on, Baba decided to take the Pontiac to Egypt. It meant that instead of the annual two-hour flight from Kuwait to Cairo where our family spent summer vacations, he had to make a road trip from Kuwait, across Iraq, and through a part of Syria to Lebanon, where he shipped the Pontiac from Beirut to Alexandria. The car had to complete the last leg of the trip in that little Mediterranean Sea cruise, because otherwise Baba would have had to drive through a Palestine that was increasingly becoming Israel, by way of a scalding regional conflict. The Pontiac crossed the whole Fertile Crescent in about three days. Baba made that road trip a few times in different cars, with the boys joining him on only one of them, in 1973. They still remember how the heat of the arid dry desert of western Iraq was unbearable, like the hot air coming out of my mother's hair dryer. Baba drove while they slept, snacked, and listened to a tape recording of the comic Egyptian adaptation of *To Sir, With Love*. The desert frightened them in the night; they dreaded the fierce dogs when Baba stopped once to nap in the car. They were not dogs but Arabian wolves. Once they reached Mount Lebanon, it was like the AC had been suddenly plugged in, and a totally different scene emerged, one with white-tipped mountains and an evergreen carpet of cedar trees. Driving through the mountains on narrow roads at nighttime was exciting only for the boys. It was a terrifying ordeal for my mother, who recalls nothing of the scenery, because she would be busy praying and reciting verses from the Quran with her eyes nervously shut. She did have fun in Beirut, though, where they would visit Lebanese friends, who were also fellow expats in Kuwait, and go out at night in the swinging city of the Arab world. One time she recalls, they were about to ship a car when the port workers went on strike so they got to spend the extra day boating around the caves of the Jeitta grottos.

The Pontiac arrived in Egypt in the late sixties and stayed there. For their annual summer vacation, my family of was joined by extended family, and the Pontiac would squeeze in as many aunts and cousins and grandparents as it possibly could, and they would all drive north from Cairo to the beaches of Alexandria. After a few days, they would head westward along the southern Mediterranean coast, almost all the way to the Libyan border. It was worth the extra drive, because the farther west you go to the beaches of Marsa Matroh and Sidi AbdulRahman, the whiter and finer the sands become, and the deeper the azure color of the sea, trimmed with sparkling streaks of turquoise.

One day Baba was sitting in his Pontiac, stuck in Cairo traffic, when a man dangling from a nearby streetcar yelled at him jokingly, "It's a socialist country now, and tomorrow we'll all be riding like you!" Baba laughed and shot back in true Cairene street spirit: "It's a socialist country now, and tomorrow I'll be riding with you!" Despite the fancy cars Baba bought, we really weren't the kind of people that were hurt by nationalization, for we were neither landowners nor industrialists in the ancient regime. Baba actually supported Nasser and his socialism, his pan-Arabism, and his anticolonial battles. I think he would have been amused to know that the Pontiac was named after an American Indian chief, who, like Nasser, revolted and fought against British occupation. In any case, things started to get bad for us as a family around the time I was born in the mid-seventies, and it was not because of state socialism.

Baba's enterprise based on buying cars in Kuwait and shipping them to Egypt wasn't a very good idea. Other families were investing their petrodollar savings in real estate or other businesses. Baba would not admit to himself that he just loved shopping for a car and driving it across borders and spending time customizing it. He told himself (and his wife) that his affair with cars was a business investment, and that the plan was to rent the American cars out to the police force and the film industry, and the Ladas and Fiats to the taxi drivers. However, an operation like this needed to be overseen, and Baba was in Kuwait most of the year and not that interested in business management either. He probably rented out one or two for a year so and that was it. He didn't even resell them. At one point he had eight or eleven cars (my parents debating the correct number usually resulted in a long shouting match). Baba's cars became a money pit, or a curse, as my mother prefers to describe it. They all met their demise one way or another, one of the more painful losses being that of the fancy 1971 Oldsmobile. The Cairo municipality removed it in the early eighties, when they were replacing gas pipes in the street where it was parked. Its papers were missing and somehow Baba never saw it again.

The recreational road trips stopped too. Wars were breaking out here and there, and the days of open borders between Arab countries came to an end, as did the ideology that proclaimed it. The last road trip Baba made across the Fertile Crescent was when my mother was pregnant with me. Her water broke as civil war erupted in Lebanon, and a few years after that the Iraq–Iran war started, followed shortly by the Israeli invasion of southern Lebanon. The invasions and the wars never quite ended from then on. That is why I never went on any of those legendary trips; I never got to eat masgouf on the banks of the Tigris, nor drive across Syria and reach Mount Lebanon.

It's not fun to be born during the years of decline and only hear stories or look at pictures of past glories. It made me relate to Detroit in the way I'd like to slow down when passing through its decay, hoping to capture a trace or hint from its golden years. Another war much related to the wars that ended my family's road trips caused the oil crisis that cast a dark spell on the Motor City. It became impossible to continue manu-facturing cars like the Pontiac and the Oldsmobile. The gloom started to descend on both parts of the world around the same time.

Baba left Kuwait altogether when I was six. My brothers followed him to Egypt, one after the other, to attend college or boarding school in preparation for college. I stayed on for a few more years with my mother, who had started covering her hair like most women there at the time. She taught math in a middle school and was quite happy at her job. I thought there was something particularly wrong with my family, divided like that between two countries and only getting together during summer vacations. Recently though, I realized that it was not just us. Many expat families living in Kuwait were similarly dispersed. The rush to the Gulf was not for permanent settling. Even if their kids were born in Kuwait, expats didn't have the right to send them to the public university, unless one of the parents was on the faculty there. Also, no matter how much experience these expats had at their jobs, there were some positions that could only be filled by Kuwaiti citizens. Expats also weren't allowed home ownership. Apparently, a lot of guest workers adapted to these conditions or didn't mind them, including my mother, who defended Kuwait, saying,

It's such a tiny country! On the other hand, the only thing a disgruntled expat could do was to turn his back on the high salary and the things it could buy and opt for a poorer lifestyle, an uncertain restart, or an early retirement back home. And that's what Baba did when he was about forty-five.

Back in Egypt, Baba spent most of his time and much of his savings decorating his private law office in downtown Cairo, but he never quite practiced law. In the eighties and nineties, all of Baba's cars were old and outdated. American cars were not popular in Cairo. Egyptians preferred European and Japanese cars. We mostly drove the humble Fiat or the Lada and I didn't like them. They looked like a small fridge or a stove on wheels because they were white, boxy and pretty basic. Our big red Vauxhall was better looking, but still way past its prime. As a teenager, I was embarrassed by our old ugly cars. I often wondered why Baba did not sell them all and buy just one new car, even a small one. A car that would be less chunky, less noisy, and that would have a little more padding. I was so used to slamming our heavy car doors shut with such might that I terrified the owners of newer, lighter cars.

Yet instead of selling his old cars, I saw Baba spend considerable amounts of time and money going from one mechanic's garage to another, fixing this car and repainting that one, and even replacing whole engines. He still had the Pontiac, but it was probably not very sensible or practical to drive a 1962 convertible around 1980s Cairo traffic (even though it was repainted into a mood-appropriate grayish white). So he didn't, as far as I remember, except for once, and it was the only time I was ever in the Pontiac.

Late one summer night when I was maybe eight, Baba and Mama for some reason went out in the Pontiac and I happened to tag along. The top was open and I sat silent in the distant backseat while Baba drove away from the city, upwards to the much quieter Muqattam hills. I just sat there staring at the vastness of everything: the backseat of the Pontiac, the night sky above, and the limestone ridges we were driving along. We stopped to have dinner at a restaurant called The Black Horse on the corniche, at an outdoor table that felt terribly close to the cliff despite a protective fence. From up there, we could see the glimmering lights of Cairo, the citadel, and the minarets. I remember that I just hovered between the table and the fence, never quite sitting in my chair, and that I ate all the pickled cucumbers, which to me were tastier than the grilled quail my parents were having. It must have been a rare, spur-of-the-moment date night at this point in their deteriorating marriage and, weirdly, I was there to witness it. On the drive back, Baba sang loudly. He was a heavy smoker and had chronic asthma. He used to give a disclaimer whenever he was about to sing while driving: *I sing because it loosens the phlegm in my chest and helps me to cough it out.* I don't know why he couldn't just admit that he liked to sing. That evening he sang a song by Abdel Wahab called "Cleopatra," a romantic poem written in standard Arabic about nighttime, a boy whose skin is the color of beer, the queen he's in love with, his boat made of dreams, and the river Nile.

My very last memory of the Pontiac is from the early nineties, when it was a dirty, abandoned relic parked in front of my late grandfather's house. Even though the house had a garage, no one thought the old Pontiac deserved to be kept inside. Instead, it was left on the curb, half covered with a ragged discolored canvas, the way people like to do in Egypt; they cover their cars with canvas the way they cover the furniture in their homes. In this case, it was very fitting because the Pontiac did become home and bed for many families of stray cats and dogs. I was scared to get anywhere near it. There were always little animals scurrying around it and sometimes one big dog sitting very authoritatively on its top, guarding God-knows-what inside. This was around the same time that most of our Egyptian friends returned from Kuwait in the wake of the Iraqi invasion. On TV, the images of Iraq were so different from what had settled in my mind from the stories of the road trips my family used to take. From CNN and Al-Jazeera war footage to more recent films like *The Hurt Locker*, I never saw a trace of the water buffaloes, green fields, clear rivers, or boats. As if my family's life before me belonged to a long-gone mythical past.

Living in automobile land for the past few years constantly reminds me of Baba, who died from one of his asthma attacks in 2004. I am sure he would have liked to come and visit one of the heritage car fairs they have here. I would have stood beside him, translating his conversations with the exhibitors and car owners. He didn't know a lot of English, but he used the little he knew impressively, almost theatrically, delivering lines like those from classic Hollywood movies. One particular line he recited a lot was from *The Ten Commandments*, when King Seti who loved his adopted son Moses yet had to banish him to save his own reign over the kingdom says, *What I did I was compelled to do.*

The last car Baba drove is known in Egypt as "The Monkey." It was a secondhand 1960s Fiat 1100 that he bought from a friend for a very low price. It was so quirky that it was cute rather than pitiful. Its doors were hinged at the center, also known in the industry as "suicide doors," so every time I'd open the front door I'd do a little twirl to get in. The gearshift was a stick mounted on the column of the steering wheel. I broke it once when I was still learning how to drive, and it was the first and last time I tried to drive one of Baba's cars. He defended his odd little car, saying, *It's an old car for an old man*, and he liked to point out its original light blue paint color and interior that were in *fabbrica* shipshape.

Having learned from his horse lesson, I never asked Baba to buy me a car. After a few years in my first job, I saved up for a down payment on a new 2001 Fiat Uno. It was a budget supermini car, manufactured in postcommunist, postsocialist Poland. Baba liked to drive it sometimes too. I liked having a car as a single woman living in Cairo because of the independence and the protection it provided me, but I was never too attached to any car I bought. Strangely, it was Baba who advised me to be practical when choosing one, saying, *It should be no more important than a shoe.* I think he was afraid that I might fall under the spell of a beautiful car that would eventually control me through debt or devotion.

Two months before he died, Baba sold his Pontiac for the equivalent of five hundred dollars. It's a mystery why he waited that long to sell it, and why he finally got rid of it like that. My brother, who inherited Baba's passion for cars, had helped Baba fix the Pontiac and clean it up, but he too was caught by surprise when Baba suddenly sold it. My other brother grew an aversion to Baba's cars early on; he swore never to touch one of them and he never did.

I don't care much for cars, but I do love road trips. It is what I think I've inherited from Baba: the way he would suddenly decide to take the slower countryside road from Cairo to Alexandria, rather than the faster desert highway like most other vacationers. The way he would stop at crummy roadside hash houses to try truck drivers' food, and the way he would suggest going into one of the small villages to pay a visit to an old distant relative and look at old buildings. My mother did go on those unplanned visits either reluctantly or because he appealed to her sense of social duty, but he was never able to convince my mother to leave the car and join him in his culinary adventures. Maybe that's why I haven't made as many road trips as I would have liked—I'd either have to go alone, or hold others captive to my desire, depending on the kind of power I hold over them.

During Egypt's short gleam of revolution in 2011, I was easily convinced by friends to start planning for a road trip across the Arab countries newly liberated from dictatorship. Our freedom caravan was supposed to start out from Tunis, where they had toppled their dictator first; then head to Libya, where the dictator was hiding in a hole; drive through Egypt, where people were still dancing in Tahrir square; and make it all the way to Syria, which we thought would be the next dictatorship to fall. I imagined the time had come for me to drive across borders the way Baba once did, but the idea was as short-lived as the revolution that inspired it. The road trip plan never went beyond the social media group where it was incepted, liked and shared. Sometimes I trick myself into consolation by touring the Arabic restaurants and grocery stores in Dearborn as if they were living souvenirs from Iraq, Syria or Yemen. At least I got to taste the black date molasses that my brother raved about.

ıI|Iı

Last summer in Ann Arbor, I discovered that old car smell at a heritage car fair. I was struck by how a familiar smell could linger on inside a car for decades and become the starkest difference between new cars and cars like Baba's. Every time I stuck my head through an open car window, the car owners thought I was admiring the interiors of their classic cars and went on proudly describing how they maintained all the details and accessories. The truth was, I didn't notice any of these details. My eyes were shut while I caught whiffs of hazy memories.

I walked through the fair scanning over the cars hurriedly, as if I were on a mission, asking if someone had brought a 1961 Pontiac Parisienne. Then the rain forced me to sit behind a glass window of a cafe on Main Street, and my gaze shifted to the old wrinkled faces of the exhibitors. I wasn't interested in the specs of their cars, I just wondered if they had stories similar to Baba's. Maybe there's something near universal about how men from that generation loved their cars. I wished I could ask them why they kept their cars for so long, and what it had cost them, or what Detroit was like when it was the rich car capital of the world. Baba's cars had seen a rise and fall too, and because of that unglamorous retirement, we got to spend time together, and I listened to his stories. The stories were free, and they outlived the cars.

◻ ◻ ◻ ◻ ◻

9

LAYLA AZMI GOUSHEY

Profile of a Citizen

Generations Then and Now

I can't get over the death of 13-year-old Hamza Al-Khatib, tortured to death in May 2011.

My first experience with brutality and oppression happened in my own home at the hands of my mother when I was eight years old. My mother was American with British ancestors in her genealogy. She had grown up in a strict Baptist town in Lake Worth, Texas. She held latent colonialist views of the native and the colonizer. Indigeneity versus an assumption of Manifest Destiny. Savages versus Civilization. East versus West. She would rip the labels off pork products and put them in the refrigerator for my Muslim father to guess at and avoid. Each of my parents oppressed the other with their cultural expectations of right and wrong. These were our private family struggles.

My father was a Palestinian refugee who owned a tailor shop in Dallas, TX. He brought me to work that day because he wanted me to wait on customers. Tall, imposing men would come into the shop and he would tell me to go and see what they wanted. I was very shy, and at one point, I started to cry. I did not understand the importance of this cultural tradition to my father, who once spent time in his own father's butcher shop in the old city of Jerusalem. No one had explained why I was there or provided any guidance for me to follow. My father called my mother to come and pick me up.

She said nothing on the ride home. I had expected a slap or a telling off, but she offered neither. Once in the house, I went to the family room and started playing with my toys. Without warning, my mother emerged from the hallway with a belt, pushed me onto the floor and began to mercilessly, silently, beat me. I cried, and I screamed *I love you Mommy, please stop*. She did not stop until she was exhausted. Her face was red, her hair was unkempt, and she was breathing heavily when she stopped, but she did not cry. She was beating me because of her own psychic wounds: her parent's divorce and her upbringing in a small judgmental town north of Ft. Worth, Texas; her failed expectations that marrying my father would get her out of Lake Worth and into exotic new lands; her disappointment that because of the drudgery of caring for me, her dreams of exotic lands had been sidelined. My back and legs were red from welts. Life went on as normal from there, but I made a pact with myself to leave her someday. Even at that age, I knew I would grow into my personal power. I would be able to get out from under her brutality. I knew her brutality was a choice, and I vowed to choose a different path. Most of all, about that day, I remember the silence.

I can't get over the death of 13-year-old Hamza Al-Khatib, tortured to death in May 2011.

Hamza was from al-Jizah near the southern city of Deraa in Syria. He was brutally tortured and killed by Syrian security forces in May 2011. He had attended a protest with his father and they became separated. His family had no news of him for a month. Then, his body was returned to them in horrific condition. His arm was broken, he was covered in burns, and his genitals had been mutilated. Some may wonder how an adult can inflict such brutal wounds on anyone, but especially on a child.

According to CNN's Arwa Damon, Hamza wanted to be a policeman, but he changed his mind when he realized the brutality that Syrian police inflict on the population. He was at the protest because his cousin had been killed by security forces.

Hamza's school picture, released by his family, shows a baby-faced boy with a hesitant smile. This picture melted my heart because I saw my own sons in his cheeks, his smile, and his eyes.

I am a mother, and I can't get over it.

In the report titled *Education for Citizenship in the Arab World: Key to the Future* by Muhammad Faour and Marwan Muasher, published in October 2011, the authors state that "The recent uprisings have irrefutably demonstrated that Arab publics are no longer willing to be silent about the failure of their political systems in providing both freedom and bread." They also say that "Students need to learn at a very early age what it means to be citizens who learn how to think, seek and produce knowledge, question, and innovate rather than be subjects of the state who are taught what to think and how to behave."

I can't get over the death of 13-year-old Hamza Al-Khatib.

As the mother of two boys near Hamza's age, I picture the confusion and fear that Hamza must have felt during the month he was held. Also, as the mother of two teenage boys, I know that he already was a thinker, an innovator, a seeker. More heartbreaking is the realization of the betrayal Hamza felt when he realized that adults could inflict merciless pain, that the police and government authorities he once admired were malevolent, that there was no one to save him.

I can't forget.

1985. Syria. My father, 13-year-old brother, and I were walking along a dusty road near a vacant lot in Damascus. My father left us for a moment to relieve himself. When my brother asked where he was I said, "He's probably saluting the president." My father, overhearing me, said. "Hey! Careful! You don't know who's listening." He looked from side to side as we walked back into the city.

I had developed sarcasm to manage my mother's disgust with me, but I didn't yet realize that a bawdy joke about the Syrian president was a pretty dangerous thing to do, especially in the aftermath of the destruction of the town of Hama. That was only a few years out from the 1982 obliteration of the Syrian town by Syrian President Hafez Al-Assad's forces. At least 20,000 men, women and children died at the hands of their own military. This type of loss within the population of my home country, the US, was unimaginable and so I was not aware of the personal risk of my sarcasm. As a US citizen, I had a false, foolish sense of safety that was bred in suburban shopping malls and beneath the new steel skylines of the south-central United States.

I can't forget the death of 13-year-old Hamza Al-Khatib.

The symbol of the father, the patriarch, is everything in the Arab world. The concept is mixed into symbolism and reverence of a country's leader. There is a paternal presence to which everyone pledges loyalty. Ordinary people, however, are not always powerful. The structures of patriarchy that emphasize honor and shame also breed fear to step out of the norm. Humiliation is always a risk for men and women due to poverty and lack of opportunity and the pressure of those social norms. Humiliation by government workers and politicians is common. Many times, people bring those humiliations home to foist onto their own families. It is a dangerous, heartless brew.

But fostering humiliation is not exclusive to Arab culture. One only need to consider the scandal of Abu Ghraib prison in Iraq—where in

2003 US soldiers raped, humiliated, and tortured prisoners—to know that the capacity to humiliate and wound is in every human. One only need consider my mother's psychic wounds and the way they bled onto me.

1985. Syria. Later, we took a cab to the Bloudan area west of Damascus. The cab was a cream-colored 1960's-era checker cab built in Kalamazoo, Michigan. The driver was so proud of his vintage American car. As we drove into the surrounding hills, I looked down on the valley. The sun set behind the mountains, and I saw glowing windows like stars in the valley that matched those in the sky. Lebanon lay beyond that horizon. I idealized it: a beautiful land, despite its civil war, its massacres.

The hotel was a Swiss hotel. There were hard rolls, butter, and jam for breakfast. The beds had thick mattresses with heavy blankets, although for some reason I was still chilled all night. I can still see the graveled road outside of the hotel the next morning. I often hear and see Syria in my mind. I hear the traffic in Damascus. I see the Bloudan valley lit with the lights of homes and businesses. On the way back to Jordan, by bus, a woman was reaming out the driver and people just kept sitting there as if in a daze. She was shaking a booklet at him. I assumed it was her passport. I was impressed because, while I had lived through many of my mother's rages, I had not seen a woman take anyone on in public like that.

I had not yet heard of Nawal El Saadawi, an Egyptian doctor, feminist, prolific writer, and activist. A seeker and producer of knowledge who in 1975 had written *Woman at Point Zero*, a novel about an Egyptian woman who endures abuse, prostitution, and imprisonment before meeting her ultimate fate. This is the same El Saadawi who in 2014 said "the root of the oppression of women lies in the global post-modern capitalist system, which is supported by religious fundamentalism." Capitalism and patriarchy have a common cause, it seems.

I had not yet heard of the brave innovator Tawakul Karman, a 2011 Nobel Peace Prize winner from Yemen who founded a group called "Women Journalists without Chains." She has led non-violent protests, and has been imprisoned for her dissent against the government in Yemen.

I had not yet heard of dissenter-protester Ahed Tamimi. Palestine. 2017. Ahed Tamimi is a 16-year-old Palestinian girl who slapped and punched Israeli soldiers at a protest after her cousin was shot in the face. She was arrested, and later, so was her mother.

I can't get over the death of 13-year-old Hamza Al-Khatib.

1985. The border between Jordan and Syria. The latent threat of oppression. My privileged, scarred reading of life versus my father's desperately hard-earned refugee's knowledge. As we came back into Jordan from Syria, the Jordanian security agent asked to see what was in my luggage. I guess by that point I looked disheveled and definitely not Jordanian in posture or attitude. I opened my suitcase and there was a small box containing a gilt picture frame I had purchased from a shop in Jordan before going into Syria, but I did not pay attention to the person in the picture. The agent roughly gestured for me to open the box, and I did. Inside was a gilded-framed picture of King Hussein of Jordan, beautifully wrapped in cheap black velvet. Our collective patriarch of that moment. The agent told me to wrap up and we could go. They did not check the rest of our luggage. My father told this story for years. "He thought he could cause trouble, but we were better than him. Heh!"

That was the same trip where I drank a cup of tea at the Syrian border as we went back into Jordan. I developed a terrible stomach reaction and was sick for days. My mischievous 13-year-old brother took a picture of me; sick in bed. That is what 13-year-old boys do.

1986. Palestine. I was so enchanted with my experience in Jordan and Syria that I saved my money to visit Palestine a year later, when I was twenty-one. I was beginning to think, to seek knowledge. I wanted to learn about Palestine, to see it firsthand. As a seeker of knowledge, I found a willing teacher. Although Jordan and Syria have oppressive regimes, I was protected during my travels by my father and by my Arab heritage. I went alone to Israel to visit family. The Israeli government first taught me the bare realities of state-sponsored oppression. I was held in detention on arrival in Tel Aviv. While in Ramallah and Jerusalem, young Israeli soldiers, culturally American men and women who held dual American-Israeli citizenship would stop us and ask for my identification, I would watch them harass other Palestinians on the street, looking for trouble. In the short time I was in Palestine, I learned about structural racism, and how Palestinian teenagers could be imprisoned for years for writing graffiti on a wall, or for just being in the wrong place at the wrong time. How people could be injured and killed by Israeli soldiers and police with no redress from any government. I was astounded that the dual American-Israeli soldiers I met, my cultural peers, who I could have easily been joking and jostling with in my dorm at college, could participate in such a farce.

I can't get past the death of 13-year-old Hamza Al-Khatib, tortured to death in May 2011.

1986. Dallas, Texas. I joined The Arab-American Anti-Discrimination

Committee (ADC), a civil rights organization. My first attempt at organizing the Dallas ADC chapter came to an end at a Denny's Restaurant during coffee with several others who were Palestinian Muslim immigrants from South Lebanon. As we discussed plans for outreach to other Arab Americans in Dallas, some members felt that we should exclude Christian Arabs. My Palestinian friends were still rightly outraged and deeply wounded by the massacre of Palestinians in the Sabra and Shatila refugee camps in Beirut, Lebanon in 1982. The perpetrators of the massacre were Phalangists, a political group populated by Maronite Christians. In my naivety born of privilege as a Westernized, suburbanized Arab American, I could not understand why all Arab Christians were being ostracized. I did not understand the visceral pain felt by my companions. After all, one of my father's best friends was a Lebanese Presbyterian man named Munir Bayoud, a retired Southern Methodist University math professor who also was an Arab American community leader in Dallas, who advocated for justice in Palestine.

As a young man, Munir Bayoud had earned a math degree at the American University in Beirut. He went to teach in Jerusalem. It was there he witnessed the battles for Palestine and the partition of Palestine into two states: Israel and Palestine. When he immigrated to the United States in the late 1950s to work at Southern Methodist University in Dallas, he met his wife Katy, an American woman of similar heritage to my mother. Katy was also a teacher. She possessed a calm southern drawl that belied her hardheaded quest to liberate Palestine through education and activism. Think, seek, produce knowledge, question, innovate.

I cannot get over the cruelty of the world's indifference to Hamza's fate.

Faour and Muasher also say "The challenge of replacing both leaders and regimes with ones that follow democratic norms is huge and certainly not automatic. As the Arab world starts this long transformation, a self-evident but often ignored fact is that democracy will thrive only in a culture that accepts diversity, respects different points of view, regards truths as relative rather than absolute, and tolerates—even encourages—dissent."

1986. Accept diversity. Tolerate dissent. When I realized my ADC Chapter friends were serious about excluding Christians in our group, I walked out in a huff, furious at the lack of expression of democratic values. Before I left, I gave an impassioned speech on listening to multiple views, on embracing diversity, on the value of multifaith conversations. I was developing an awareness of my own secular nature, my own biases against religious fervor. A couple of weeks later, I heard from a member who said the other members realized I was right, and to come back, but I could not manage the anger that stirred within me during those conversations. I decided to focus on my own work and studies. I now realize that deep wounds lay beneath our emotions during that time: the massacre at Sabra and Shatila, the twice-displaced Palestinian peers who were reconciling themselves to their fates, and my mother's psychic wounds that had been passed down, beaten down, really, into me. I could not tolerate too much injustice. I did have enough awareness to marvel at the young Lebanese Druze man, a cook at that Denny's restaurant, who could hold a job in a seemingly normal manner after having lived through the carnage and destruction of the Lebanese civil war. It was painful to feel that others were being harmed in the slightest way, yet I could not yet see past my own pain and privilege to understand that Palestinian and Lebanese immigrants, after Sabra and Shatila, after the Lebanese civil war, lived with deep almost unresolvable pain that blocked their democratic aspirations. They were not expressing religious fervor, but distrust, resentment, and fear which led them to turn to faith as a protective shield. I could not see that the politics and pain from those regions followed us into the diaspora. There are visceral psychic wounds that lead to chronic conditions of mistrust one must endure after becoming fully aware of cruelty.

I keep trying to rescue 13-year-old Hamza Al-Khatib.

1990. Dallas, TX. My first public protest was near the state fairgrounds. This was toward the end of the year. Iraq had invaded Kuwait on August 2, 1990. My awareness of US foreign policy in the Middle East had been growing, and I remembered that earlier in the year the Saudi government had sponsored a cultural exhibit that had been curated by the Dallas Art Museum. The exhibit had toured the country. I saw this as too convenient, and I smelled a rat. I was deepening my thinking. I wondered if the Saudis had known a manufactured crisis was coming. I wanted to share my growing awareness of politics with others.

After a few years of stumbling, the local ADC group had been reborn when Katy Bayoud took up the mantle of president of the Dallas chapter. Katy Bayoud, the seeker and producer of knowledge, the retired Texas teacher who was referred to as an honorary Arab because her embrace of the culture was sincere and true, held the torch for Palestine when no one else would touch the subject. She kept asking me to come back to ADC, telling me that everyone was now working in tandem. Finally, after Iraq invaded Kuwait and I began to see the political machinations that had led to the invasion. I said, *OK. I'm in.* That is how I learned of the protest to stop the United States from its military action against Saddam Hussein's army in favor of diplomacy. That is how I ended up on the corner of Grand and Second Street in Dallas holding a sign someone had handed me that said *No Blood for Oil*. I noticed that the back of the sign said *US out of Nicaragua*. I was with the pros. I learned that dissent was a right and a responsibility.

I can't get over the death of 13-year old Hamza.

1991. January. My second protest was in Dallas, TX at John F. Kennedy Memorial Plaza. Kennedy is famous for the quote, "Ask not what your country can do for you, ask what you can do for your country," but most Arabs know Khalil Gibran said it first. The memorial monument is a giant open-air cube that is meant to represent a tomb. When I got there, the interior of the tomb was silent, but soon the dubke-playing percussionist from Southern Methodist University was there, keeping it real. This was during Operation Desert Shield—the first US Gulf War. As protesters gathered, I held a poster that said *Wage Peace*. Munir Bayoud and his wife Katy were there, but there were few others from our ADC meetings. I knew that participation in protests was dangerous to middle and upper-class Americans' reputations and careers, but for immigrants from Arab countries, they were dangerous to life and limb. Fears of reprisal, irrational or not, follow them into the diaspora. As my uncle once notably said about participating in Arab American events, immigrant Arabs fear that everyone is a spy. Truths are relative rather than absolute.

I can't forget.

1991. February. The Highway of Death. The US military targeted a retreating army. I can only think of those Iraqi soldiers who were once youngsters, like Hamza in 2011, like myself, like all of the young persons in the Arab diaspora in the 1980s, who found themselves in a predicament not of their making, but who bore the brunt of state brutalities and international brinkmanship. Young people = cannon fodder. I was an American, and these people were not my enemies. I was becoming aware that the state could be the enemy of many people. Reports describe a horrible scene of retreating soldiers being picked off from above by US military planes. Truths are relative rather than absolute.

I can't get over the death of 13-year-old Hamza Al-Khatib.

So, patriarchy is not my thing, but then I think of Libyan leader Muammar Gaddafi, when captured in a drainage ditch, saying to his captors, *What did I do to you? Don't shoot me. Don't you know right from wrong?* He was humiliated, finally, by having a bayonet shoved into his rectum in his hometown by his metaphorical sons, rebels, twenty-first century citizens, who he had called rats and cockroaches. Truths are relative rather than absolute.

2017. People, especially young people, want opportunity. Many of today's Arab youths are educated but without jobs or a stable future. Many more are on the move as refugees fleeing war and poverty. These young women and men: where are they to go? They must have cultural spaces to think, produce knowledge, question, innovate, accept diversity, and dissent. We must create those spaces for them.

I'm not over it.

2017. St. Louis, MO. I teach freshman college students who strive to think, produce knowledge, question, innovate, accept diversity, and offer dissent. There are separate yet connected griefs. We are only three years out from the summer of 2014 when in St. Louis Palestinian Americans and allies protested the Israeli siege of Gaza and then later in the summer joined the protests over the police killing of Mike Brown in Ferguson. My class is a mix of African Americans, heritage students of middle eastern or Muslim descent, and white students, some of whom have served in Iraq or Afghanistan. Most understand the definitions of neoliberalism, imperialism, and neocolonialism. They understand there is more than what we see in the headlines, but there are also some who are just learning more about their place in the world.

Philando Castile, Hamza Al-Khatib, Mike Brown, Muhammad Bouazizi, Trayvon Martin, they are all in my mind as I teach my classes. One day in class, I show the documentary *How Facebook Changed the World: The Arab Spring.* We watch a scene that describes Mohamed Bouazizi's humiliation at being slapped by a police officer, and his subsequent self-immolation-as-protest in a small town in Tunisia. An African American student from impoverished north St. Louis begins to cry. She sobs openly and loudly. The rest of us are taken aback at her outburst, and at first I don't know what to say. Minutes pass. Finally: "I never knew," she says, "that other people also lived like that."

Nope. Still. Not. Over. It.

My father was a good man. He was an intellectual, although he had not completed formal schooling. From an early age, I attended academic lectures on the culture, history, and politics of the middle east due to my father's interest in the politics of his homeland, Palestine. He was also a humanitarian, often offering what small aid he could render to those less fortunate than us.

There was the time I was in car accident in Dallas, Texas. I T-boned a car as it illegally crossed into an intersection. As I got out of the car to exchange insurance cards, several men jumped out of the other car and started to run. Drivers who had stopped to help looked on in amazement. Finally, someone shouted "Hey! They're illegals!" Someone else muttered *wetbacks*. The police pulled up and jumped out of their cars. They chased the Hispanic men and caught three of them. Later, the police asked if my father wanted to press charges against the driver because the accident was his fault. He said no, those guys have enough problems. Truths are relative rather than absolute.

Since 2011, I keep trying to rescue 13-year-old Hamza Al-Khatib.

Profile of a citizen: my sons know the difference between a first world problem and a developing world problem. I am so proud of them. My mother once marveled *You are so nice to your kids!* after I rebuffed her advice to slap their toddler hands if they kept grabbing objects to chew on. But according to Abraham Maslow, if our basic human needs for love and security are not met, it is harder to develop into fully actualized human beings. My greatest joy is that my sons feel free to express their innovative talents. They are seekers of knowledge.

I can't get over the death of 13-year-old Hamza Al-Khatib. I keep trying to save him. I am there with him in his moments of panic and fear.

There are many, like Hamza, who will never get to express the values he mistakenly believed Syrian police officers and state agents possessed.

There are also many quiet, hardworking young women and men in our global society whose imperfect, all-too-human families struggle to help them gain skills and education that may not lead to jobs. Reports that examine the data on education of Arab youth paint a grim picture of few opportunities. Judging by the data on graduation rates at American community colleges, prospects in the US are equally grim. Yet, we have the knowledge to do better. This is a call for us all to think, produce knowledge, question, innovate, accept diversity, and encourage dissent. Truths are relative rather than absolute.

I've met many of these young people as they navigate Arab and Western worlds. They are family members, friends, and students in the classes I teach. I sponsor the Global Studies club at my campus. I meet so many smart and articulate students from St. Louis and from all over the world. Right now, I am concerned about one young Iraqi woman. She is the breadwinner for her family. She is eighteen, and her mother suffers from post-traumatic stress and paranoia because of her experiences in

Iraq during the 2003 US invasion. A doctor had suggested her mother have another baby to focus on something new and move on, but the plan did not work as intended. Her mother stays home with the new brother, still afraid to leave the house. The eighteen-year-old daughter works full time and attends community college. She must be the strong one in their new land, in St. Louis, Missouri. Near Ferguson. The birthplace of the new civil rights movement. Her father does odd jobs in the city of St. Louis to make ends meet. When I speak to her, she must interrupt to answer her mother's text to let her know she is with me, her teacher, and that she is OK; there are no spies or security forces to harm her.

I am a mother. I'm not over the death of 13-year-old Hamza Al-Khatib.

Hamza Al-Khatib: twenty-first century citizen. That Hamza's role models in law enforcement—who should have been models of respect and honor, who should have been representatives of a benevolent patriarchal state (is this possible?), or should have been representatives of a fair and just democratic state (this is possible—tried to emasculate this young man by beating him, shooting him in the arm, imprisoning him alone and without access to a parent, by putting out cigarettes on him, and by mutilating his penis demonstrates that humanity possesses so deep a psychic wound, one wonders if we can save ourselves. This event has passed into history with only a few murmurs of outrage from Western and Arab leaders. In truth, for eons, young people have met a similar fate. Unfortunately, brutality is nothing new, but we must work to minimize its strength in the world.

Imperialism, state-sponsored violence, and thinking in absolutes: These demonstrate our leaders' impotence and shame. Sometimes that violence is replicated in the home, as it was in mine. Like so many children and young people who are displaced and on the move now, or who live in societies with diminishing opportunities for education and personal development, Hamza's ideals were pure, vital, and alive, until they weren't. I am a mother. I am a teacher, an educator, a mentor. I rely on my life lessons from my failures and shames, to build positive structures that help others develop their potential. However, the grip and global reach of the amoral, immoral state continues to tighten. I operate on hope for my children and for our next generations, but I also have anger on their behalf because they deserve better. We must build social, political, and educational structures to help them navigate this world. Tyranny, oppression, brutality: they are all a choice, and we must help our youth choose a different path.

10

〇 〇 〇 〇 〇

TARIQ AL HAYDAR

Machine Language

She wasn't calling me a sand nigger. Not exactly. Nothing she said was directed at me, per se. I was just the overweight guy leaning against the glass wall of the arcade, smoking a Marlboro Ultra Light. My best friend, Rashid, wasn't even trying to pick her up. He was just flirting with one of her friends. Seattle in 1996 didn't seem like a racist place and time, but there I was, trying to keep my corpulent self out of the way, inhaling carbon monoxide in the fringes while Rashid engaged a gregarious blonde. Meanwhile, Aziz, Rashid's acquaintance, was chatting up her Asian friend, who had her arm in a cast. They were all in earshot, but I tried to focus on what Rashid was saying. Whenever he interacted with girls, he would transform into a different person, one who spoke in non sequiturs that they would find charming for whatever reason. Sometimes I suspected that they were actually laughing at him, which made my face red and sweaty. Embarrassment by proxy. More often than not, however, I'd realize that they were not ridiculing him at all. His conquests always seemed inexplicable to me.

He ambled back to where I was standing, a prominent pimple occupying the center of his forehead and a shit-eating grin adorning the rest of his face. "She likes me," he announced.

"Who doesn't?" I sniffed as I stepped on the butt of my cigarette. "Can we go now?"

"Aziz is talking to her friend," he said as he adjusted his little eyeglasses that were much bigger than his little eyes. "What's burning your rice?"

"Nothing," I mumbled. I glanced at the blonde girl, who had gone back to discuss the encounter with a third, slightly overweight girl. I didn't even notice her at first, which caused me to immediately identify with her.

Aziz walked back to us and said, "If I knew how to speak English, I'd be the crusher of maidens' hearts." He exhaled loudly.

I had just met Aziz that day, so I nodded. Like us, the group of three young women had convened on the other side of the exterior of the arcade. They were standing at the exact point where the sidewalk merged into the beginning of the parking lot, but I could still hear what they were saying, more or less. The girl with the broken arm didn't have much to say about Aziz, but the blonde kept going on and on about how funny Rashid was. That's when I heard the third girl say it. I don't even know how it fit into the conversation, but I distinctly heard her refer to us, with a modicum of disgust, as "those sand niggers."

That was the first time I had ever heard that phrase. I was familiar with "nigger," of course, although at the time I associated it more with the raging East Coast–West Coast rap war than with a national history of violence.

"I think that fat chick called us 'niggers,'" I told Rashid and Aziz.

"Us?" asked Rashid. "Are you sure? But we aren't black."

"She said 'sand niggers,'" I replied, half-wishing I had said nothing. "You know, like niggers from the desert."

This sent both of them into a frenzy. They walked up to the three young women, trying to appear as menacing as possible. "What did you call us?" shouted Rashid.

I lingered, staring at the cigarette butt I had stomped earlier.

The slightly overweight girl straightened her back and walked up to Rashid. She was taller than him. "Why don't you get on your magic carpet and fly back to Saudi Arabia?"

How did she know we were from Saudi Arabia?

The three of them started screaming at each other: Rashid in broken English, Aziz mostly in Arabic and the girl in an accent I couldn't quite place. I walked up and put my arm between Rashid and the girl and pleaded, "Let's go. She's not worth it."

"Yeah, you go," she said with a smirk.

Back in the car, Aziz discovered that I spoke fluent English. "Are you kidding?" he said, turning to me in the backseat. "If I spoke any English at all, I would have damned the good out of her."

Rashid and Aziz went on and on about how I should have utilized my language skills to the belittlement of this racist. Did I not have enough self-esteem to stand up for myself? The more they talked, the more convinced I became that they were right. I couldn't sleep that night, my mind awash with the litany of profanities I could and should have hurled at her.

Redemption beckoned the very next day, as Rashid and I walked out of the QFC carrying bags of ice. The slightly overweight girl was right there. She had spotted us and was walking towards our car with both of her middle fingers raised. The obscenities I had rehearsed in my mind the night before came flowing out of my mouth: suggestions for sexual favors she should offer; speculations on the possible shallowness of her gene pool; and, of course, put-downs of her appearance. Mainly her weight.

Rashid was pleased. He patted me on the shoulder and laughed approvingly before he drove off in his rented Ford Taurus. But I didn't feel any satisfaction.

I've always spoken some kind of liminal language; equipped with the basics in both Arabic and English but perpetually miscommunicating, or at least not entirely satisfied with what I ultimately say. As a boy growing up in Richmond, Virginia, I insisted on rolling my Rs. I refused to pledge allegiance to the flag of the United States of America, or to the republic for which it stands. I'd just stand there every morning, silently waiting for my classmates to finish their ritual. Maybe it wasn't that strange, considering I've never been a US citizen anyway. Then again, citizenship didn't mean anything to me then. My world revolved around *Transformers*, which I watched every weekday afternoon at four o'clock. My favorite was Jazz, not only because he was Optimus Prime's second-in-command, who ordered Sunstreak and Sideswipe to transform into a Lamborghini and Ferrari before every battle with the Decepticons, but, more importantly, because Jazz was a Porsche. Only years later would I discover that Jazz was supposed to be black. An African American robot from Cybertron.

We moved back to Riyadh after I finished second grade. I could vaguely understand Arabic, but I couldn't fathom how I'd be able to study science, history and geography in that language. I had to take an entry exam to get into Ma'had al-Asima Schools. The large man with the large mustache told me to write *elephant* in Arabic. I did, slowly drawing the circle of the *F*, the little saucer with two dots underneath that was *Y* and the umbrella handle that constituted *L*.

"You forgot the dot on top of the *F*," he said.

I looked at him, afraid that they would send me back to Richmond. "It's OK," he laughed.

A lot of my time in elementary school was spent deciphering words I had never heard before, often to comic effect. I thought *nation* meant *mother*. In my mind, *Hathal* wasn't just a name, it was the person who sang the *athan*, the call for prayer you sometimes hear in Hollywood movies like *The Exorcist* or *The Hurt Locker*. When my cousin told me that I'd *regret* not giving him my Super Mario Brothers cartridge, I thought he'd said that I would be *filled with blood*.

The worst part about Riyadh was that I couldn't play with other kids during the week. Everyone lived in isolated concrete villas. All my friends and cousins were car rides away. I found myself missing how I could navigate our entire neighborhood in Richmond by bicycle. In lieu of the basketball games I couldn't play anymore and the frogs I couldn't hunt in the pond that was now half a world away, I watched VHS cassettes filled with American sitcoms in an infinite loop: *Family Ties*, *Alf*, *Webster*, *Night Court*, *Mr. Belvedere*, *Cheers*, *Perfect Strangers*. I guessed at what language they spoke on Mypos, theorized about Bruce Willis's true feelings toward Cybil Shepherd and wondered why Theo kept getting into trouble with Dr. Huxtable.

"Why don't I understand anyone's jokes?" I asked my mother abruptly one day.

"Your classmates?" she asked. "Do they understand your jokes?"

"I keep quiet for the most part."

"You need to watch Egyptian films," she suggested, and took me to a video store on Thalatheen Street, where she bought me *The School of the Mischievous*, a black-and-white play starring Adel Emam and Saeed Salih. It took me a few viewings, but I began to understand the humor, though I didn't understand what Younis Shalaby meant when he said, "Spell it and drink its water!" The audience went crazy though, so it must have been funny.

Mr. Bassam was a Palestinian high school teacher who tutored me. Every day, he'd start our Arabic lessons the same way: "Write an *H*."

I'd try to draw those two not-quite-concentric circles, but Mr. Bassam would sigh and tell me, "Don't lift the pen up. It's all one motion."

It took me a while, a frustratingly long while, but I eventually mastered the *H*, which seems simple enough in retrospect. Mr. Bassam would later tutor all my younger brothers, and when they all outgrew his expertise, he'd come by and play table tennis with us and watch La Liga or World Cup matches, chain-smoking all the while.

"So when will you quit smoking?" I'd ask.

"As soon as the school year ends," he'd say. "Teaching dumb Saudis is very stressful. I need my fix."

Once the school year ended, we'd ask him again and he'd reply: "As soon as the school year begins."

"Why?" my brother would laugh. "It's summer vacation."

"Son," he'd say, "I have to drive all the way to Nablus and endure those motherfuckers and their endless checkpoints. You can't talk to soldiers. Teaching dumb Saudis is a lot less stressful."

After graduating high school, I majored in computer science at King Saud University in Riyadh. I chose computer science because it was not medicine. The first semester was a breeze because we had to take six English language credits, which I aced. Then we had to learn C and Java.

The most terrifying entity I've ever come across is the compiler, a program that translates source code from programming languages to binary code. Typically, after the Algerian professor told everyone what kind of program he wanted us to design, I'd scribble the little I understood of whatever programming language I had to grapple with. Once my program was done, I'd run it through the compiler, which would inform me that I had fifty-four errors. It never specified what they were. Sometimes, a single misplaced semicolon produced twenty different errors. After an hour and a half of searching through my sorry excuse for a program, line by line, I'd finally find a semicolon that shouldn't have been there. I'd delete it and run the program through the compiler again: Ninety-one errors.

I've always loved getting lost in bookstores: exploring different sections, examining covers, sampling pages, discovering authors. I was on Olaya

Street at Jarir Bookstore, which isn't there anymore, leafing through Joseph Conrad's *The Secret Agent*, when I noticed a middle-aged man with a potbelly staring at me.

"Is that for class?" he asked.

"No."

"So why are you reading a Joseph Conrad novel?" he asked, apparently amazed for some reason.

"Because I like Conrad," I replied, putting the book back on the shelf.

"Are you in college?" he asked. "What do you study?"

"Computer science," I sighed.

He took a stack of papers out of his breast pocket and mumbled, "Let me give you my card." But then he shuffled the papers for five whole minutes, muttering, "I know it's here somewhere." Suddenly, he stuffed the papers back into his breast pocket and triumphantly produced his wallet from one of his other pockets.

"I think it's in here," he beamed. It was, and he extended it to me, urging me to contact him if I ever thought about transferring to the English Department. I can't remember his name, but he was an assistant professor. As soon as he left, I threw his card in the trash. I don't know why I did that, and I'd waste a couple more years torturing myself with that damn compiler, but in the end I did transfer to the English Department.

I moved to Washington, DC for graduate school, where I met a bunch of newspaper columnists and intellectuals. Many of them were Arab nationalists who had thick mustaches and listened to obscure (to me at least) Iraqi singers and found my love of Wu-Tang Clan and Guns n' Roses off-putting. We organized gatherings at local community centers where we could get together with other Arabs and discuss Marx or Arendt or Said and debate whether or not Arabs were too primitive and barbaric for democracy.

Salah was a Kuwaiti who had caterpillars for eyebrows and always showed up in jeans that were ripped at the knees. He never spoke Arabic. The English he spoke reminded me of my own: the kind news anchors from Minnesota spoke once they'd beaten the specificities and regionalisms out of their tongues. Most of my friends didn't like Salah.

"Why does he speak English all the time?" they'd ask. "It's not like we have any Swedes or Alabamans in attendance."

I tried to stick up for him, even though I secretly disliked him just as much as they did. One of the few things I remembered from linguistics classes I took as an undergraduate was that speakers of a subordinate language spoke a dominant language for one of two reasons: either it facilitated communication, or the speaker desired some kind of prestige through association with the dominant language. I tried to argue that Salah belonged to the former group, even though I suspected he fell into the latter.

"Well," said one of the Arab nationalists, "he can speak all the English he wants. He's still a sand nigger to them."

I don't know how true that is, or who this *them* referred to. It seemed like such a massive pronoun. I closed my eyes and imagined ripping *THEM* up into a thousand little *thems* I could scatter into a river.

Then I imagined diving into the river, separating myself from everyone else, and allowing the stream to take me to where the ocean began. The salt water carried me to some distant land, where I emerged from the sea and rested on the sand. As the last rays of sun flickered, a group of women and men in strange purple and yellow clothes approached, holding spears and speaking in tongues. I couldn't recognize the languages, but I understood that they were asking me to identify myself.

I opened my mouth.

□ ▯ □ ▯ □

11

RANDA JARRAR

Biblioclast

1.

My father. He wanted me to become a writer, but when I did, he didn't like what I wrote.

He hated my first novel and called it pornography. It features lots of teenage sex and masturbation, as well as an unsavory portrayal of a narcissistic and selfish father. He insisted it was the sex scenes that offended him and not the depiction of the father character, whom I had based loosely on him. Finally my father stopped speaking to me and said he would start again only if I publicly burned every single copy of my book. I love to imagine myself doing this: my transformation from rejected pornographer to redeemed daughter and biblioclast.

2.

Most burned texts are destroyed because they've been deemed heretical by one religious group or another. Torah scrolls were burned by ancient Romans. The Talmud was burned in medieval France. In 2010 an American pastor named Terry Jones threatened to burn two hundred Qurans on the ninth anniversary of 9/11. He didn't do it, but dozens of Qurans were set on fire by other people.

My novel was a blasphemous text in our household, where my father was God, and his word was Truth, and anyone who talked back to him, or even just interrupted him during breakfast, was a heretic.

3.

I've started indulging in this fantasy of myself as a biblioclast. Here is how I imagine it:

I round up all the copies of the book in my house. I have two paperbacks in my office, six hardcovers in an old chest, and two advance-reader copies on a shelf in the dining room. I burn them all in my backyard barbecue pit.

Next I begin to contact people who I know might have copies and ask them to mail the books to a P.O. Box in Kyle, Texas—the town in which I began writing the novel, where I rented a trailer for three hundred dollars a month (including all utilities). The readers, baffled, comply, because I explicitly state how important it is to my father that they do this. Friends who have heard my complaints about my father—that he was so strict I wasn't allowed to socialize, that he struck me, that he often made me feel as if my large body were unworthy of love—don't understand why I would burn my book for him. I tell them that my father did his best to love me, that he praised my writing, that he took me on a trip to New York City when I was thirteen, that he used to sing with me and laugh at my jokes. I tell my friends that, as I near the age of forty, my empathy for my father has deepened. I work in a place where I am a minority, and I can finally imagine what it must have been like for him, a Palestinian, to immigrate to the US and work at a place where he was the only Arab, perhaps the only person of color. I tell them that I miss my father. This makes it a bit easier for them to understand.

4.

The Quran was passed on orally in the years after the prophet Muhammad's death, and it was not written down until two decades later, between 650 and 656 CE. In Arabic the slightest mispronunciation can change the meaning of a word entirely. (When my father was a boy and heard the muezzin's call to prayer—*Hayya ala salaa*—he thought the word *hayya*, which means *come* was actually the word *hayya*, which means *snake*, and so he would imagine a snake on a prayer rug, which confused him greatly.)

After the Quran was fully transcribed, the caliph ordered that all manuscripts containing any excerpts from the Quran be burned, so that there would be only one official version.

But many people had learned verses by heart, and those may have differed from the official Quran. I always wondered how those versions could be destroyed. How do you erase memory?

5.

In my fantasy I order every single copy of my book from bookstores and warehouses around the country.

Then comes the tricky part: the book is in several public and college libraries. I try to check out every single copy of my book through inter-library loans. If that's not possible, I fly to the libraries and steal their copies. If I can't steal them, I set fire to them in the library bathrooms and try to escape before the alarm goes off.

Now the expensive part: the copies of my book in China, Taiwan, Italy, Germany, and Palestine. I ask readers for help burning the books, but they can only do so much. So I purchase a multicity plane ticket: Berlin, Rome, Beijing, Taipei. I don't bother to fly to Tel Aviv, which I tried once. I was questioned for hours because of my Palestinian last name and wasn't allowed to enter Israel. So I call a journalist friend of mine, and she rounds up all the Hebrew copies and burns them in front of a settlement that had once burned down her family's olive orchard. She takes photos so we can show my father proof that those copies are burned.

In Berlin I snort coke and go clubbing for forty-two hours straight and then drunkenly collect all the German copies of my book in a sack and carry it on to a flight to Rome, where I drink lots of espresso and do the same thing all over again. I find every copy of my book in China, and in Taiwan, too. I bring all these copies with me on a flight to Austin, Texas.

When I arrive in Austin, I get nostalgic, because I can't afford to live there anymore. The airport is full of transplants: women in expensive cowboy boots who don't deserve to call my old city home. I rent a car and drive twenty miles to Kyle, go to the post office, where the rest of the books wait for me, and take them all to a field a few miles outside of town, by the five-mile dam where my son and I used to swim because it was free. I pile the books into a kind of pyre. In my hand I carry long, dramatic matches. My best friend stands beside me and asks if I'm sure I want to do this, and I say I do because, despite everything, I love my dad. Then I light a match and touch its bald, burning head to the base of the pyre.

The books go up in flames. The flames last for a while. The bibilo-clasm gives me a small bibliogasm. I take pictures with my iPhone and text them to my mother so she can show my father. After an hour of burning, I check my email on my phone. I have three junk emails from Netflix, PEN American, and Change.org.

A few minutes later my mother texts and says that my father wants to know if I also deleted all the files of the book on my computer.

I fly to my house in California, pull up all the files on my laptop, and delete them. Then I find the files I had sent myself as backups in 2001, 2003, 2004, 2005, and I delete those, too. Every single trace of my first novel is eliminated.

6.

In the thirteenth century the armies of the Mongol Empire, led by Hulagu Khan—Genghis Khan's grandson—stood outside Iraq and asked its caliph to surrender and pay his respects. When the caliph refused, Hulagu and his men attacked Baghdad, ravaging the city. Nearly a million people were killed. All the libraries were burned down, including one called the House of Wisdom. It is said that the water of the Tigris River ran indigo with the ink of books that had been hurled into it.

7.

My novel is completely erased. That's when I imagine my father arrives at my rented bungalow to tell me that he loves me again. We hug. Then he tells me that, while we were hugging, he noticed I have back rolls, and that my skin is dry, and if I really loved him, I would lose weight. As in shrink. Become smaller.

And that's when I have to admit to myself that my father might want *me* to disappear, too. He might want to erase me. To throw me, and not my book, onto the pyre.

8.

In 1948 Israeli soldiers ransacked Palestinian homes and looted family libraries. Sixty thousand books and manuscripts were stolen. The eight thousand books that remain are now housed at the National Library of Jerusalem. The other fifty-two thousand were pulped or burned. My father was burned—no, born!—in 1950 and grew up in the West Bank. His biggest crime, like that of all Palestinians, was his birth, and the sentence for this crime is disappearance. The main problem with Palestinians is that they continue to exist.

In 2007 the Hamas-run Ministry of Education threatened to burn a collection of Palestinian folklore that it had deemed pornographic, but Palestinians protested this decision, saying the folktales, though sometimes crude, were a cultural treasure. They'd been transmitted orally for centuries. They needed to be preserved. The ministry swiftly revoked the decision to set the books aflame.

9.

Recently I met an elderly artist in West Texas whose daughter didn't talk to him for years. We sat together by a natural pool, and he told me that he thinks my father wants my respect. He told me that sometimes, though it seems strange, we have to apologize to the people who have wronged us.

Another man, a lover, told me that having a father is better than not having one. His own father died six years ago.

Then a good friend of mine lost her father.

And that is when I decided to contact my father—for real—to see if he still wants me to burn my books.

He doesn't.

I fly out to New York to see him, and when we meet, I apologize. I tell him I'm sorry that I hurt him. We hug. Seven years after we last spoke. We are both on our best behavior. He isn't critical of me, but he also doesn't apologize. I ask if we can agree not to talk about the hurtful things we've said and done in the past, and he says yes, let's not mention the times you've shamed and disappointed me. He laughs, and I try to laugh, too.

That afternoon we go for a walk and stop at the shop that carries his favorite Arabic newspaper. He buys it, and I hug him again while he holds the newspaper written in his mother tongue.

My father now has Parkinson's, and his body is curled slightly inward. His socks are pulled up too high, and his mustache is completely white. Seeing him changed like this stings. And I understand that I need to let go of my old image of my father—tyrant, bully, biblioclast—because he no longer exists.

⬚ ⬚ ⬚ ⬚ ⬚

12

FADY JOUDAH

Your Name Is on the List

On August 2nd, 1990, I became a born-again American. I didn't know it at the time. I was a college sophomore in Athens, Georgia, on my way two years later to medical school in Augusta. My parents and siblings were visiting from Riyadh. The news of the Kuwait invasion on the evening screen surprised us. Our lives were about to change but how and when? Dad kept his cool as pretense in our presence. Soon the Saudi and US governments would play their cards and expose him. Back in Riyadh, in the first days of November, dad received a letter from the intelligence branch of the Saudi Ministry of Interior informing him that his contract at the university was terminated, effective immediately, and that he and his family had seventy-two hours to leave the country.

A week before the Saudi letter reached him, Dad got a call from an American friend at the embassy. At the time, Mom was an Arabic instructor there. A résumé that would later help her and dad to land jobs when the family resettled in Clarksville, Tennessee in 1992.

"Ahmad," said the American voice, "I'm calling to let you know the Saudi government asked us to supply them with the list of residents we have files on. Your name is on the list. They called a second time and asked for your file specifically. I could do nothing about it, of course, but give you heads-up. I'm sorry. They also asked about Zarifah, whether we had reason to be cautious with her. We told them there was nothing there."

The reason the US had a file on my dad was not because he was the husband of the language teacher at the embassy. The file dated back to the 1960s, dad's graduate days in the States. Hoover's FBI kept tabs on Arab students, especially those who had leanings toward Nasser's Egypt and the Palestinian cause. After Stokely Carmichael's visit to campus in Austin, dad was interviewed by FBI agents. They wanted to know whether he and others had anything to do with the invitation. They wanted names, and to let dad and friends know they were being watched.

"Did they ask about anything in particular?" dad asked his friend at the embassy.

"Yes, they wanted us to confirm whether you were an Arafat advisor."

"What did you tell them?"

"That we knew what they knew. That you used to visit with him whenever he came to the city. Your name was on the sign-in sheets. No secret. And that if you did have his ear, we considered it a good thing, a possibility for a backchannel one day."

I'd met Arafat once on one of those visits. I was sixteen. He was a short, energetic, effusive man, a person in meta-longing—a longing beyond the present—entrapped in what became, with time, a perilous yet necessary conversation. And as much as anyone of us is made up of photons, Arafat was a beam of light that bent with the arc of justice. Or he was a moon that reflected the light others projected on it. In certain parts of the world and for many people, he was the dark side of their moon. In other parts and for many more, he was the light they saw in themselves. He was better than a man on a twenty-dollar bill. Or another who dodged a leather shoe.

Dad knew Arafat in the 1950s at the University of Cairo. All Palestinian students, refugees, displaced, or threatened with disappearance knew each other. Their relationship was always superficial and wouldn't have led to a functional backchannel, as the American embassy man suggested, perhaps to sugarcoat the Saudi obsession. Dad thinks it was a letter he'd sent to Arafat months before the Gulf War that did him harm. In the letter, he proposed the establishment of an international union of Palestinian intellectuals. The letter must have been intercepted, dad thinks, by some petty banality of evil. I think dad was wrong. The Arafat incident was a farce of national security in paranoid times. It was also a part of the chronic persecution of Palestinians for daring to stand up to the gravity of their loss. His American record was evidence of this. After Dad immigrated to the US and he was up for citizenship, an FBI agent paid him another visit, "to close the book on this, once and for all," the agent said in reply to my father's disquiet with the nonsense of the visitation.

The meeting took place in my parents' residence in Clarksville.

"Mr. Joudah, would you clarify the nature of your relationship with Arafat? I know it's all here," the agent pointed to the file in his hand, "but would you, in your own words, one last time, for the sake of this interview?"

"If it's all in there, I have nothing else to add."

"Mr. Joudah, is it true that you used to report to him about internal US matters in the 1960s?"

"I had access only to public things."

"But did you report to him?"

"This is absurd. I have nothing more to say."

From Hoover, or is it Truman, to a Saudi King. From Balfour to now and through one of his graduate professors in the 1960s who told him, "Ahmad, I want to be frank with you. I don't like Arabs. Find another path away from me." From my days as a young American watching my dad pulled out of the customs line for questioning at JFK airport. Fingerprints collected in a glass-walled room so that transparency's meaning is a double-edged sword in case dad, within his rights, didn't offer his fingerprints voluntarily, which he didn't. There was always someone who believed his file needed updating.

Dad, through good friends and calm heads, didn't leave Saudi Arabia in seventy-two hours. He was granted reprieve. Still he was forced to resign his post at the university. There was no staying for him after that. And he began to plan another departure. In January 1991 he sent me a letter with all his and Mom's confidential information enclosed, should anything happen to them while Scud and Patriot missiles consummated their romance. He ordered me and my older brother to file for their immigration. They were granted entry to the US without their children, all three of them minors. My parents flew my three siblings to Derna to be with their two aunts. Who else would Mom trust more than her sisters? In a few months, my youngest sister would turn four. Her mom would part ways with her soon thereafter. Another severance that nearly dissolved my mom in its boiling oil. To say that my parents were distraught is an understatement. To say that their Palestinian wounds were exhausting and inexhaustible is to undermine their beauty which they called upon throughout their lives.

What did Mom and her sisters talk about in case she died away from her children? Did they have another howling goodbye when she left her three kids in their care? Dad suppressed his pain, went about his world as he had done, methodically. He was about to enter the darkest, most hurtful days of his adult life. It was his PTSD at last that would hit him like a freight train for all to see. Betrayed and persecuted, displaced a second time, he found his gaze, head and neck, fixed on the past while his torso was given its marching orders. To look ahead he had to turn his body toward the past. To keep his torso toward the future, he couldn't see ahead of him.

To bring my siblings over from Derna and out of their aunts' care, a congressional humanitarian parole was needed. This would come through the office of a black Congressman in Texas who would later lose his seat in reelection. His warm welcome of my parents was unconditional. They came to him through an old friend, from the Austin days, the same woman who had secured a spot for Mom in the Austin Daily as a *bride from Palestine* soon after I was born.

The Austinian woman was now well-to-do. And yet it was her housekeeper who knew how to get to the Congressman on more personable terms, through family ties. Whatever the serendipity, it was about women, mothers talking and standing up for each other. The humanitarian parole was obtained in October 1992. The letter was sent to me. As a first-year medical student, I had the most stable address in my family. I called my parents, heard their relief like steam simultaneously coming through every manhole in a metropolis. My parents had spent a year away from their younger children, the youngest of them had celebrated her fifth birthday an ocean and continent away.

"Three hundred and seventeen days," Mom corrects me.

My parents' Austinian friend was the first person to greet my parents at the airport when they landed in the US after immigration was granted. They went straight to Austin, to be in her reassuring company. On the way to her house, a demonstration across a bridge slowed down traffic. The demonstrators were vociferous, Mom recalled. She was curious about their grievance. "They're protesting for the rights of bats to continue their residence within the city, under bridges. Their colonies make for spectacular sunsets," said their friend.

"I wish I were a bat," Mom sighed.

An ant, a bee, a termite.

An albatross, a heron.

A colony.

Mother, your sunsets are stunning.

Forbidden Fruit

"What's the matter, dad?"

"I reached the part where I had to walk back alone in the wee hours that dawn," he said. "I was just a boy. I'd forgotten how scared I was."

My youngest sister walked in on our dad one day in the basement in Clarksville. He was at his desk writing down his memories as we had urged him to do. She found him in tears.

It's a cut-out portion of the story in 1948 that dad has repeated to us throughout our lives. He was forced by none other than his illiterate mother to return in the dark and get his school papers after the migration south had begun. It was always the same truncated narrative, told as if it were the story of a boy whose mother had sent him to fetch eggs or bread before the neighbor ran out, the shop closed, or the sun set. Did he cry along the way and never tell anyone about it?

It was afternoon. Dad saw the Egyptian commander leave town in his vehicle. The troops were readying for *strategic withdrawal*—leaving town without notifying the people so as not to spread panic. Everyone panicked. The people were defenseless. Dad ran to tell his family. The word spread like fire in dry wood. In an hour, nearly five thousand people were marching out of town with barely anything on their backs. There was no time to pack or load. Some forgot the cash they'd been saving in the lining of their bedsheets.

A couple of hundred men, mostly young, stayed behind to claim what belongs to the people, should anyone care to listen to them. Of our family, my paternal grandfather stayed behind.

The exodus scarcely traversed a handful of kilometers in the sand before darkness fell. The people were on the outskirts of Hamameh, a small town north of Majdal-Askalan. They were thirsty and hungry. There was a huge field of sugar cane. Its owner stood at the entrance to ward people off like flies. Dad laughs at this. The landowner succeeded in protecting his crop but a few days later he lost everything he owned to the Israelis when their dispossession crept further south, and the man ended up another refugee in Gaza.

In Hamameh they camped overnight. The adrenaline and despair had left so many depleted. Dad was in deep sleep when his distressed mother woke him.

"Did you bring your school certificates with you?" she asked him.

"No" was his reply.

She sent him on the double back to Isdud to get the papers.

"Now?" the exhausted boy protested.

"Yes. Go straight to your dad. He's at the house. You can't risk losing all those years of education on top of our losing everything else," Halimeh said.

"I'm hungry," Dad said.

"I have no food, and there's no time. Go," she commanded her youngest and favorite son.

Dad walked back in the dark of the wee hours. His listening was dazed with random gunshot echoes, jackals howling, hyena giggling, and dogs barking. He got to Isdud and his father opened the door. Startled, my grandfather told him to get his papers and skedaddle out of town as fast as he could. "But I'm hungry," the boy pleaded. "There's no food here." Famished, my dad knew where to go. He sought an old, large lotus tree at the edge of town where he used to rest and play. He ate his fill of its figs then packed his pockets for the trek back.

He got to Hammeh late. The masses had already left further south. Caravans of the displaced had to make room for other caravans on their heels from other towns in the area. Dad joined whatever flow had raised itself up for the uprooting, a pilgrimage to loss, linear on the ground, circuitous and borderless otherwise. He reached Majdal-Askalan and went straight to the Egyptian Military attaché. A young boy of fourteen years, my dad was eloquent and intuitive. He had gained the respect and friendship of a senior Egyptian commander who would later become a lifelong friend. The Egyptian man issued ten flour sacks for my dad to take to his family. Eight of the sacks went to other elders in the clan. Dad was left with two for his immediate family of fourteen individuals. To get the two sacks to Gaza, he hired a cameleer. Each bag weighed about fifty kilograms. The cameleer's fee was one sack.

The hordes of the dislocated were omen bearers for the towns they passed through, tremors of flight, messengers of dreams and nightmares of return and exile. Each town the displaced visited on that migration path would later be sacked and depopulated. Each town they passed through they cursed as they left behind their ghosts in air and cactus.

The caravan that my dad and his cameleer joined to Gaza left at night. That's all he remembers. Throngs of people, their crepitus and clanking under a waxing gibbous moon. In Gaza my grandmother, her children, their wives and children, stayed in one room at a friend's house. He was an ex-soldier who had fought alongside my grandfather in WWI in the Ottoman army. In a few days, my second uncle would go back into cleansed territory and get his family a massive camel hair tent for them to move into.

In Isdud, the Israelis split the few hundred men who stayed behind into two groups. The young became prisoners of war and were sent to labor camps to assist the looting effort. The old were sent south to Gaza. My grandfather was among those.

"Ahmad, do you remember Avraham, the shoe smith?" My dad's friend, Batrawi, asked him. Batrawi, three years older than my dad, was among those imprisoned for staying behind, forced to help in the plundering of the depopulated villages and towns.

Avraham had no family or at least none that anyone knew about. He was the only Jewish man who lived in Isdud. His shop was his home. He slept, ate, worked there. He was the best at what he did, had taken in a few local apprentices, taught them his trade well. During the war, he disappeared only to reappear as a guard in one of the prison camps.

"He treated us well," Batrawi said of Avraham. "He brought us tea and other small comforts he had access to. He would reminisce with us about the old days as we sipped hot drinks together. But he kept coming around to one question. A question about that guy who once looted his shoe shop and was not caught or punished. 'Do any of you know Musa's whereabouts?' Avraham would ask us repeatedly. But no one knew where Musa was. Then we lost track of Avraham. Work got in the way. There was furniture and livestock to expropriate, books to shelve in Israeli libraries and tag as *Abandoned Property*."

As for dad's night journey to retrieve his schooling documents, it wasn't necessary after all. But he got to eat the figs of the lotus tree one last time, against forgetting. He took one last look at his town, whole, against erasure.

Wormhole
Bonfire, Oleander

Come back, butterfly, I'm only a post on your migratory path, a settlement that doesn't become a nation. I'll be your residence for as long as you need. *Come back. Home is gone.*

Since I was a child my dad would tell me fragments of my second-oldest uncle's story about return. Dad never began the telling in the same place and never picked it up from where he'd interrupted it last. Only he knew the triggers that brought the splinters alive within him. Even when I asked him to tell it whole, from A to Z, I'd notice a missing loose end or an omitted digression. Here I gather what I can knowing fully well: how incomplete the tale is. In some instances, I know what I leave out. In others, I don't.

"After migration from Isdud, refugee camps popped up all around Gaza," said Dad, "but your uncle wouldn't give up going back to town. He rejected tents and couldn't accept that all was lost. Once, sometimes twice a week, he'd go back. At first your uncle said that his returns were practical, to retrieve our belongings that we had left behind in the panic of that final afternoon. The village stood there vacant like a body waiting for us, its organs, to repopulate it. But all your uncle did was empty the town further. He brought back mattresses, blankets, clothes, utensils and who knows what else, women's accessories and small toys for kids. Then he started hauling the rest of our stored harvest, the last harvest we'd ever taste from our land, sacks and sacks of wheat we kept in a cellar, as most people did in those days.

"For a small fee, your uncle often enlisted Bedouins to help, a portion of the wheat or some clothing. They provided the camels when his donkey wasn't strong for the load. Were it not for your uncle we would have suffered brutal cold and hunger that first refugee winter when no UN agency came around. I remember the intense bonfires, how I'd tend them till the last ember," Dad said, "and how frequently a kid tripped and fell into a fire, suffered severe burns. None of this happened before when we lived in mud houses and kept warm with braziers.

"Your uncle," Dad continued, "didn't return to town alone. He mostly went with a cousin or two. It was a risky affair. There were landmines along the road. There were patrols that roamed the streets and alleys of our town, apparitions that shot at strangers who, weeks prior, had been the rightful residents. Once, while coming back by the shoreline, a land-mine blew up and took the life of his cousin and the donkey he was riding on. You know that dead man's son. That tall businessman who married the pediatrician you liked so much as a boy in Riyadh.

"And when there was no more wheat stored up in the belly of our houses, and no one else from other clans was going back to collect their stuff, your uncle started to bring back other people's wheat and kept it for himself and us. The owners of those homes protested. Our family was divided. Your mother's father, a kind and just man, suggested a fifty-fifty split. My father refused. His son, he said, was risking his life while others had risked nothing.

"Then our oldest brother, a pious man, chose against sin and refused to eat any food with the family that wasn't wheat-free. Luckily for him, the UN commenced their canned provisions shortly thereafter.

"He was imaginative, your uncle. He brought back an irrigation pump and a massive camel hair tent. And when there was nothing left of this paradoxical return, he persisted to visit the town. Your grandmother begged him to stop. 'Listen to your younger brother,' she told him. He would mock me: 'What possibly could he, a teenager who hangs out with Communists, know about the world?' But I knew we were simple villag-ers with limited agency. Your uncle was a wounded dreamer. Sometimes he went back just to walk the empty alleys, sit in the café alone, sleep under the roof he'd slept under for so many years, or in the open fields he used to tend, and watch the stars, a dose of home, a medicine that doesn't heal or cure. Then it got too dangerous. Surveillance increased. He had to camp out in the oleander grove outside town by the railroad the British had built. The same track that he fought to destroy in 1939 with other men in town. The same railroad your pious uncle worked on for years, and when he suffered a hand injury on the job, the British paid him workman's compensation for decades. They can respect a contract, those British, but not land or its people.

"There in the oleander grove your uncle dreamed of being the first one in town to return when return would be announced. From October to February," said Dad, "your uncle kept returning and dreaming, dream-ing and returning, and rolling his tobacco until February 24 when the armistice was signed. I sent for him through a Bedouin: *Come back. Home is gone.*"

On February 24, the treaty of Yandabo marked the British disintegration of the Burmese people. On February 24, the treaty of Dancing Rabbit Creek was proclaimed, under the Indian Removal Act, during Andrew Jackson's presidency, and became the first removal to be carried in effect. The Choctaw swapped land for peace and ended up with neither.

On February 24, a bounty on Salman Rushdie's head.

And Fidel Castro relinquished the Cuban presidency at long last.

"When you were born," said Dad, "your uncle was serving a jail sentence for peddling in rifles and plotting for return twenty-two years after our departure. And when he died nearly thirty years after that, he died a refugee vomiting blood in a hospital that had no more blood bags to give to old men."

Invisible Shrine

The desk at which my youngest sister found my dad crying, while reliving his fear of the dark on that exodus night, was the same desk he worked on in his study in Riyadh, the desk that shadowed much of my childhood.

In his study, his books were his companions, documents that preserved his scent, the dead skin on his fingertips, the potpourri of his life, his pressed flowers, and portals of time.

Dad's books were sacred property to him. Everyone in the family knew it. This hallowed bond dates to 1956 when the Israelis invaded Gaza. Dad was in Unaizeh, Saudi Arabia. His family put his books in a wooden box and buried them. If found, through search and seizure, they would incriminate him and the family. After Israeli withdrawal, the books were never returned to their shelves. They stayed in the box. The family knew it was a matter of time before they'd need to rebury the books, those forbidden things with unharnessed powers. That time came in 1967, the year my parents were married. The box was forgotten in the ground. When it was remembered, the courtyard of the house had been rebuilt.

In Riyadh, Dad had to sell his library. He needed the cash. To slow the hemorrhaging of his life-savings that awaited him in the coming years as he embarked on another resettlement. A few thousand books, hundreds of them collectible, he sold them to a private library. The section that housed his books bears his name. I remember his library as a boy, its towering shelves, solitude in columns and rows, a place I would enter to imagine my dad where I know him least, admired him most, a man whose heart was after *the history that history neglects* as he was fond of saying.

After Riyadh, he didn't teach college again. He would take nearly twenty years to pick up a pen to write another article or book. The job he and Mom locked into, the only job they could find to combine their income, was as language instructors for the 101st Airborne special unit in Fort Campbell. They had mouths to feed. Dad swallowed his shame. Mom, on the other hand, gave each soldier she taught an Arabic name, occasionally served them delicious food and, in turn, they called her mom, helped her around the house, built her a deck, chopped the fallen willow and maple when hurricanes felled them.

"Maybe, at some crucial moment in a stranger's life, Arab, Muslim or not, here or faraway, one of these boys would hesitate to pull the trigger because of what we shared with them," Mom would say in existential mode, to counter the indignity her husband felt, or the cringe inside her as her soldier sons were deployed to invade Iraq in 2003.

Of Saints and Dreams of Escape

In December 1998, I took my dad and his US passport to Isla Mujeres. After eight years in the chrysalis of his defeat he was emerging into triumphant life. The sea, I thought, would take him back to childhood, to the Mediterranean, Isdud, Deir al-Balah, and Gaza. In the transparent blue waters of the Yucatan he stood in his swimming trunks, water lapping his knees. He'd been talking for a while, scene after scene, act after act, about his second exodus, the Riyadh expulsion, exorcising demons. I asked him if he remembered the dream he had on the night of the day he took us to see his village twelve years earlier. My brother and I were teenagers then. No longer his village, forever his and ours. His face went blank for a moment. I tossed in a few headlines to entice his recall, but he was somewhere else already. He said, "In Clarksville, I had another dream.

"I walked in on the King in his court in Riyadh and I objected to what he'd done to me. 'Why did you expel me?' I was terse with him. A shouting match ensued between us. Then I approached him with the intention to strike him. My arm was raised. His guards stepped in and I started running. I ran harder and harder, couldn't shake them off. And just before they could catch me I started flying."

He became the light at the edge of a black hole. To escape he flapped his arms. "It was hard to get off the ground," he said. "I'd overcome gravity then struggle with it again. I kept flapping my arms until your mother woke me and held me for a while." Then he chuckled: "I must have wing-beaten her during my flight."

A vivid dreamer, I inherited my dad's sleep. I startle my wife with groans through the gates of my grinding teeth, a horn in my viscera blowing to alert a herd of one.

Not all my chase dreams end in paraplegia before my screams wake me among the living and the well. Sporadically my floundering for survival and escape transforms into a capacity to walk in air. Submerged in Lethe, the terrible anxiety of the chase is instantly wiped out. It dissolves into my lower limbs climbing a staircase in space where gravity has ceased. No one can reach me there. And each time, to suspend or interrogate my disbelief, I tread deeper into this bliss, a bliss that opiates me. I bounce around in all directions until a simple thrust levitates me, like a bird riding a high current barely needs to flap its giant wings. When I wake, I remember nothing of the chase and, for a few seconds, am unable to distinguish reality from dream, gravity from its abeyance.

I can never predict the elements necessary for this rare recurrence. But it does come in other varieties, most notably when the dead reappear to me in my sleep. By dream's end my dead become so alive that their death is what's unreal for a while after I wake. This is loveliest when I fall quickly back to sleep until the morning. I safeguard their resurrection for a few hours more.

In November 1990, when the letter of termination from his job was posted, Dad was fifty-six years old. It's an age I dread. Sometimes we imagine the age of our parents' death as our destiny. And if not their death then the age they suffered their first debilitating ailment, the one that flings mortality at one's face like no previous illness had done. No doubt this is an exaggerated belief in the potent precision of genetics that humans had adopted over millennia. We are animals addicted to pattern. Pattern as the mother of science and the inexplicable.

After great pain a formal feeling comes. And within that formal feeling, beyond a certain threshold, there is no hierarchy of suffering. Who measures that threshold? What science? Will it always be a science coupled to power? For Dad, home had been pulverized, reduced repeatedly to its nuclear constituents. As if he'd been gulagged to the Big Bang of belonging. An imaginary time, without boundary, without beginning or end.

Prodigiously we are full of praise for, and awe of, those who have surpassed this annihilation of home. We revere the energy they emanate, the sum of histories they cancel out inside us. Those who have overcome identity are either heroes or saints. The hero, a singularity, overcomes identity by subjugating and employing it to maximum utility on a collective scale. The national scale is one example. The saints succeed by transcending place and conventional time.

Sometimes the hero and saint merge into one. Joan of Arc, for example, or Saint Genevieve. Or the Palestinian-born Saint George, an apparition of Khidr, the mystic who lives across epochs.

My father is no hero and no saint. He stared down his deletion and resisted it. I had grown up with his struggle, as I did with my mother's and that of numerous family and friends who colored my life. Dad is always writing Isdud into the world. One village as synecdoche of Palestine, and one people beyond metaphor for the human condition. His erased home whose remains live on inside him, offered him an alternate cosmos, a shuffle between order and disorder, a gift the dead, who are the past, sometimes share with the living to soothe their woe, to teach them how to live.

What death awaits me at fifty-six? What will eat at me until then, until I survive it, if I do? Will it be the death of place or profession? Or will I feel I had nothing to fear all along?

Year after year my father walked Isdud alley by vanished alley, field by disappeared field, and one neighborhood after another he entered its houses. The first time I saw him perform this magic, impersonate a state none of us could see while standing on the same piece of earth as he was, was on the day he took us, my brother and me, to see his village. I was fourteen, the same age Dad was when he last lived in Isdud.

To Be Continued

That day in Gaza, a family friend picked us up in his car and drove across the checkpoints to Isdud, now a coastal city in Israel, a modern port. We passed a large prison camp, its sterile, sinister walls. Isdud, the ghost town, three or four kilometers inland, where farmland was best, was our destination. A police officer stopped us, issued the driver a ticket over a license plate technicality. "You people need to learn the rules," he said.

Where the town once stood was a field of almond and orange trees. Around its edges and in its interstitial spaces, grass and cacti were overgrown. Dad started pointing things out. There was his elementary school at one end of town. A stone building, roofless, with gouged out eyes for windows. We walked its grassy floor. Here is where he sat in first grade. His best friend sat over there. And behind the stony partition was his third-grade classroom. We followed his footsteps and voice. The girl's school was further. Its construction was completed the year they were driven out of the village and was never inaugurated. We walked toward the mosque and the main café or what remained of them. The café had a staircase like an ancient scaffolding that led to the roof. A radio used to broadcast its sounds. Men played backgammon. Then off we went to two of the three shrines in town.

The older shrine had a grotto that hosted children, graciously, for games of hide-and-seek, especially on holy days. It belonged to Salman, a Persian disciple of Mohammad. The Prophet had made him part of his bloodline, through divine ordinance, after Salman advised the Prophet to dig a trench during a critical siege, and this proved crucial to victory. Other versions suggest that the shrine housed the remains of another disciple, the first admiral in Islam who managed to defeat the Byzantines at sea. He lived in nearby Askalan, where Saint George had slayed the dragon, but the admiral died in Isdud. The shrine was consecrated in 1268 by decree of the Mamluk Sultan Baibars.

The second shrine was for Matbuli, a Sufi Imam who lived in Egypt under the auspices of another Mamluk Sultan, Qaitbay. Through his dedication to the poor and disenfranchised, Matbuli's popularity grew. Whether he moved to Isdud willingly or was expelled by the Sultan through the influence of sycophants is irrelevant. He outlived the Sultan and died in Isdud circa 1499. His shrine was better preserved, as it had been instated more recently, in 1858.

The least known of the three shrines belonged to a local man. Not much is known about him. His death was the most recent, within a century or so. As kids, Dad remembers they were cautioned against playing too close to the tomb. The shrine possessed a life force that transformed the strong emotions and feelings of those within its domain, happy or not, into incomprehensible, unpredictable states.

Twenty-six years later, when my parents visited the town's ruins again—this time with my youngest sister, the one they had to leave behind in Derna after leaving Riyadh—they found both older shrines had been leveled.

Almond and orange trees were now wheat fields. The orange trees that my dad and his nephews had carved their names on during one of their returns to the grounds, were uprooted.

The local imam's shrine, the smallest and lowest to the ground, could not be removed.

A Bedouin man stood guard at the grounds. As he asked them not to linger too long, Dad inquired about the shrines. The guard told him that after Caterpillars were done with the two older sanctuaries, the bulldozer came to a halt when it approached the third one. At first the driver was unable to operate the machine, as if it were a donkey responding to a higher presence, it didn't budge. Then the driver himself became paralyzed, briefly immobile and bewildered. Terrified, the crew rejected further orders to demolish the tomb.

Did the driver suffer a mini-stroke, a transient ischemic attack that served as psychic illusion for those around? When is the history of desecration a transhistorical event and when is it a universal phenomenon? Are ruins a prerequisite for return?

I remember how trapped I felt within the mysterious clouds of that afternoon. My dad's excitement as he reanimated Isdud for his two sons' blind eyes. It was incongruous with the pain I knew he'd felt when he spoke to us of Palestine. This joy, of having brought us back to absence, the indelible proof of his past, didn't fit. His was an outer body experience. That was the only explanation. He had gone beyond memory.

I grasped this most clearly when we came upon the sycamore tree of his childhood. We had arrived at the family's part of town. Here stood our house. There our mother's parents lived. Here was the threshing floor. There was a winter pond, and on and on, I became dizzy and disoriented while he was thriving in virtuality.

He found the sycamore tree exactly where he'd left it the last time he saw it whole, forty years earlier. Only its thick wide stump remained. An old matriarch of the landscape, it had been amputated.

Twenty-six years after he brought his boys to Isdud, he returned with his wife and youngest daughter. The latter took photos of the town's bones: the two schools, the café, the mosque. In front of the boys' school was a large sycamore tree. Dad says it wasn't there when they fled in 1948.

Did a wind carry the seeds of my father's sycamore tree to the boys' school? Did the two trees talk with each other before the elder one was hacked? Did the stump have anything to say afterwards? Did it speak of watching mud houses decay then get bulldozed? The new sycamore at the boys' school is still waiting for children to climb it.

I stood in front of the stump and Dad stood behind it, with his back to where a house wall would have been. The stump knew whose son I was. It followed me for years until I could recognize it. It was 2005 when I did. I was in Darfur. In the plain that separated Nertiti from the slope-gates of Jebel Mara. There it stood, a giant sycamore in semidesert, old as my father, and whole. I greeted it each time I rode the jeep past it into the mountain to deliver medical care to a besieged people once a week. And I greeted it each time I came down the mountain into town.

Event Horizon

On the night of the day my dad took my brother and me to see his village, all three of us slept in one room on thin foam mats on the floor. Deep in the night my brother and I woke to my dad making terrifying noises from the caverns of his consciousness. He was dreaming. The noise didn't let up. It heightened as if a wizard was calling the forces of darkness to the light and risked his own demise in the process. It was a nightmare. My brother and I watched as Dad waltzed with apnea. His moans grew louder like an aphasic man trying to will an alphabet into being.

"Shall we wake him?" my brother asked

"We should wait," I said. "It will end soon, and if it ends without his waking, he won't remember it in the morning, and we won't have to either." This was no comfort to my brother.

"And if it doesn't end?" The look in his eyes wanted to arrest a dream before it commits a nightmare, or arrest the nightmare before it commits a murder.

Yes, I thought to myself, people have been known to die from their dreams, in them, all that panting and adrenaline. The hesitation on my face while my secret soliloquy went on was all my brother needed as he nudged our father awake. I felt relief and defeat at once. I didn't want to know what the dream was about, and had hoped to spare Dad that knowledge. But that knowledge was nothing new to him. His face wore the calm of an experienced dreamer.

"What was it, Dad, what was it?" we asked in unison to justify our action and express our concern.

"Oh, nothing," he said as he cleared his throat. "Some Israeli soldiers were chasing me. I was just sorting out my run," and he went back to sleep.

13

⬜ ⬜ ⬜ ⬜ ⬜

JOE KADI

The Saving Grace of a Favorite Cousin

4 May 2018
My most favorite of favorite cousins—
sending love as I write—

I can't believe Jameelah did that. It seems so intentional and clearly thought out . . . and I always think of her as so sweet. You did express your belief that there were other personality traits lurking beneath the surface. She had access to dozens of things and yet she deliberately chose to shred that sweet little hummingbird's nest Duncan gave you on your six-month anniversary! So sweet of him. So nasty of her. Ouch ouch ouch. Of course you were upset. Did she seem to grasp what you were saying when you threatened to take her back from whence she came? And what was Oscar Wilde doing when all this was happening? Looking wide-eyed and somewhat alarmed, I suppose. You do have your hands full with them.

Speaking of him, I couldn't sleep two nights ago, and got myself on YouTube, looking for a suitable old movie to put myself to sleep with. *The Trial of Oscar Wilde* popped into my head, for some unknown reason. So I watched the first hour and fifteen minutes. It's amazing what can happen when your adored cousin has done a standup comedy schtick on that terrible line about street Arabs. "What did you expect? Did you think I was some kind of common street Arab to be bought with cheap trinkets and an occasional supper in some Soho restaurant?" (youtube.com, *The Trial of Oscar Wilde*, 21:18). It didn't bother me at all! I laughed hysterically, remembering you standing on the wobbly chair in your kitchen, copying the line in your terrible British accent, and then giving your best

Jack Shaheen *Reel Bad Arabs* explanation. (Bless him; what a gift for our community.) This is the way to deal with racist stereotypes!

Seriously, though, I hope that Jameelah's momentary lapse of good judgement isn't going to stop you from moving ahead with the Bast tattoo. I so love the idea of two queer Arabs cousins with Bast tattoos, visually stating our commitment to carrying on the fine upstanding Arab tradition of cat worship. I think the left shoulder is a perfect spot. It won't hurt as much as the back of the neck.

First the irritating story of the week, so I can get it out of the way. You know how relieved I am not to be at the same school as you-know-who. Relief isn't quite the right word—not strong enough. No more painful encounters in the hall, no more marching into those monthly meetings like a soldier going off to battle—from which he knows he might not return. Well, this week, she ended up at my school, for some meeting with some set of unfortunates. And of course I had to run into her, on the fifth floor of Social Science. I lied through my teeth, responding with the same "Yes, it's good to see you too." Should I have been honest? Are social pleasantries a tradition worth holding onto? Are they the glue that holds our barely civil society somewhat together?? You tell me, you've got a better handle on those things. As she and the unfortunate colleague who was accompanying her made off down the hall, I distinctly heard her say: "Oh yes, that's Women's Studies! A white man teaching!"

This has gone on for years. And yes, I corrected her, sometimes in the group setting, sometimes one-on-one. Do you know how I fought to stay calm during these encounters? And of course I had to speak calmly and respectfully—no more righteous anger from the Arabs or queers or women in these enlightened times. Ha ha. Yes, of course you remember. You've heard about all 437 of them! And right now you're wondering if I managed to hold on to my sense of self through this latest attack on my racial identity. No I did not. I came home with that shrinking feeling, like our dear Lily in *The Incredible Shrinking Woman*. My version would be *The Incredible Shrinking Arab Canadian Transgender Man*, and of course I wouldn't be as funny as she is. Not that there's much to laugh at, as far as I can tell. It's my perennial struggle, here in Calgary. In a city with all these Arabs, all of us ostensibly falling into the category of visible minority. But when you're light-skinned, and the name is Joe and not Mohammed, and the accent is absent because English is your first language, good luck. The system grinds on diligently and efficiently, in a no-nonsense manner.

Racism has a million ways of creating hyper-visibility and invisibility on the same day, at the same time, with the same people.

Remember the gray Formica table, the chairs we squirmed into with our short legs, two chubby Lebanese kids with mouths watering? Gram maneuvering the wooden paddle to take the Syrian bread out of the oven. Working to avert another scar on her forearm that sometimes came from touching the hot wire rack. How on earth did she come to think rubbing butter is the way you take care of a burn? Don't we have better folk medicine traditions? Must have been something else we lost on the way over.

For you Syrian bread at the top of the list, for me grape leaves. We both pretend-smoked them, then got into the serious business of fingering them with utmost tangible pleasure, playing with the bits that fell out onto the plate, letting the lemon taste melt. BTW, have you noticed how many non-Arabs think there's too much lemon in our dishes?! Ha—how is that possible? The look of utmost satisfaction and just-rightness that lit up Aunt Rose's face as she sucked the juice of a half-lemon, then immediately picked up the second and finished the job. It took me a while to work up to it but I can do it now. There might be a bit of puckering but it's minimal.

No concern then about Racial Identity—capital R, capital I. None. Just two earnest children responding appropriately when a loving grandmother filled up our plates. In that tiny bungalow with two tiny bedrooms, Gram and Aunt Rose each with their single bed. The striking cleanliness of the house, the simplicity, the few possessions. Same as all of ours, basically. How small everything was, how little we had. Navigating the vagaries of working-class existence in southern Ontario within the global capitalist system, circa 1960s. How many people alive today use a word like vagary? I wish we hadn't lost so many words. I wish our language wasn't weakening. Please—don't let me start in about my students' writing skills. Or lack thereof.

I know what you did the minute you picked up this letter from the mailbox. Got yourself inside, prepared the tea, and lit up. Sprawled out on the couch with this letter. At least we're doing our best to keep that particular Arab tradition alive. We haven't gone over to the other side—with organic wine or beer from a local micro-brewery. Cannabis it is, and while Trudeau and his team have dropped the ball on way too many important promises, at least we're moving toward legalization of our favorite herb! We have to figure out a way to get ourselves together to celebrate, on the day it's finally legal. Why are you on the other end of the country? Why are you on the East Coast? I know, I know. The real question is how did I end up in Calgary? Exactly. It's a question I ask myself on a regular basis. Where was I—oh, racial identity. Who cares about it, who thinks about it, when you've got enough people around who see you? Even one. If you and I lived in the same city, and regularly hung out and ate and smoked and drank tea with great abandon, I would not feel this way. Invisible, that is. I would not feel that I had to prove anything. I would feel part of something, and it would be a physical thing, an embodied thing, that was just there, that I didn't have to talk about or name or explain or create a fucking theory about. Now I sound like some kind of biological determinist (is there such a word?) but you know what I mean—and you know I know it's not biological. But there's something embodied about it because I've felt it, when I've had it. And it hasn't been an intellectual thing. They're simple elemental activities that the body responds to. And when they're gone the external world's approval takes on such meaning. I wouldn't care about you-know-who if I was coming home to you and we could laugh about it and make fun of white people and remind each other that dear old Marilyn Frye did us a favor when she came up with the birdcage metaphor. Here in Calgary circa 2018 there are too many wires for me to fly around. There's the white world and its desire, maybe even its need, to know who's who as soon as they look at us. If it's not visible, it's not real. If your racial identity is not visible, it's not real. And of course then we've got the wires that come from our own community, from inside as it were.

I did take your advice. I showed up at a workshop planned by three local groups, where we learned about media representation of Arabs from an earnest—and yes, dark-skinned—thirty-year-old who no one had a problem identifying, and a white man with the same research topic. Which is great. What white person would have taken that on twenty years ago?! Guess what happened? From out in the hallway I saw the usual greetings amongst the folks who know each other, the simplicity and straightforwardness of the Arab-to-Arab greeting. With me, it was the highly excited, overly polite, and far too enthusiastic welcome of the Arab greeting a white person who has done them the great honor of coming to their event. I sank into a depression, which got worse when I saw the Styrofoam plates they were serving snacks on. Styrofoam! Yes, the stuff that takes half a million years to break down, the cocktail of toxins that should have been outlawed decades ago. Somehow these insults to the earth hit me harder than they used to, as climate chaos becomes more real with each passing day. Did you see the flooding in New Brunswick? Could just one weather reporter include just one sentence at the end their report on the latest flooding/hurricane/tornado/earthquake: "This appears to be part of the pattern of the intensification of extreme weather events that climate scientists have been warning about for thirty years." But who's counting? And I know, I know. You're right. It's time for me to light up. Consider it done. And thank Allah and the Creator and the Great Spirit and the Buddha for medical cannabis, that's all I can say.

Did you know E. M. Forster dedicated his book *Maurice* "to a happier year"? I like it—think I'll adopt it for my new slogan. Just tell me there is a happier year coming. Invisibility is a hard thing to reckon with, especially when you're doing your best to be visible. Can racial identity be taken away, can it be lost? Does it mean I'm letting others define me? Who has the power here? I don't know, I sure don't feel like I have it. Is one steady local connection with someone who knows who you are enough to sustain identity?

Whose perceptions about race matter? Who gets to decide who's who? Think about the range of understanding of racial identity within our own community. I've lived in places where I was part of the community —it was a group that understood our skin tones vary, our name patterns vary, and yet that didn't make anyone less than. It meant we operated from an inclusive definition of racial identity, an inclusive definition with the understanding that there is a diverse spectrum of Arabs.

So it happened again today. I was walking home, along 26th Ave., and a car drove by with a Manitoba license plate. You know what happened . . . that tiny bit of unusual green coloring on the plate that happens to be the exact same unusual green paint that Aunt C had in her kitchen, on the south wall. I know we have the same reactions when we see the license plate. Our three-hundred odd connections that no one else in the world shares. That green color, Gram's kitchen, the Capitol yellow-and-orange 45 label for the Beatles *P.S. I Love You*, the thick lilac bush in Uncle M's backyard we smoked our joints under. Don't ever ever ever ever ever go away. I've lost every other family member. You have to stay. Make that HAVE TO STAY.

I'm really OK with you still having the same positive thrill when you see the green; I want you to have that. I want you to have a positive connection with her. Even though mine's gone. When I see the license plate I have this dismally flat smack to my heart. She really has rejected me, and that relationship is gone. Even after everything that has happened in this family of ours—things that go beyond even the typical Arab fucked-up family dynamics—I can barely grasp this loss. There were three people I thought would stick with me through this life. Three. Out of that massive extended family. Whatever it was—a hundred of us? At least. Down to three. Aunt C, sibling, cousin. Three that I seriously believed, utterly knew, was so reassured by, the presence of the three of you and the earnest belief the three of you would stay. And in 2018, you're the only one still standing.

News flash: I confess, I do like to believe that I don't fall prey to the same mistakes other people make. Laugh as hard as you want. You know this about me. Fine. Laugh away. Lots of people are rejected by family members when they transition. These family members may have stood by them during things like same-sex relationships, disclosures about family violence. Like, for example, Aunt C. She stuck with me through thick and thin. I knew on an abstract level that none of that guaranteed support through a gender transition. I thought I knew it on a deeper level. But I didn't. I'm still in shock that she dumped me. And there's no doubt anymore, ten years into her rejection; now I understand that's connected to being on such shaky ground, racially speaking. Part of this gradual withering away of my racial identity is a direct result of that loss. Sitting in that gray kitchen with the unusual green paint on the south wall affirmed me in ways that go beyond speech.

And not to worry. I have totally let go of what happened last year when you were visiting Aunt C, and could not ignore the large elephant in the room, that is, me. You weren't doing that typical dysfunctional Arab family dynamic thing where people talk about other people without consent and cross all kinds of boundaries. Which is not your style—thank the Creator! The moment was there, you had to say something. Only to have her shut it down. "I have nothing to say about HER," she said icily and emphatically. The same tones she used during our last phone call.

Enough of that. How is the novel coming? We need the great Canadian love story between an Arab man and an Indigenous man. And you're the one to write it . . . . . . the two of you were so adorable together. Arguing over the merits of bannock versus Syrian bread. Why on earth did he decide grad school in New York was his heart's calling? And who says long-distance relationships can't work? Bad decision, Duncan, that's all I can say. I know, I know, it's all water under the bridge and you're happy he's doing environmental law for his people up north and you haven't thought about him *in that way* for years. (Liar.) That's alright, I find myself in the same position. It's the age thing. Who thought we'd end up here, single and not a prospect in sight. Even after suffering through the indignities of online dating. At least you have it somewhat easier as a gay man. Try being a trans man looking for a relationship with a woman. Good fucking luck, is all I can say.

Special request, special request. Please call at least once this coming week and fill up my voice mail with your best imitation of your mother's voice when you came out to her. The way you nail that note of shrillness coupled with fear when she said *There are no gay Lebanese!* I need a good laugh. Or two. Or three. How many gay men's coming out stories have to do with an extraordinary effort not to laugh at their dense parents swearing up and down that people like us only exist in other racial communities? Honestly. Not to mention that family members who could have been named at that moment . . . I mean, thinking about Cousin Johnny. Straight? I don't think so. . . . And we could name a few others here.

I do feel better, after writing this monologue or epistle or long-winded letter to you. I assume we are the only two queer Arab cousins in existence who write long letters to each other—in handwriting—with purple fountain pens. No texting for us!

Sending love, and more love, habibi. Pet Jameelah and Oscar for me, and give them catnip. Tell Jameelah you forgive her for destroying the hummingbird nest. I myself will wait for the special Halifax organic catnip that you are packing for Bronwyn.

Your most favorite of favorite cousins of all time, and of all lifetimes (if you were to believe in reincarnation which I know you do not, although I myself remain on the fence, given the fact that the Buddhists have an awful lot of things figured out correctly), I remain,

Joe

◻ ◻ ◻ ◻ ◻

14

MOHJA KAHF

I Cannot Go to Syria

If you want to piss me off, ask me when I last went to Syria.

I cannot go to Syria; I cannot go to Syria; I cannot go to Syria. For a lifetime, I cannot go to Syria. Born in Syria to Syrian parents, I did not create the conditions that have resulted in my never being able to set foot in Syria so long as the Baathist dictatorship rules. My parents became exiles when I was a child, so I became an exile as a child. I cannot go to Syria.

I cannot go to Syria, and my Syrian authenticity is questioned by US progressives who support the regime in Syria. I cannot go to Syria, and my authenticity to speak as a Syrian is questioned by some of the Syrians inside Syria who participate in the Syrian Revolution to protest the regime, which bars me from going to Syria for a lifetime. If these Syrians were forced to leave Syria with their children, if they were exiled by the regime for a lifetime, what do they think their children would be one day, but me? And will these new exiled Syrians question their children's authenticity to speak as Syrians about Syrian experiences, a lifetime from now?

If you're a friend and want to show how little you know me, ask me when I was last in Syria. Show surprise when I say it was the 1970s.

My family, with its array of moderate Islamist leanings, dissents against the Assad regime. I dissent against my family's particular type of dissent, but I still dissent against the Assad regime, and I still stand by my family's right to dissent without having their existence threatened. At least these folks to whom I am related and with whom I disagree so much got one thing right: the Assad regime is a police-state dictatorship guilty of atrocities. Because the regime brutally punishes the exercise of freedom of speech and regards direct criticism of the president as criminal, because its security apparatus has immunity and the power to override any pretense of due process or rule of law, none of us can go to Syria.

Syria began this decade with a population of twenty-three million—but with seventeen million more in diaspora. I wonder how many of us seventeen million are exiles.

I resent my Syrian friends and relatives who go to Syria. Syrians call it *going down to Shaam.* "We're going down to Shaam this summer" trips off their tongues, "Nazleen a'l shaam." I get it, they're not in any trouble with the regime and they still have the ability to visit home, so why wouldn't they? I still wonder, *What have they had to deaden inside themselves to ignore the routinized torture of prisoners and the normalized pain of people living under a brutal dictatorship?* Then I think, *How judgmental are you being, Mohja?*

Somehow, I never resented my Syrian relatives who live inside Syria for visiting me as a child. But part of me judges them too—what have they had to shrink inside themselves to endure, to survive there? *Look, cut that out*, I tell myself; I love them and they risked something to visit my family.

I resent my American friends who go on Syria excursions when they know I can't. Some of them have gone to study at institutes and, ultimately, I am sure, have benefitted the regime, which gets a cut of everything. Why aren't they in solidarity with me, and with every Syrian the regime hates so much that it deprives them of home soil under their feet?

I resent my non-Syrian professional colleagues such as those I meet in the Syrian Studies Association, who come and go to Syria on professional trips. Don't they know the fucking dictatorship allows no freedom of speech for Syrian intellectuals such as the leftist Yassin al-Haj Saleh, who remained in an Assad prison for sixteen years, while these academics have gone about being, some of them at least, regime apologists?

Maybe it isn't so black and white, I tell myself, *let me look and listen for a while.* I consider that maybe they went to do research that could one day help human rights in Syria, or could help to rebuild Syrian culture on a healthier footing than with the thick fog of fear, suspicion, and resentment that has permeated the country under the Assads. Some of them do, I'm sure. Still, after a few newsletters and correspondences, and a meeting or two sitting around a table listening to several of my professional colleagues offer scholarly apologism for a brutal regime, I've had enough; I leave the Syrian Studies Association.

Around 2000, I am busy creating a new course, a special topics seminar on Syrian literature. For research, I travel to Quebec in the dead of winter to attend the Musee de Civilisations' special exhibit on Syria to see artifacts on loan from the National Museums in Damascus and Aleppo. I salivate over objects I will probably never get to see in their original settings: bas reliefs of Assyrians on a chariot and of an early Christian girl on a tomb, busts of Palmyra women in their jeweled headdresses. I come home from Quebec and write a children's play on Palmyra's Queen Zenobia, which my daughters and their friends perform in a local park that summer. I read Hanna Battatu's thick tome on Syrian demographics and politics, and Lisa Wedeen's book on the cult of the Baathist leader and what it did to warp Syrian culture. Nizar Kabbani's poetry sets me on fire, as does Muhammad Maghut's, and I devour Zakaria Tamer's astonishing, surrealistic fiction, and Ghada Samman's, which is so Syrian in its dark humor—Syrian exiles, Syrian exiles. All these are part of my research for the course but also profoundly part of my life, and that's why I created the course: to understand why, and how, and what, Syria had been, and might be.

I build the course around a panel I have organized on Syrian literature at the Middle Eastern Studies Association conference in Washington, DC, in which I present a paper about how none of Syria's great authors treat the 1982 Hama massacre directly, and how self-censorship for survival produces strange gaps in Syrian cultural production.

A woman stands up after the panelists finish presenting to the audience of forty people, and asserts, "There was no Hama massacre."

"What?" I exclaim.

"There were some criminals assassinating people, and the regime protected the people. That's all it was. No massacre."

I almost think I've heard her wrong. Because I cannot go to Syria, it is my first encounter, in the flesh, with head-spinning Syrian regime doublespeak.

"What the—what—*what*?" I sputter. "How dare you deny the blood that was shed. People *died*. How dare you—?" An older Egyptian man glances up with shock—at *me*. What in hell is going on here?

My copanelist, a graduate student on Fulbright from Syria, whispers to me, "Do you know who she is?" She pushes a note toward me. *She's Bouthaina Shaaban—Assad's translator at Camp David.*

My other copanelist, a major scholar, knows exactly who Bouthaina is, having worked with her both during Bouthaina's spell as a guest researcher at the scholar's university, and when the scholar was doing her research in Syria.

Neither copanelist responds. Not a whisper. Which, for the vulnerable graduate student, is utterly understandable—the terms of her Fulbright scholarship require that she return and serve in a Syrian institution. If she speaks out, she will not be able to go to Syria without risking prison, torture. Even just by being on a panel with me where regime atrocities are mentioned, she is in jeopardy. And the major scholar later gives me some explanation about needing Bouthaina's good graces to get a visa in order to finish a book she is writing.

I look around the room, expecting many other attendees to stand up, scandalized by the enormity of Bouthaina's massacre denial. Not a puff, not a word. I wonder if I've gone through a looking glass and entered a wonder-world where it is some horrifying opposite day. Heavy silence. For a second I doubt—am I living in a massacre narrative that only exists inside a Syrian dissident narrative? But wait, no, there is the *fact* of the massacre—I knew people who died in it, real people.

Then a Lebanese academic, my former professor, stands up. "Of course there was a Hama massacre. It was huge. It was committed by the government. Tens of thousands of civilians were killed. And this is just a typical Syrian state denial of it," she says. She pours out facts and analysis for several minutes, demolishing Bouthaina's ghastly massacre denial. Restoring reality to the room.

Minutes after the panel disperses, Bouthaina comes over to the graduate student panelist, lays a hand on her arm, and inquires, "When are you returning to Syria to fulfill your scholarship obligation?" The student quakes, and rightly so. Bouthaina is issuing a threat. She is saying, in language anyone from a police state dictatorship understands, "I am reporting you." That student, now a professor, never returns to Syria.

Hafez al-Assad, the dictator who created the conditions that bar me from going to Syria, dies in 2000 and is succeeded by his dictator son Bashar. There is talk of amnesty and a lot of Syrians who have never been able to go back to Syria start going back. I wonder if I could go back. Then I remember my stand with Bouthaina at the conference. She has been promoted by Bashar to be minister of expatriate affairs.

During the years when Bashar allows some exiles to return, I am at the grocery store in one of the oil-rich Gulf states with an elder Syrian relative. "Don't look now," Auntie whispers to me, "but there's Um Flan." Um Flan ducks down in the pickles and olives aisle, trying to avoid us. Um Flan hasn't been able to meet the eye of any other Syrian in town ever since her husband ended their family's exile and managed to return to Syria. How did he, a wanted dissident, make good with the regime? He went to the embassy and humbly begged to write a confession, most likely naming his associates, because you had to give them what they wanted to go back. And then you had to pay weekly visits and inform them some more. So he turned in his friends. They would be people with relatives who still lived in Syria, of course, vulnerable to the reach of the regime, who would now be disappeared by its brutal security forces. He betrayed his prior principled opposition to the regime in order to be able to summer in Syria again. He and his wife were pariahs among Syrian exiles now.

My cousin goes to Syria. My cousin who is just like me, with a life-time outside, visits Syria sometime in the early 2000s. She is not an activist or someone who has ever formally taken a stand against the regime and then reneged on it. Her I can forgive for going to Syria, because I loot her of all her Syria images when she returns, and they concern an overlapping set of family memories I need back. Like a locust swarm I pluck her clean, I make her give it all to me, every street she has trod. Before she'd gone, she had her name checked on The List at the Syrian embassy in DC. They told her my father was still on The List, and would be detained by the Assad regime should he ever set foot in Syria *or even countries adjacent to Syria*—hinting at Lebanon—where Syrian regime authorities also have pull. Certainly any of his children landing in Syria would be taking a big risk. I consider going to Syria anyway, then I think of my children.

Banah, my younger daughter, is in the second grade. Her school, with an all-white faculty and a smattering of black and brown children, boasts of its diversity. Every single girl in my daughter's class is in the Girl Scout troop. My daughter begs to join.

When I register my daughter, the troop leader says to me in a certain tone, "The Girl Scout Promise mentions God, you know."

Guess what, I've been a Girl Scout myself. I still have my frayed laminated copy of the "Girl Scout Promise" from my girlhood. My elder daughter was a Girl Scout a few years earlier, at a troop across town.

At first I don't connect what the troop leader says to the fact that we are living in post-9/11 America.

She goes on, "We meet in a church." Again with that strange tone. The church in question is right around the corner from my house. Convenient.

"I'm not sure if you'd have a problem with that." She wants me to have a problem with it.

She is unwelcoming me.

I put the tone aside. There are many bigger post-9/11 tensions in the air, and I have not yet begun to process the smaller ones.

During Banah's first year in the troop, I help out with the international fair exhibit on France, teaching the girls to perform "Un, Deux, Trois, Soleil." The troop leader, who adores France and decorates her home in what she deems French Provençal style, appreciates my help. The next year, when she requests suggestions for a country they could do for the international fair, I volunteer Syria. I go around my house gathering mosaic boxes, which my children call *Syria boxes*. With some of their tiny wood inlay pieces warping, the boxes are just about all my children have of Syria by way of physical artifacts. Amman is the closest my children have ever been to Syria, the closest they are likely ever to be in my lifetime.

The troop leader approaches me in the school parking lot, where all the parents and girls have gathered before we drive to the mountains for the troop's Saturday camp.

"Some of the other mothers are concerned about your suggestion that the troop do a Syria booth for the Girl Scout's annual international fair," she says. The other mothers gather around her. "I don't know if you know this, but the Girl Scouts is a patriotic organization," she continues.

It seems like such a non sequitur. I haven't put together what she means.

"Syria is on the State Department list. It's an Axis of Evil country," she says.

"I have no intention of celebrating Assad's government with the booth at the fair," I say. "That's not what Syria is all about. To me, Syria is—is—"

How am I to explain? That I cannot go to Syria. That I have nothing left after all these years to show my children of Syria except a few broken-down mosaic boxes. That I want to manufacture Syria-related memories for my daughter by having her make a lame-ass Syria booth in Girl Scouts. That I've interviewed my parents over the years about the street where we lived, about what snacks the peddlers sold (*'irk sus* and boiled nuts), and about family members I don't know because they would never be able to come here and we would never be able to go there. How am I to explain, even to myself, why I pore over maps of Damascus trying to find the streets my parents named in the new shape of the city? Tongue-tied, I have flashes of memories of men and women speaking the horrors of the Hama massacre, their faces obscured on VHS tapes I helped translate into English as a teen in the 1980s. This woman thinks I am endorsing Assad's Syria? The state Syria of the massacre-denying Bouthaina Shaaban, Syrian regime doublespeak, chest-thumping official Syrian discourse about resistance against US imperialism and Zionist expansion? How the hell am I supposed to explain Syria, my Syria, to a bunch of white women in a school parking lot in Fayetteville, Arkansas, five minutes before a Girl Scout camping trip?

I back away. It feels like a scene out of eighth grade when the popular girls bunch up in the hallway and say something obliquely ugly, and you can't think of an answer on the spot, but think of a really good one when it's way too late. I scramble into my car to hold back tears, hating myself for letting it all get to me. How would the troop leader know anything else about Syria, anyway? It isn't her fault. I try to let it go.

"Are you OK?" asks the mother of one of Banah's friends, bending to peer through my car window.

"No," I say.

I take my little girl to that camp, because her heart is set on it. You can't do that to a child, take away something you promised, without a damn good reason, and in that moment I'm not sure that denying her the camp wouldn't be more about my hurt feelings than her needs. So you allow your child to be around people who look askance at her because of her origin and religious affiliation, and you watch your child look up to those people. Because their disdain goes over her second-grade head. Or does it?

After the camp, I write a note to the troop leader withdrawing my daughter from their troop and telling her why. Because you also can't subject a child to people who look askance at her for where she comes from, not when you can help it. The troop leader writes back a long letter explaining that she is not a bigot.

"I bet she thinks she's not racist because she's been to France," Banah says a few years later, nailing it.

Over a decade later, the Syrian Revolution begins as an unarmed grass-roots protest movement uniting Syrians across religious affiliation and ethnicity. Hundreds of thousands of Syrians find it in themselves to express dissent against the regime at last, astounding me and overturning any resentment I harbored about Syrians who stayed home. A road to Syria opens up for me for the first time in my life. I begin imagining an actual return to Syria, a really real, real one. I go to southern Turkey to see what I can do for Syrian refugees—years before the media starts paying attention to Syrian refugees. I get close enough to see Syria across grain fields. My life divides into time before that moment and after. I feel ready to give up my house, my job. My life, if it comes to it. The young nonviolent protesters are ready to risk everything; why shouldn't I? I have prepared for a lifetime for this life-changing moment.

The Syrian Revolution starts, and my right to speak as a Syrian about Syrian conditions gets questioned by white people in the United States—by some people of color too, but mostly by white people—who have never been to Syria but seem to know better than Syrians what it is all about. It's about Iraq, most of them seem to think, unable or unwilling to distinguish one Arab country from another. Or it's all about US geopolitics. Just never about Syria itself, or Syrians, our bodies, our lived experiences. *But you haven't been there in years, right?*, progressive US peace activists say, denying massacres in Syria. Progressive US pundits dismiss Syrian exiles as regime-haters. Well of-fucking-course we are. We are right to hate a police-state dictatorship. I'm sorry that the lives of Syrians exiled by a brutal regime are not authentic enough for their scrutiny, but that doesn't make the regime any less a brutal dictatorship. Such so-called progressives would rather give the regime a pass, and mock exiles who condemn the regime for being exiles who condemn the regime. Syrian exiles are not the Syrians who have suffered under bombs and been starved and sarin gassed, so who needs to hear from us? I not only understand but support prioritizing the narratives of Syrians inside Syria—but meanwhile, go ahead and publish work by any white man or woman who ever lifted a leg in Syria.

The Syrian Revolution starts, and I begin attending conferences on Syrian opposition—mostly suits trying to make politics out of the enormous risks taken by the protestors on the ground. Then I meet some of these protesters who escaped on foot from Syria, and I want to do anything that will help them be heard over the Syrian-opposition politicos. Some of them immediately recognize and respect the solidarity and bitterness of a Syrian sister-dissident. Still, others ask, *How long since you've been to Syria?* I am tongue-tied. I cannot go to Syria. All my life I have been living in Syria nonetheless.

◻ ◻ ◻ ◻ ◻

15

PAULINE KALDAS

Walking Home

Twice a week, I take the three-mile walk home after teaching—from downtown through neighborhoods, past vacant lots, unkempt yards, and front porches with no railings to enclose them, their borders edging into the street.

Houses stretch along this main avenue, staring into the pavement of road with cars passing in transit. The neighborhood is punctuated by clothing and gestures—a woman sweeps a porch, a woman wears a sari—where refugees approach the city, a new life begging entrance into this world. And my own history tucked inside my pocket—a small studio apartment shared between my parents and an aunt and uncle for six months, sleeping on a bed that opens in the evening, laid out in the kitchen where I'm bound into covers by an aunt whose laughter echoes against tight walls.

My steps continue, leaning into the incline of uphill sidewalk. A dog wanders a front yard with a sign that says to keep off the grass; I learn to look for him on my way home, his loneliness cornered against the fence. No brightly formulated green lawns here, the edge of grass meeting concrete blending the view from house to street.

Only the black men I pass acknowledge me. One man offers a barely perceptible nod; another gives me a clear good morning, his gaze direct; one waves from his seat on a front porch. I nod, respond, wave back.

Years of walking inside city streets, my appearance elusive to each gazer, I've learned the etiquette of acknowledgment. Return the greeting of black men—it's only recognition of our mutual existence that is requested/ keep my eyes low when passing white men—better my look not be misconstrued for an invitation/ keep an even pace against the Spanish coming from other men—no way to explain it's a case of mistaken identity. Always keep a steady beat of movement.

I'm a short dark woman with an ethnic appearance not easily identified, but it's enough to exclude white. The dark color of my skin is the luggage I carry with me. It marks my steps through these sidewalks that take me home.

Nothing to guide me but air-wind-breath—I inhale each city, learn to move in this new world, firmly grounding myself in constant motion.

To Walk Cautiously in the World

Monday morning, I wake up bleary eyed, pour my first cup of coffee, sit at the kitchen table, and unfold the day's newspaper. *OSAMA BIN LADEN DEAD* in all caps, large font, stares back at me. The headline is at the top of the page above the name of the paper. I blink—Is it April Fool's? No, it's already May. I repeat the headline as a question directed at my husband. "Yes," he answers, "It's been on the news all morning." I read, taking in the information—this man we have been trailing for ten years captured overnight. I turn the pages and stop at a short column. NATO has killed one of Gadhafi's sons and three grandchildren. How old were these children? Why were they killed? Is this really ok? But there is no more information. Most of the articles are about Bin Laden. On one of the inside pages, there is a picture of a crowd of people outside the White House celebrating, fists shooting in the air, their faces open in smiles, an American flag wrapped around one person, the white house a small brightly lit icon in the background. My husband tells me the celebratory crowds raised their hands and shouted *U S A*. What does this mean? Is this our triumph as a nation?

My brain is waking up slowly as I pour the second cup of coffee. I'm not sure how I feel—I'm glad that Bin Laden is gone, that he can no longer hurt another person. His death makes me keenly aware of the tragedy of his life, the destruction that he has caused to others. But is it ever OK to celebrate a death? Something in all this unsettles me. My mind calls up the image of those who gathered to have picnics and watch lynchings.

Beneath the headline, there is a picture of Bin Laden on one side and a picture of Obama on the other. My husband points out the similarity —skin tone, features. My daughter says they have the same nose. I look back and forth at the photos. Yes, visually, they could be cousins. The trick of circumstance that creates us—our parents, the country of our birth, the religion we are born into, the range of choices we are allowed in living our lives. Pull one thread and we can unravel into a different life. We are not so distant from each other.

I fold the newspaper and put it in the recycling bin—my attempt to push the news aside, to remove it from my daily life. At the dinner table that evening, Celine tells us that one of her friends said she thought of her when she heard about Bin Laden. What does this mean? How does Bin Laden's life intersect with my daughter who is Egyptian/African American, born in the United States, and a fourteen-year-old middle school student? She goes on to tell us that her classmates were joking around, claiming they had killed Bin Laden. Something about all this disturbs us, yet none of us can quite pinpoint the source of our feelings. Yasmine says no one said much at her school, but she also explains that she had made a decision that morning to tune it all out. It's a protective shield that I know she has used before. Inappropriate remarks, ignorance expressed by others—she lets them slide past her, skimming across her surface to keep them from penetrating and harming her.

Just yesterday, one of our daughters was trying to convince us that racism today is not as bad as it was in the past, and our other daughter was arguing that racism can be expressed by a variety of people. My husband—who is African American—and I gave them examples of the way that history seeps into the present, and the way we must remain on guard—that as a minority, you must develop that keen sense of aware- ness, be somewhat cautious in your interactions with others. No, they argued, it's not right to be suspicious of certain people, and everyone experiences discrimination. They believe that some things remain locked in the past, and the present we live in is a better place. We rallied back and forth—they find our views almost prejudiced and we find their per- ception of the world to be naïve. Yet, a part of me hopes they are right, that the world they grow into will indeed be relieved of its heavy past.

After dinner, I decide to walk to the grocery store to pick up a few things. It has been a warm day, and the evening breeze makes the walk pleasant. I'm enjoying this neighborhood where we have recently moved, a middle class area of mostly single-family homes and also a number of apartment complexes. I see a young boy riding his bike, a woman dressed in a sari pushing a baby carriage, and two other women talking. There are so many newcomers to this country who start their lives in these kinds of apartments. My aunt and uncle lived in a similar place, the building occu- pied by immigrants from various countries, everyone complaining about the distinctive food smells seeping under their doorways. I'm wondering if these immigrants will eventually move out and buy homes in a more secluded suburb, if they will miss the community of these buildings. I approach the store and note a few young boys sitting on one of the tables outside. As I walk by, one of them yells out, "Osama Bin Laden." His body has turned in my direction and his voice is aimed toward me. I'm the only one walking past them. A hard rock in the pit of my stomach—fear even here in the open sidewalk where it's still daylight. From the corner of my eye, I note how young the boy is, barely in middle school. I continue walking, my steps in the same beat, carrying the hard edge inside me. My steadiness pushed by the need to survive, to protect myself.

Once inside the store, I look out to get a closer look at the boys, but they are already gone, perhaps running away from their own attempt at bravery. I linger, making my selections slowly. The truth is I feel slightly embarrassed at the way I've been shaken by the boy's shout. I call my husband to ask whether I should buy strawberries or raspberries even though I have already placed the raspberries in the cart. I call two more times, asking mundane questions. My husband's response grows irritated. I know the ring of the phone is disruptive. He might be reading, listening to music, or just following his thoughts. But right now, I'm grateful to simply be his annoying wife. The truth is I just want to hear the voice of someone who cares about me, who does not see my ethnicity every time he looks at me, the comfort of being perceived as a person in its purest term.

What did those boys see when I walked past them? Do I look like Bin Laden? Maybe it's the eyebrows—those thick, curved lines outlining our faces and making us look suspicious. My physical appearance is elusive—I've been identified as Italian, Spanish, African American. The combination of my darker complexion, brown eyes, black hair, and sharp-angled nose lends itself to multiple interpretations depending on the onlooker's gaze. Egyptian is not the first possibility that comes to most people's minds. But when an incident occurs that highlights Arabs in the media, people's assumptions shift, and I'm defined in relation to the day's news. We are chameleons transformed by the political events of our time. I'm reminded of the Sikh man murdered shortly after 9/11, presumed to be Arab at that moment in history. Was this those boys' attempt to imagine themselves as heroes? Shouting at me, labeling me the enemy—how far would their aggression go?

Entangled in the thread that connects all of us are also these young boys. We exist at the same time and in the same place—their shout only brought us closer. I wonder if I should have responded. I could have said, "Yes, he's my long lost cousin." But the sarcasm of my comment might have diffused before it reached them. Or maybe I should have sworn at them in Arabic, taken refuge in words whose meaning they cannot understand, scaring them with those guttural sounds, using their own fears against them. But that might have only escalated the situation instead of letting it sift back into dust.

The next morning, there is another short article about the attack on Gadhafi's compound. The grandchildren who were killed were one infant and two toddlers. They were too young to know what they had been born into, still unable to recognize their inheritance, or decide what to do with it. What sense does it make to destroy them? And to cause agony to those who loved and cared for them? The rest of the paper is filled with details of the attack that killed Bin Laden along with three men and one woman.

I'm not sure what we are left with at the end of all this. But I tell my children that after the day's events, I'm not quite ready to let my guard down. They nod in acknowledgement. And this is what we have—the politics that reach into our lives, the history that will not release itself from the present. I still hope for a future where my children do not have to build a protective shield, where they do not have to walk cautiously in the world.

A Sense of Direction

My husband claims I have a bad sense of direction. He presents the following evidence:

- The belief that whenever we find ourselves at an intersection trying to determine whether our destination is to the right or left, the turn I suggest is inevitably the wrong one. This gives my husband the pleasure of saying he was right—an accomplishment he rarely achieves.
- The story I told him about driving to a job interview in a small town in southern Massachusetts only to be confronted with the *Welcome to Rhode Island* sign. My attempts to convince him that this was simply a premature welcome to the small state where we would one day live have failed.
- The fact that my method of driving requires me to take the longest route to my destination. I don't like driving on highways, which I define as any road with a speed limit above thirty-five.

I remind my husband that the responsibility for my fear of highways is a direct result of misplaced confidence in his directional abilities. When we did move to Rhode Island, we had to transport some of our belonging from his parents' house in Massachusetts to our new home in Providence. I followed him as we drove back to Boston, navigating the myriad highways and the drivers who calculate two inches as a sufficient amount of space between their car and yours. As we approached our exit on the right, my husband signaled to move into the left lane. My instincts told me this wasn't right, and I remained in my lane, trying to communicate telepathically with him. He didn't budge, so I suppressed my instincts and switched lanes to get behind him. Two seconds before the exit, he switched back to the right and took the exit. It was too late for me to follow him, and I found myself on a five lane highway in the middle of Boston during rush hour. By the time I managed to get out of the steaming traffic, I had vowed never to drive on a highway again.

My husband needs to believe that he knows where he's going, even when he doesn't. The advent of the GPS has done little to help the situation—he argues with Carmen, as we fondly call our GPS, and claims she's telling him the wrong way. My daughters have surrendered their social lives after spending an hour in the car while my husband drives, trying to get them to a friend's house for a party, claiming he knows where it is when he has been going in the opposite direction.

ılılı

I may have acquired my sense of direction from my parents. When we immigrated in 1969, the plane tickets clearly listed Los Angeles as our destination, yet we ended up in Boston.

My parents' failed attempt to make it to our original destination may have resulted from the difficulty of transitioning from the Arabic-speaking world to the English one. Arabic moves from right to left, and this serves to establish our sense of direction from the moment we perceive the written language. After spending six months in Cairo, this movement became so ingrained in my children that when they returned to America, they flipped their books and notebooks around and to the other side so the pages could turn in the direction of Arabic. When I arrived in America at the age of eight, learning to go from left to right with the English language must've permanently damaged my ability to move in a straight line. Given a choice, I'm most likely to turn right, moving back to the origin of the first language I learned.

I have lived in Michigan, New York, Rhode Island, and Virginia, but the West Coast still eludes me. Now, both my daughters are applying to colleges in California—perhaps they have retrieved those original tickets.

ılılı

I never panic when I lose my way. My faith remains unshaken—if I keep walking or driving, I know I will end up in the right direction. It's only when we get lost that we find our destination. I present the following evidence:

- We are young, spending a month backpacking in Europe. The heat from the sun subsides as we meander through the narrow corridors of Venice. There is a continuity of architecture that makes it difficult to decipher one street from another, and we can't be sure if we have already walked this way. We are lost. My husband's nerves become agitated; he's eager to find some sign in this urban forest to guide us back to our hotel. "Don't worry," I assure him, "if we just keep walking, we'll find our way." But he's impatient, unable to enjoy the scenery of this city framed by water. There is nothing he can hold onto, so he lets me lead, and my footsteps carry us from one turn to the next. The sun is setting and a gray light envelops the small city. The approaching dark heightens my husband's anxiety, and he's even willing to ask someone. At one turn, we come face to face with a group of travelers, but they are also lost and have no direction to offer us. The sun descends as we make another turn and find ourselves standing in front of our hotel.

- We are in Martinique. My husband has received a grant to pursue his research on the Martiniquan writer, Aimé Césaire. When I ask him if he'll try to meet Césaire while we're in Martinique, he says he'll just see if it happens. My husband is definitely not a planner. A few days into our trip, we're standing on a street corner, about to embark on an afternoon walk. The plan is to go in the direction of a garden we've read about. "I think it's to the left," my husband says. "No," I respond, "I think we go straight down that street." Our two daughters stand between us, unsure of which parent to trust. My husband acquiesces, perhaps hoping to revel in proving me wrong. We walk alongside fan palm trees and hibiscus flowers in this island vibrant with colors and people who move with firm footsteps. Yasmine notices a large building with a sign indicating that it's a theatre. Her love of drama enables her to find her way to a stage even in foreign lands. We enter into the building, my husband immediately noticing the numerous posters of Césaire. We wander up the steps to discover that the second floor holds the offices of Aimé Césaire. Asking a few casual questions of a woman sitting behind a desk, my husband finds himself with an appointment to meet Césaire the next day.

My sense of direction eludes the logic of someone like my husband who takes the most direct route from point A to point B. I tell him that there is more than one way to get to your destination—side streets and zigzag turns that can lead you to unexpected places as you travel. Perhaps it's the history that brought his ancestors from Africa to the shores of America that makes him resistant to my logic. Such history demands a clear sense of direction—the ability to trace the path back to your origins, to find the trail that moves North, to carry a drum beat from one ear to another—a triangulation of lines that must be followed for survival.

I cannot deny that my husband is correct when he says I can get lost anywhere. Once I step outside my door, there is no way to know where I will end up. I might take a right instead of a left; I might let my curiosity guide me down a street I've never walked; or I might decide to lengthen my steps by making a circle that inevitably doesn't lead back to my starting point.

My ability to get lost solidified during my study abroad trip to Oxford during the summer of my junior year in college. I didn't know the other students and often found myself with extra time. On days with no classes, I took the bus to London alone. When I got to the city, I walked. I didn't visit any museums or historical sites. Instead, for hours, I walked the streets of London; through neighborhoods and squares, I wandered with no plan and no map. I wanted to see the houses and streets where people's lives happened. So I walked and I got lost and I learned to have faith.

I trace my wandering footsteps to the streets of the largest market in Cairo: Khan el Khalili. The narrow alleys of this market are filled with myriad shops and kiosks selling everything from belly dancing outfits, backgammon sets, and Pharaonic gods to pots and pans, copper trays, and rugs. If you don't buy something when you see it, you will lose yourself as you try to retrace your steps through the winding paths back to the same shop. One night, as we searched for a backgammon set from one shop to the next and then decided to return to the first one, we were led into a pattern of spirals until, I hate to admit it, my husband returned us to the original shop. Past midnight, we found ourselves with our friends, Maggie and Ayman, bargaining for a backgammon set inlaid with mother-of-pearl. After an hour of back-and-forth offers that attracted at least six people, each choosing their side, we left with our successful purchase. Our shopping expedition concluded with eating fetir at a place that Maggie and Ayman knew, tucked alongside the shops. Our daughters watched the cook stretching and twirling the dough into a thin layer threatening to tear. It remained intact and arrived at our table, one filled with sharp cheese and another sweetened with powdered sugar.

I've learned to get lost with ease, certain that I will arrive at an acceptable destination. Unfortunately, Celine has not inherited my ability to keep calm when she loses her way. Now that she has been awarded her license, whenever she goes out, my husband and I remain in a state of suspended panic until she returns. If the phone rings and it's her, we have to decipher, through her shrill cries and sputtered words, where she is and how to guide her back to a familiar place. My attempt to tell her that all she has to do is follow the road and trust her instincts does little to help.

ı|ı|ı

I disagree with my husband's assessment of my sense of direction. There are certain places I can always find. I present the following evidence:

- Early morning in Egypt, Yasmine and I walk to Tseppas pastry shop. I know that we can step out of our apartment building, take a right and then a left by the car always parked on the sidewalk and another right after the small kiosk selling fresh pita bread and then walk past the fruit seller where we buy the small yellow guavas to arrive at the same time as the truck delivering the pastries. The young man who works at the shop hands each of us a piece of konafa with cream, fresh and warm from the oven, his silent gift offered like a communion.

- We return to Egypt every eight years or so. Each time, we are invited to my relatives' homes and I have to find my way. Addresses are elusive in Egypt—when I address Christmas cards to my family, I have to write things like "9 Mahmoud Ismail Street / From Abd el Aziz Ali Street or 43 El Gazair Street, Building 7/4." Street signs are rare, and as we walk through a neighborhood, I have only the imbedded memory of my past visits to guide me. Hunting by instinct, I walk, my husband insisting that the house we're looking for is one way or the other, but here I demand that he follows me. Inevitably, I look up to find my Uncle Fouad's apartment building, tucked down an alley barely visible from the main street. My husband flounders, having been certain that the building could not have been here, but his logic is no match for the streets of Cairo.

ı|ı|ı

There are no highlighted lines on the map for me to follow. I was born to a life in the crowded city of Cairo, to repeat the pattern of each generation's hope—a doctor husband, an apartment in Zamalek, shopping trips to the City Stars Mall in Heliopolis, children at the British

International School. I should have witnessed Sadat's assassination, Mubarak's demise, Morsi's election, El Sisi's victory. Instead I find myself living in a Tudor home, writing and teaching at a small college in southwestern Virginia, tying threads across the passage of ocean to my African American husband, to my children born of this unexpected journey, all of us unwinding the path from one continent to another.

□ □ □ □ □

16

LAILA LALAMI

So to Speak

Not long ago, while cleaning out my bedroom closet, I came across a box of old family photographs. I had tied the black-and-white snapshots, dog-eared color photos, and scratched Polaroids in small bundles before moving from Morocco to the United States. There I was at age five, standing with my friend Nabil outside Sainte Marguerite-Marie primary school in Rabat; at age nine, holding onto my father's hand and squinting at the sun while on vacation in the hill station of Imouzzer; at age eleven, leaning with my mother against the limestone lion sculpture in Ifrane, in the Middle Atlas. But the picture I pulled out from the bundles and displayed in a frame on my desk was the one in which I was six years old and sat in our living room with my head buried in *Tintin and the Temple of the Sun.*

A great many of my childhood memories, like this photograph, feature books. Every night, my father would sit on one end of the living-room divan and my mother on the other, both of them with books in their hands. Neither of them had gone to college, but they read constantly— spy thrillers, mystery novels, science fiction, comic books, the newspaper, magazines, biographies, memoirs. I don't know how or why my parents came to love books so much; perhaps books provided them an education about the wider world, a sense of adventure that was missing from their lives, or an escape from the dreary official speeches that were regularly broadcast on state radio and television during the reign of King Hassan.

It was perhaps only natural that my siblings and I learned to do the same from an early age. I remember how we passed copies of *Astérix* to each other, how we lent to or borrowed from friends the latest issues of *Pif* magazine, how we fought about whose turn it was to read *Boule et Bill.* When I began to read children's novels, I found in Rabat's many bookstores regular new offerings from the Bibliothèque Rose or the

Bibliothèque Verte, which included series by the Comtesse de Ségur, Jules Verne, Alexandre Dumas, Georges Bayard, and many others.

Once, when my best friend Nawal and I finished reading *Les petites filles modèles* by the Comtesse de Ségur, we wondered why the title page said "née Rostopchine." After much discussion, Nawal surmised that this must have been a disease with which the author had been afflicted since birth. It hadn't occurred to either of us that women in France might take on the names of their husbands, since our own mothers, following Moroccan tradition, kept their maiden names. After reading *The Three Musketeers* and *The Count of Monte Cristo*, we used our bedsheets to make capes, pretended our plastic rulers were swords, and faced off while screaming *en garde!*

Of course, none of the characters in these books looked or spoke like anyone I knew. In those days, in the late 1970s, nearly all of the children's literature that was available in Moroccan bookstores was still in French. The characters' names, their homes, their cities, their lives were wholly different from my own, and yet, because of my constant exposure to them, they had grown utterly familiar. These images invaded my imaginary world to such an extent that I never thought they came from an alien place. Over time, the fantasy in the books came to define normalcy, while my own reality somehow seemed foreign. Like my country, my imagination had been colonized.

I began to write when I was nine years old. Unsurprisingly, the stories and poems I wrote were in French and featured characters who said things like *en garde!* I had just started the fifth grade when Mère Elisabeth, the school's director, pulled my father aside one morning and asked him which junior high school he had in mind for me. She suggested the Lycée Descartes, where much of Morocco's elite—business leaders, doctors, lawyers, intellectuals of every persuasion, government ministers as well as their political opponents—sent its offspring. My father said no; he could not afford the school fees at Descartes. In fact, he had only agreed to send me to Sainte Marguerite because it was relatively inexpensive and because my mother had insisted. When my father saw that I was upset about not going to the same school as my friends, he tried to explain his decision. "Your father is not a minister," he said in a soft, apologetic tone. Oum el-Banin, the public junior high near our house, would be fine.

At the new school, I excelled in all the subjects that were taught in French (mathematics, physics, biology) but struggled with the ones taught in Arabic (history, geography, civics). Still, the change meant that I finally started to receive proper Arabic-language instruction. The curriculum focused on excerpts from the classics of Arabic literature—the *Mu'allaqat*, al-Mutanabbi, al-Khansaa—and slowly moved on to modern authors like Naguib Mahfouz and Taha Husayn from Egypt, Khalil Gibran and Elia Abu Madi from Lebanon, and Mahmoud Darwish from Palestine. Because our school did not have a library, some of our teachers set up their own lending clubs. This involved each student donating one book—any book—in order to form a classroom collection from which we could borrow Arabic novels. I don't remember ever being assigned fiction by Moroccan authors; perhaps Moroccan authors were being taught to Egyptian, Lebanese, or Palestinian schoolchildren.

It was not until the age of fourteen, when I started to read adult literature on my own, and independently from school, that I came across novels and stories featuring Moroccan characters in a Moroccan setting. The first of these was Driss Chraïbi's *La Civilisation, Ma Mère!,* which featured a heroine that was so much like the women in my family—feisty, funny, and with a sharp sense of repartee. I have a very vivid memory of my cousin Hamid giving me a copy of Tahar Ben Jelloun's *Harrouda,* a book that felt deliciously transgressive because of its frank treatment of sex. The work of Leila Abouzeid was also a revelation. To read *'Am al-Fil* was to discover that the ordinary stuff of our lives was as fertile ground for fiction as any other.

And yet, because of my early exposure to French in literature, nearly everything I wrote in my teens and early twenties was in French. This did not seem to me especially odd at the time; after all, many of Morocco's writers used the colonial tongue: Abdellatif Laâbi, Mohammed Khaïr-Eddine, Tahar Ben Jelloun, Driss Chraïbi, Fouad Laroui. My parents thought that my writing was adorable, and praised it the way one might praise a child for a particularly good magic trick or a well-told joke, but they made it clear that writing was not a serious option for the future. I was expected to do something sensible with my life, and train in a profession that could guarantee a decent living in Morocco: medicine, engineering, or business.

Of course, their warnings did not stop me. I continued writing poems and stories and reading anything I could get my hands on at the Kalila wa Dimna bookstore in downtown Rabat or from the used booksellers in Agdal. Still, my parents' pragmatic talk had all but convinced me that writing could merely be a hobby and not a vocation, and so I went to college to study linguistics. Since I could not make a living from using words in a creative way, at least I would be able to do it by using them in an analytical way.

After a bachelor's degree at Mohammed V University in Rabat, I applied for, and received, a British Council Fellowship to do a master's degree at University College London. I arrived in Britain shortly after Saddam Hussein's army invaded Kuwait. I had been fairly apolitical until then, but the dislocation and racism I experienced in London, the classes I took at the School of Oriental and African Studies, and my exposure to the work of people like Edward Said changed all that. Every time I went back to Morocco, I couldn't help but notice how much and how often we moved between French and Arabic. All of us, whether we wanted to or not, went through life switching codes: Moroccan Arabic or Amazigh in our homes, with our friends, in our places of worship; but in job interviews, in fancy stores, in formal soirées, French was *de rigueur*.

Two years later, I arrived in Los Angeles to do a PhD in linguistics. I spent most of my days working on research articles and conference papers that had to be written and delivered in English, which made me think even more about the relationship between Arabic and French in Morocco. French was not just a prominent language in Morocco. It was the language of power; an indicator of social class; a means to include or exclude people. The education I had received had emphasized the importance of French to the detriment of Arabic. French was used in our media, our government, and our businesses. Nearly half of the shows on Moroccan television were bought from and dubbed in France. There were no neighborhood public libraries, so we often had to depend on cultural centers, like the one sponsored by the French government, for free access to books. The role of French in my life became clearer. Writing in French came at a cost; it inevitably brought with it a colonial baggage that I no longer wanted to carry. I started to suffer from a peculiar case of writer's block: if I could not write in Arabic, perhaps I should not be writing at all.

I went about the business of living. I had a degree to finish, after all, and I needed to find a job after graduate school. I tried to steer clear from writing, but writing wouldn't steer clear of me. I think that in some way we do not choose stories, but that stories choose us. A braver writer—a Ngũgĩ, say—might have immediately cast aside the colonial tongue and returned to the native one, but my literary Arabic was not good enough to allow me to produce a novel. The Arabic language is often referred to as "al-lugha al-'arabiyya al-fusha" or "the eloquent Arabic language."

I sorely lacked that eloquence. One day I thought, *Why not try my hand in English?* I was already spending my days writing my dissertation in English, so perhaps I could use English for my fiction too. After a few tries, I noticed that the linguistic shift enabled me to approach my stories with a fresh perspective. Because English had not been forced upon me as a child, it seemed to give me a kind of salutary distance. The baggage that, to me, seemed inherent in the use of French to tell a Moroccan story seemed to lessen when I used English to tell the same story.

I have always written, because I have always had the urge to tell stories, but I cannot pinpoint the exact time when I decided that I should try to be published. I know now that it had something to do with reading work after work in which men of my race, culture, or religious persuasion were portrayed as singularly deviant, violent, backward, and prone to terrorism, while the women were depicted as silent, oppressed, helpless, and waiting to be liberated by the kind foreigner. I think I had had enough of "surrogate storytellers," to use Sherman Alexie's phrase in his introduction to Percival Everett's *Watershed*.

The surrogate storytellers told a version of Morocco—mysterious, exotic, at once overly sexual and sexually repressed—that seemed entirely removed from my reality or indeed the reality of others around me. Until I came of age and started rereading the works I had approached with great innocence as a child—books such as *Tintin in the Land of Black Gold*, for instance, or *Tintin in the Congo*—I had not had the desire to go through the trouble and sacrifice it takes to be a published writer. Still, as I was finishing graduate school, my writing path became quite clear to me. I had always told stories, but now I wanted to be heard.

□ □ □ □ □

17

LISA SUHAIR MAJAJ

Journeys to Jerusalem

For almost forty years I have been going to Jerusalem. Although I grew up in Amman, my earliest memories tap into the hills and stones of Jerusalem, splinter in its rocky soil. This is true even though my coherent recollections of Jerusalem begin later, after I turned seven, the biblical age of reason, and the eastern part of the city fell under Israeli occupation. Who is to say at what point experience turns to memory? Traces register at the deepest layers of consciousness, and we are heir to things we cannot always name.

Before 1967, my older sister recalls, we could drive for lunch from Amman to Jerusalem and back in a single day, untrammeled by checkpoints and borders. Now, when Palestinians cannot even go the short distance from Ramallah to Birzeit—much less from Amman to Jerusalem—without being forcibly reminded of their occupied status through multiple checkpoints, ditches dug across the roads, and barbed-wire fences, this is wondrous to contemplate. That this earlier time of unhindered Palestinian access to Jerusalem exists, for me, before the onset of clear memory, residing instead in a shadow realm of impression that is almost mythical, seems only appropriate. After all, despite their support in a long legacy of UN resolutions, Palestinian claims to justice appear to have taken on the characteristics of a fairy tale—a story of wish fulfillment told at night to credulous children, but dismissed by the powers of the world in the light of day.

I have no explicit recollection of those early family visits to Jerusalem, of the drive down into the richly fertile Jordan Valley, past fields of banana and tomato, and then up again, toward the dun-colored Palestinian hills that formed the base note for Jerusalem's symphonic walls. But subtle impressions of light and shade, the smell of freshly turned earth, the springtime syncopation of poppies and wild mustard by the roadside, the off-white facades of stone buildings rising on the eastern approach to the city—their chipped facets holding light like an internal glow—must have made their way into my subconscious, emerging later as a sensation of mysterious familiarity, till it was as if I had always been traveling this route.

Mingled sights and sounds and smells of the city itself must similarly have registered on my earliest awareness: the majestic vista of the Dome of the Rock, its golden hemisphere casting a glow over the city; the worn bulwark of the Old City walls, eloquent with antiquity; the streets filled with snarls of cars and people and sometimes donkeys; blaring horns, drivers shouting at each other, vendors calling out their wares; and the proliferation of odors, as car exhaust and perspiration collided with the distinct aromas of za'atar and freshly roasted coffee.

In contrast—for Jerusalem has always provided a study in contrasts —my relatives' house off Saladin Street, near Herod's Gate, must have provided then the oasis of calm that it does in later memories: the cacophony of the street falling away as we passed through the tiled corridor leading to the internal garden fragrant with lemon and jasmine, and then to the house itself, where we were welcomed with kisses and exclamations. For if Jerusalem was a city rich with historical legacies and sensory texture, it was also an emotional space, one resonant with familial warmth and familial claims. For me, child of an American mother and a Palestinian father, reminded too often of my anomalous status in Palestinian culture, the embracing welcome offered by my Jerusalem relatives was a comfort, proof that one could be different and yet still belong. I might be *Americaniyeh*—my brown hair and hazel eyes might set me off from my black-haired, black-eyed cousins, whose fluency in English, German, and Arabic put my monolingualism to shame—but within the familial space we were all *beit Majaj*, of the house of Majaj. And when my aunt called us to lunch, to a table groaning with kusa mahshi and wara' dawali and baba ghanouj, no distinction was made between the cousins: we were simply *the children*, expected to behave properly and eat well.

Within the context of Israeli occupation, moreover, we were all— American passports or no American passports—Palestinian. As a child I did not fully understand the words *occupation* and *military rule*. But I could see how my father's face froze to an impassive mask when we approached Israeli officials at the bridge crossing between Jordan and the West Bank; how soldiers gave orders and we were forced to obey. It did not escape me that although we made the crossing along with other foreign passport-holders—our documents processed in air-conditioned buildings instead of in the sweltering (or, in winter, freezing) tin-roofed areas where West Bank Palestinians spent long hours waiting to be cleared for passage—we were invariably treated differently: called to one side, searched and questioned while the tourists moved through unhampered. Most unsettling, from my child's perspective, was the extent to which my father, at home the epitome of power, was drained of his authority by these Israelis with guns riffling through our documents. As we waited for transportation away from the bridge into the occupied West Bank, I stared out at the Israeli flag blazoned onto the Palestinian hillside like a tattoo on raw flesh, and wondered what Palestinians had done to deserve this treatment.

When we finally reached Jerusalem and the haven of my aunt's house, however, these humiliations seemed in some way badges of honor. The more harassed we were on our journey to Jerusalem, the greater was our sense of being Palestinian. Even my American mother participated in this sense of communal belonging, as if by marrying a Palestinian she had not only married into a family but into a national experience. Years later, this sense of belonging was hammered home when my mother checked into an Israeli hospital, seeking a diagnosis for the mysterious and debilitating skin problems that later proved to be manifestations of cancer. The Israeli nurses, who knew she was married to a Palestinian, did not change her blood-stained sheets: after she had asked for fresh linen for days, they finally tossed the clean sheets on the floor and told her to make the bed herself.

Even at an early age I could see that to be Palestinian meant being part of something larger than the immediate family and its expectations. It meant being connected to a land, a people, and a history, all of which were symbolized by a single city: Jerusalem. If Palestine was the homeland whose echoes reverberated through our lives no matter where we lived or how we sought to distance ourselves, Jerusalem was the emotional center of this homeland, the focal point of Palestinian longing. And despite the fact that I grew up feeling in many ways distinctly American—and, like so many Americans, distinctly lacking in political awareness—on some level I too wanted to be included in this national definition.

I recall one winter day in Jerusalem when I was around nine. In the morning we walked through the Old City over cobblestones slick with rain, drinking in the sensory rush as shoppers bargained for vegetables and fruits, vendors pushed carts through the crowded streets, and food stalls enticed passersby with the scents of schwarma and falafel. After lunch we went for a drive to an outlying area of the city studded with olive groves and stone fences. After the tumult of the Old City, the open spaces of earth and sky seemed like a lyrical pause at the center of a musical score. My father and uncle stopped to talk to a farmer while I wandered a muddy path beside a low stone fence, drinking in the landscape of green and brown and gray, the olive trees pruned to simple lines, the intricate balance of stones laid carefully atop each other to form the orchard's bordering wall. Something about the landscape's energy, the careful industry of the olive grove and its surrounding wall, stayed with me, a small kernel I quietly harbored. On our return to Amman I tried to capture those perceptions in a painting, laboring to render the complexity of individual stones, the stark beauty of branches etched against a sky swollen with rain. My art teacher, a gentle Palestinian man whose name, as he loved to remind us, meant *friend*, leaned over my page to ask me what I was painting. When I told him it was a scene from my recent trip to Jerusalem, he patted my shoulder. "You love Palestine," he said warmly, as if it was a secret we shared. Although I sensed that the emotion he had in mind was larger than I could really comprehend, I nodded.

As experiences such as this one poured, wave by wave, over my consciousness, they laid down traces, so that even before I could recall specific trips to Jerusalem, the place had become part of my mental landscape. Going there seemed a bit like visiting a grandparent: something natural and inevitable, a right as well as an obligation. Jerusalem—and through Jerusalem, Palestine—lived in me the way a grandparent's genes live on in the body of a child: a mysterious habitation linking generations. It lived in me, too, like a destiny: something one might at times prefer to escape. (Sometimes I think that the melancholic strain in my personality comes from Palestine's proliferation of stone: I have never managed to raise my head under that weight.) No matter how much time passed between my visits, Jerusalem echoed through my consciousness, and with each arrival I was transfixed by that deep chord of familiarity: summer heat beating on stone, the drumming of winter rain.

Since childhood I have been testing my voice against this echo. And for almost forty years I have been making this journey to Jerusalem, the way a musician rehearses a melody, the way a swimmer goes to the sea.

||||

Throughout my childhood, going to Jerusalem was a descent and an ascent: the downward journey through the Jordan Valley, the actual passage across the river, bracketed by tedious waits on either side of the bridge, and then the upward passage through the Palestinian landscape to the final destination: Jerusalem. At the heart of this journey lay the Allenby Bridge.

In my childhood recollections the bridge, Jordan's only portal to Palestine, was a simple wooden structure across a murky channel of water that seemed wholly unworthy of its mythical reputation. Was this muddy stream really the famous River Jordan, the place of Jesus' baptism, the river celebrated in literature and song? Even on winter crossings, when the water moved more swiftly, swollen with rain, and rushes laced the surface like camouflage, the river seemed disconcertingly unimpressive. Gazing down at it as we rattled across the bridge in a bus or, on occasion, walked across, suitcases in tow, I marveled at the importance granted this seemingly insignificant body of water. And I marveled at the fact that this stream was all that separated Jordan and Israel: Would these muddy banks really hold enemy tanks at bay?

I knew that *crossing the Jordan*, whether in American culture or in Bible stories, was supposed to signify a passage from slavery to freedom. After all, I attended an American school until I was a teenager, and my best friends were missionary kids. But in the local Palestinian context that I also inhabited, the Jordan River stood, instead, as the demarcation line between dual oppressions: exile and occupation. On the eastern bank of the river Palestinians lived in forced separation from their homeland, often in desperately poor refugee camps. Although we lived comfortably in a middle class neighborhood of Amman, I knew that there were alternate universes to my own small world: that only a few-minutes-drive away were refugee camps where children with dirty faces and hungry eyes begged for food. On the western bank of the river Palestinians lived under the boot of military rule, again often in refugee camps forgotten by the world. Between these two banks flowed the river itself, spanned by the insubstantial web of wood named after General Allenby, the commander who led British troops into Palestine in 1917, starting, one might say, the whole Palestinian tragedy.

On the western bank of the river, my father was a Palestinian under occupation: his land confiscated, his identity denied. On the eastern bank, he was a Palestinian in exile: his future held hostage, his identity denied. And when he stood in the middle of the bridge, swaying between the poles of injustice, what then? Perhaps, beneath the facade of righteous anger that made him such an imposing figure in my childhood memory, he was like so many other Palestinians: simply bewildered, caught off-balance by history.

I turned seven in October 1967, soon after the June war that placed the remaining land of Palestine under occupation and made hundreds of thousands of Palestinians refugees, many for the second time. That fall my father brought home an oil painting of a man carrying his children across the Allenby Bridge. The painting, which now hangs in my study, was rendered with thick, nervous brush strokes in tones of black and yellow, the choppy paint surface evoking a sense of uneasiness. The man portrayed in it stands stiffly, leaning slightly to one side as if braced against his load. He hoists a small child in the crook of one arm, gripping the sleeve of another child, who clings to his back, between his teeth. His gaze is directed vacantly off to one side, as if there is no point in meeting the viewer's eyes. Behind him, seen through the framework of the bridge, are indistinct figures in a long line: other refugees waiting to cross.

Taped to the back of the picture is a black-and-white photo of the scene the painting replicates, along with a scrap of paper bearing a few typed lines: "The Israelis drove approximately a quarter of a million people out of their homes on the West Bank during and immediately after the war of June 1967. Here a father brings his children to safety across the River Jordan." (UN estimates place the number of refugees resulting from the war at up to half a million.) In the photo the man looks downward, as if focused on nothing more than the next exhausting step forward. In both photo and picture he carries nothing but his children: his free hand is splayed open, as if emphasizing the radical experience of his loss.

I grew up with this painting but did not really understand it. I knew it had to do not only with the presence of Israeli soldiers at the bridge crossing, but also with the war, which had entered my consciousness as fragmented shards of perception: the piercing spiral of air-raid sirens, the terrifying roar of bomber planes overhead, the dank odor of perspiration and fear permeating the protected inner hallway where we huddled for safety. I had until then largely been spared knowledge of the world's injustice. But even then I was beginning to understand that there was no real hiding from the forces unleashing violence around us. As I grew older and experienced other wars, I began to understand what could not be escaped: not so much the planes and bombs as Palestinian history itself.

If the 1967 war served as my first encounter with Palestinian history, crossing the Allenby Bridge to the West Bank on our journeys to Jerusalem provided a hands-on education in the realities of Palestinian identity. We were fortunate indeed to be able to make that journey across the river in the opposite direction, to go toward Jerusalem instead of fleeing. But we crossed the river on transit visas, our stay limited, the parameters of our journey beyond our control. And although as American passport holders we had a far easier time of it than did most Palestinians, still we could not escape the ramifications of being Palestinian. Those gray-green (later, blue) embossed US passports made a significant difference in how we were treated. But they did not make all the difference. Although our crossing might take three hours instead of seven, although we were not usually strip-searched, did not have to send our shoes to be X-rayed, and were generally spared the humiliations most Palestinians seeking to enter their homeland were subjected to, still we understood that in the eyes of the Israelis we were not real Americans: we were always Palestinian, always a threat.

For me, a bookworm and a budding would-be writer, one of the particular hardships of the crossing was that we could not take anything printed or handwritten across the bridge, for fear of rousing the censor. How I longed for a book with which to pass the interminable wait! But it was impossible. Carrying anything printed, even a novel, meant long delays while we waited for clearance from the censor. What the censor was looking for, we never quite knew. Coded messages? Revolutionary secrets? The mention of the forbidden word Palestine? These restrictions did not seem to apply to foreign tourists, however. I remember watching jealously as northern European travelers sat casually reading books while they waited their turn.

Handwritten documents were even more problematic. Once we were delayed at the bridge for hours: my sister had forgotten a letter from a friend in her purse, and we had to wait while the censor examined every word of that adolescent note for incriminating evidence. After that I developed a paranoia about having anything printed or written in my possession at the bridge. Even discovering a stray candy wrapper in my pocket with Arabic writing on it would set me into a frenzy of anxiety. And heaven forbid we carry names, telephone numbers, or addresses: these would trigger special attention, and would leave us worried over what trouble we might have inadvertently caused the persons so named, since one never knew how information would be used. For the same reason we never mentioned our relatives' names at the bridge, but told the authorities that we would be staying at a local hotel.

Once, when I was a teenager, we planned to cross the bridge in company with British friends whom my father had promised to take on a tour of Jerusalem. It was a chilly day, and we felt fortunate to be spared the long lines where West Bank Palestinians waited their turn to have their suitcases unceremoniously dumped out onto large tables. Inside the building where our documents were processed, an Israeli soldier looked up our names on a computer, and then motioned my father into a cubicle. I could hear my father's angry voice, the insistent voice of the soldier. Suddenly my father stormed out of the cubicle and told my mother that we were going back to Jordan: he refused to submit to these conditions. The official had decided to strip-search my father, a humiliation our American passports had usually spared us. My mother was in a quandary. If we turned back, we would be abandoning the guests we had promised to accompany. Finally the situation was defused: the Israeli told my father he would only be required to take off his shirt and loosen his pants, and my father, urged by my mother, grudgingly agreed. We passed through border control without further incident. But as we seated ourselves in the Arab car that would take us to Jerusalem, I could still see the set of my father's jaw.

Years later, I found myself standing in a cubicle at the bridge with my sister, my pants around my ankles. The female Israeli soldier who had ordered me to unclothe was writing something on a clipboard and had not bothered to glance at my naked legs to verify that I was not, in fact, concealing contraband. My jaw was so tightly clenched that my teeth ached. My sister, who had only been required to take off her shoes, raised her eyebrows and shook her head at me. But I was too upset to heed her silent warning.

"Why do I have to take off my pants but she doesn't have to take off her skirt?" I demanded of the soldier. "If you're worried about security, why don't you check us both?"

Without looking up, the Israeli woman shrugged. "She can hide something in her shoes, you can hide something in your pants."

I glanced at my sister, whose open sandals revealed most of her feet, but whose long skirt, unlike my tight Capri pants, could have hidden all manner of things. The point, evidently, was not security but harassment. I had revealed more resentment during our initial questioning than my sister, and I was being punished for it. I had a sudden vision of my father in perhaps that same cubicle, stripped to the waist while a bored young Israeli man wrote on a clipboard. Ten or fifteen years had passed, but the humiliation was the same.

Later, as my sister and I rode in a taxi through Jericho, I recalled how we had stopped in Jericho's central market after my father had been strip-searched to purchase large burlap sacks of oranges and tangerines for our Jerusalem relatives. The purchase, I think, was more for my father than for our relatives, as if the familiar gesture of generosity could restore his sense of honor. As he heaved the heavy sacks of fruit into the trunk of the car, I leaned my head against the cool windowpane and watched the market's swirling kaleidoscope of colors: orange and green and brown. After he paid the stall owner for the fruit, my father handed a small sack of oranges and dates through the window, to eat in the car. Although I had never liked dates much, I took one and bit into it. The taste that flooded my mouth was sweet and dense as earth. I could taste that grainy sweetness all the way to Jerusalem.

ı|ı|ı

In the El Al waiting lounge at Kennedy airport, even the babies had tiny yarmulkes askew on their round, bald heads. Orthodox Jews with long curls framing their faces mingled with women in tight shirts and skirts; men in yarmulkes pushed strollers. I was more than a little nervous about flying El Al: I had never gone to Jerusalem via Tel Aviv before, and was only doing so this time because the terms of my United States Information Service speaking tour required it. But no one seemed to notice that I was Palestinian. I was traveling on crutches for a badly sprained ankle, and when I hobbled to the back of the line for boarding, a man scolded me in a friendly tone: "What are you doing back here? Go to the front. You do not need to wait for everyone. Go."

On the plane, the woman next to me was eager to talk. She had made *aliya* a year before, she said, and was still bringing her things over. She had even managed to sneak an extra suitcase onto this flight.

"What do you mean?" I asked.

"I went up to a man with only one piece of luggage and asked him if he would carry a suitcase for me," she responded, clearly pleased with herself.

"But how could he agree to take something from a stranger?" I asked, horrified.

"Oh," she replied, "I knew he was religious, and I am too. You can tell, you know. We both knew it would be fine."

I stared at her. For a moment I thought of telling her that I had agreed to carry a suitcase for a strange Muslim, just to see her reaction.

But the image of armed marshals escorting me off the plane made me refrain.

After takeoff the woman continued the conversation. "Is this your first trip to Israel?," she asked.

"I've been to Jerusalem many times," I replied, "but this is the first time I've flown into Tel Aviv." I could see her flicker of confusion.

"What do you mean?" she asked. "How did you get to Israel?"

"I crossed the bridge from Jordan," I told her, a little reluctantly, knowing where this would lead. But she was still trying to make sense of me, trying to fit me into an unthreatening framework.

"Ah," she said a little too brightly. "You went by way of Egypt? You made the tour?"

"I've been to Egypt a couple of times," I replied, "but not as part of my trips to Jerusalem." I could see the realization wash over her face: I was not just a tourist, I crossed the bridge from Jordan the way the Arabs do. She turned and settled in her seat: our conversation was over. She did not speak to me again for the next nine hours.

At the Tel Aviv airport, light danced from every surface. Inside the arrival lounge, posters advertised the beauties of Israel. I tried to ignore them: I didn't want to see an advertisement for my grandmother's home-town. As I made my way slowly forward on crutches, an airline represen-tative came to help me drag my suitcase off the belt. "Is anyone meeting you?" she asked solicitously.

Just then I saw two Palestinians holding a placard with my name. "Over there," I said. The waiting couple introduced themselves: Mohammed and Dena.

I glanced at the El Al representative: the smile had been stripped from her face. "You won't be needing me anymore," she said coldly, turn-ing away.

Outside, the air was as mild as lamb's wool. It had just rained, and the sky was clean and blue. We drove along the road leading from Tel Aviv to Jerusalem, and I stared out the window at the chalky embankments studded with occasional poppies. "This looks just like the West Bank," I started to say, then caught myself. Of course it looked familiar. What was I thinking? One land: so close, so far. I wondered if I would recognize the Green Line when we crossed it. But before I realized it, we were in the familiar dusty streets of East Jerusalem.

In my relatives' house, little seemed to have changed. The parlor was cool and dark, as always. I drank lemonade flavored with rose water, which tasted like years slipped from memory, and listened to news about life under occupation. Conflicts were erupting over Jabal Abu-Ghnaim, a green area in the West Bank taken over for a settlement against the protests of Palestinians as well as Israeli ecologists. The daughter of a friend stopped by to collect the package I had brought for her from the United States. Perching on the edge of a chair, she told me, "Jerusalem is a dying city." That night I slept in the guest room, a room cluttered with books and photos. A picture of my dead mother looked down at me from the shelf above the television set. Her face smiled me to sleep each night I was there.

A few days later, I stood on the Mount of Olives in the predawn, looking out over Jerusalem. It was Easter Sunday. The sun had not yet crept over the horizon, and in the darkness we could see the yellow lights of Road Number One: a swathe of highway slicing the hills like an airport runway, built over the ruins of many demolished Palestinian homes. Nearby, another set of yellow lights marked a settlement bypass road. My cousin pointed out a darker area, lit with only a few indistinct lights: an Arab neighborhood. Behind us, a hymn rang out from the assembled congregation. At that exact moment, the call to prayer resonated from one mosque, then another mosque. The sounds of worship, Christian and Muslim, wove together on the cold air: there seemed no conflict between the two.

Later, I sat in a parlor, waiting for a car that would take me to Amman, listening to two relatives and a neighbor share memories. The massacre of Deir Yassin: how Palestinian survivors were paraded in trucks through the streets of Jerusalem, and my father and uncle threw jackets up to women in the trucks to cover themselves. The 1967 war: how a neighbor fled with his family on a road specified by the Israelis as a safe route, but returned soon after, alone, his entire family burned by napalm. The 1948 *Al-Nakba*: how a family fled from Lydda on a road they were told led to safety but that led instead into the desert; a road on which many died. The tellers' eyes were sunk in their faces, their voices quick and low, as if relating something they didn't want to remember but couldn't let go of: as if history could be exorcised through narration.

When the driver who was to take me to the Allenby Bridge finally arrived, he told me that the West Bank roads had been closed down. A Palestinian student had been killed at a checkpoint; there were tanks outside every town. We drove through back roads of the West Bank, passing by settlement after settlement. Stone facades claimed the hillsides aggressively, occupying the slopes above Palestinian villages, whose contours, in contrast, blended into the landscape. The driver named every settlement, every village: a litany of names. When we arrived at the bridge, my passport was processed at a high window that made me feel small: I wondered if the height of the window was intentional. My last view of the occupied West Bank was of an Israeli flag leaning out over the muddy water of the Jordan River, planted on the last possible span of earth. Above us, even the sky seemed captive.

ılılı

The first time I entered Israel through Haifa, it was not by choice. It was June 1982. I had been studying at the American University of Beirut, where my formal education centered on English literature and sociology and my informal education centered on the politics of Palestinian American identity. A few days before exam period, the Israeli army began their brutal invasion of Lebanon. I fled the city, squeezed onto an open truck full of sweaty, jostling bodies. Then I fled the country, crowded onto an open cargo boat filled with university students.

As dusk fell, our boat pulled away from shore. We were like travelers on a train pulling out of a station, watching the face of a loved one become smaller and smaller. The Israeli forces controlling the Lebanese harbor had granted our boat clearance, but an hour out of port, when darkness had fallen, we were apprehended by an Israeli gunboat. A spotlight played slowly over the boat, pinning us to the night. Then we were boarded and several students were taken off. We stood on the open deck for hours, dizzy with exhaustion, clutching our passports and waiting for the Israelis to return. When dawn came we realized where we were being taken: to Israel.

As we entered the port of Haifa I gazed, stunned, at the coastal view I had never imagined I would see: red-shingled roofs, a backdrop of brown earth. Soldiers brought bread and tomatoes on board in wooden crates while television cameras rolled. We must have made good headlines: "Israeli Army Feeds Hungry Refugees." But as soon as the reporters left, the interrogations began. The American citizens on board were taken to see the US consul and offered the choice to return home via Israel instead of remaining on the crowded, ill-equipped boat. I thought about the option all night. But when morning came the land seemed a closed fist: I could not bring myself to enter.

Sixteen years later I came once more to Haifa from the sea. This time I was traveling from Cyprus to Jerusalem with my Greek Cypriot husband and our year-old daughter. Unable to find plane reservations to Jordan or Tel Aviv, we had decided to travel instead by boat. We journeyed all night, the boat's engine a steady roar beneath our sleep, and as dawn broke we found ourselves approaching Haifa. As we disembarked, memory washed over me like the ship's wake: light beating the coast, the land submissive beneath its weight. Inside the immigration hall, a female Israeli official chatted with my husband, smiled at my infant daughter. Then a burly Israeli man looked over her shoulder at my immigration form, with its space for father's name. He said something in Hebrew, and within seconds, my passport had been stamped (which I had hoped to avoid) and I had been hustled to one side for interrogation. Who was I? What was my relationship to my traveling companions? Were they really my husband, my daughter? What was the purpose of my visit? Whom did I plan to see? To speak to? Where did I plan to go? Did I have family in Israel? Did I intend to visit them? (I wonder: Do they think we travel so far and will not see our families? That we will wander like strangers in our grandparents' land?) The questions were relentless. When my child wailed, the interrogator merely raised her voice above the cries.

By the time I emerged from the immigration hall, I was furious. Despite our quantities of luggage, I insisted we take a local bus instead of a taxi to the depot where we planned to catch a bus to Jerusalem. I didn't want to spend any more money in Israel than I had to. My husband hefted our suitcases and baby equipment onto the bus without argument. An Israeli man got on the bus with us and started a conversation. Where were we going? Jerusalem? He would show us which stop for the depot, which bus to take. No problem, it was on his way. Yes, he was going to work, but he wouldn't be late, there would be another bus he could take. No problem. Yes, this stop; he would get off too. No problem, really! This line for the bus ticket, yes, that's right, he would wait. Got it? Good. It was that bus right over there, where the line was already forming to board. Did we see it? Yes, that one. All right, good. He'd be going then, had to get to work. Have a safe trip to Jerusalem, enjoy Israel!

As our self-appointed guide took himself off, strolling away in no apparent hurry, I turned to my husband. "What was all that about?" I asked. "Why would someone on his way to work get off the bus to guide a stranger? Why was he going to work at eight in the morning from the port, anyway? And why so friendly—what happened to the stereotypical Israeli brusqueness?"

"Congratulations," my husband replied. "I'd say we were accompanied by security. To make sure we went where we said we were going to go, did what we said we were going to do. Look at it as a badge of authenticity, if you like: verification that you're Palestinian!"

Our bus wove through the streets of Haifa, the city melodious in morning light. My heart swelled as if in accompaniment to a movie score. The landscape seemed so familiar I wanted to cry out in recognition: light like a bright hand over the hills. My grandmother came from Jaffa, a seaside town known as the *bride of Palestine*. Its Canaanite founders called it Yafi, *beautiful*. Haifa lived in my mind as its sister: Palestine by the sea. Yet history had made me an outsider to the land.

The bus was half-filled with soldiers, men and women, their guns cradled casually, commandingly, their smooth faces a reminder of how youth is sabotaged in defense of the state. I held my year-old daughter close, whispering in her ear. She gazed out quietly at the coast, at the rows of white breakers punctuating the striking blueness of the sea. It was her second journey to Jerusalem. The first time, I had carried her deep inside my body, secure from the probing eyes of the security officers who wanted to know what I carried with me, whom I planned to speak to, where I intended to go. In my oversized coat, I did not look pregnant, and so she slipped across the border without being noticed: a small victory I knotted deep within me, a talisman against the humiliations of interrogation. A few days later, at a concert in Birzeit, my father's hometown, I felt her move for the first time. A female vocalist was singing lines of poetry by Mahmoud Darwish, something about longing and freedom. She hit a high note and held it: the child stirred violently within me.

As we traveled inland, the scenery shifted from brown earth to cultivated fields, orchards, houses. The sun moved higher in the sky; olive trees leaned toward each other like old men trading stories. The road curved toward Jerusalem through wooded hills that made deep swells in the land's body: a lover's terrain. Eventually my daughter grew restless, her uneasiness a reflection of my own growing ambivalence. I had only once before approached from the west, and the discord between the land's Arab past and Israeli present strummed through my body, a clanging chord. Around us, soldiers shifted position, stretched and yawned. My daughter stared at their guns, fascinated. When she poked a soldier in the back by mistake, I cringed, but he turned around and smiled.

Then Jerusalem broke upon our view like a wave cresting: stone and light on the ridge, buildings overtaking the land. The scene was resonant as sunlight, the city rising from the hills like the stone it was made of, integral to earth, inseparable from it. I felt a surge of mingled emotion: ache of familiarity, the painful atonality of alienation. As we wound through West Jerusalem neighborhoods, past stone houses that looked like those of my relatives, I saw that West Jerusalem was a splintered mirror image, part familiar, part strange. The city shone from every surface, as if breathing from within, indignities of entry and exclusion temporarily replaced by the constancy of stone, by light cascading down the hills, illuminating the gray-green of pine and palm. But West Jerusalem was a closed world. We passed through as transients only, till the bus spat us out onto a summer sidewalk near the Green Line, into history, into the present.

ı|ı|ı

Jerusalem is a mosaic. Our personal stories are small chips of stone, part of a larger picture that can only be fully perceived from a distance: The Damascus Gate at sunset; an Israeli soldier atop the Old City walls; a street crowded with traffic leading to a quiet interior garden. We come to the city bearing private histories, private sorrows, and find ourselves in the heart of a public space, one ancient as history, and as tormented. Against this backdrop, every shard is laden with meaning.

Yet Jerusalem is not just a metaphor, it's a city. I once showed a picture of a busy East Jerusalem street to an American woman who literally gasped in astonishment. "But it's a regular city," she said. "Cars and everything. I thought it would be more—you know, spiritual." Jerusalem has trash on the streets, graffiti on the walls, people of all kinds. There are love and hate, pollution and traffic jams, death and taxes. And for Palestinians, there are land confiscations, home demolitions, ID revocations—the shrinking circle of occupation. While Jewish Jerusalem expands into the West Bank—its appropriation of Palestinian land cemented through the so-called security wall built by Israel to separate Israelis and West Bank Palestinians—Arab Jerusalem contracts. In East Jerusalem it is almost impossible for Palestinians to get permits for new construction. Newlyweds are often forced to live with their families. Since 1996 Israel has implemented a policy of confiscating the ID cards of Jerusalem Palestinians, accentuating the sensation of a tightening noose around the Arab neighborhoods. There's a sense of erosion in East Jerusalem, as if people are trying to hold their own, but not always succeeding.

Last fall I traveled to Jerusalem to attend a family wedding. We came via Tel Aviv, where security officials paid special attention to my passport and that of my daughter, but did not detain us. We arrived in West Jerusalem around midnight. It was a Jewish holiday, and even that late at night the streets were filled with Hassidic Jews walking in groups down the sidewalk. The night air was soft around us. But the previous weeks had seen several suicide bombings, and every time our van stopped at a traffic light next to an Israeli bus, I held my breath. I did not relax until we arrived in East Jerusalem.

The day after we arrived, there was a family luncheon. Guests attended from several continents, as well as the West Bank, which under the current conditions of occupation seemed further than a continent away. Flying from Cyprus only took me an hour; in contrast, it took my West Bank relatives two hours and three separate cars to traverse the once-short distance from Ramallah to Jerusalem, across roads severed by deep ditches and barbed-wire fences. After lunch the relatives were anxious to leave quickly, instead of lingering for another coffee, another drink. They wanted to get back before curfew, and were worried about being caught on the roads after dark. Sitting in my aunt's garden, I realized: They are living in a war zone.

The next day we went searching for Jerusalem pottery. As it happened, it was a Friday, prayer time. Outside the Damascus Gate Israeli soldiers prevented us from entering the Old City. On the other side of the street, Palestinian men barred from going to the mosque to pray had lined up facing the soldiers. As the call to prayer rang out, the Palestinians knelt on the filthy asphalt, without even a scrap of cardboard to protect them from the street, and bowed their heads to the ground. Between the Israelis and the Palestinians, cars rumbled past; the air was thick with fumes and dust. It was the most potent demonstration I had ever seen: unarmed men facing armed soldiers without shouting, without threats, without stone-throwing, praying in defiance.

ılılı

Going to Jerusalem is like entering a wound. We go to Jerusalem like bleeding medics, helpless against the injustices of the world. We go to Jerusalem like refugees from history, bearing nothing but our children, the future gripped between our teeth. We go to Jerusalem because the city lives inside us like the stone of a fruit. We go because we have voices, although the world does not have ears. We go because above Jerusalem's ancient walls the sky still rises, leavened with light.

◻ ◻ ◻ ◻ ◻

18

KHALED MATTAWA

Repatriation

A Libya Memoir

1.

One June morning in 2002 in Benghazi, I suddenly remembered that the official Libyan ID I've been carrying was just a receipt and not the real thing. I decided right then to check if my real *bitaqa shakhsiya*, my national identity card, had been issued at last.

I had returned to Libya for the first time, after living in the US for twenty-one years, in September 2000 to attend my father's funeral. To become properly repatriated, I needed to obtain a national identity card, something I should have done at the age of sixteen. Twenty years since my departure, things had gotten so complicated in Qaddafi's Libya that I was given a receipt for my national ID to allow me to get by. In fact, it took so long to issue the card that some people got by using the receipt and never retrieved the actual bitaqa.

I went to the government building I had visited with my friend, Musbah, in 2000. The yellow walls of the narrow, dark hallways were covered with dust and cobwebs. Numerous paint strips hung and flapped in the breeze like clothes on a line. Some segments of the wall appeared to have been struck with some kind of mange that turned the mortar inside them into whitish dust, which collected round the edges of the floor.

In the offices, the same cranky, brown-teethed bureaucrats sat at their desks talking with friends, conversations that no one dared interrupt. These officers responded to the citizens' queries with a curt *upstairs*, or *downstairs*. Every now and then one of them would tell you bring another document, and then to come back tomorrow. There wasn't a computer, not even a typewriter in any of these offices. The cards and the tens of thousands of files in the building, like in an ancient library, were all written by hand.

At thirty-six, I was the old geezer among the dozens of young men acquiring the bitaqa. Dressed in knock-off football jerseys, flip-flops and jeans, these skinny boys looked like they'd just been woken up. They did not laugh or smirk or exchange gibes; they certainly didn't dare respond back to the officials who shouted at them. When an officer finally handed me my bitaqa, I walked past the thin young men crowded against a metal frame window where their applications were being received.

Outside the building, I noticed that the photo of my bitaqa is the same one on my American passport. My face bore traces of the unusual circumstances that brought about my return home. The photo had been taken on September 12th 2000, in Pforzheim, Germany, where my father had passed the previous day.

2.

In August 2000, my brother Majid and my sister Hanan arranged to fly our parents from Libya to Germany for medical treatment. The medical system in Libya had been so bad that most Libyans had to travel abroad to get healed, sometimes from minor ailments. In Germany, we'd meant to deal with my mother's knees, not my father's impending death. My mother resisted knee replacement for a long time, but she relented when it became too painful for her to do her daily chores. We went to a hospital in Pforzheim, Germany because a relative of ours had a successful knee replacement there. It was that doctor and no other, insisted my mother.

My father, my mother, my brother Majid, my sister Hanan, and her two young children traveled from Benghazi, via Athens, to Frankfurt and from there hired a van to the hospital in Pforzheim. It was a rough trip, especially for my father who had been treated only a few months before in Jordan, where his doctors failed to detect that he had Hepatitis C. Upon arrival in Germany, he started to fade and it was clear he was dying. I joined my family the day after they arrived.

At the end of that August, I returned to Texas to start teaching at a new job. Preparing the first few sessions, meeting new colleagues, setting up my new apartment, I felt detached and anxious. I had spent a month with my family watching my father die and all the while sensing my presence unnecessary, not that I was not wanted, but that I made no difference. In throbs and bursts that feeling of uselessness began to color my view of the years I spent away from them, my whole life appearing inconsequential and frivolous to me. Two weeks of this in Texas and I could not take it any longer. I returned to Germany on September 8th to say goodbye to my mother once again and to take another last look at my father.

In Pforzheim the second time, I learned that no airline would fly my father home. He had to be either dead or well enough to travel, they said. We needed a special medical plane to take him home. Majid, my brother, and I started calling around to hire a plane from Germany. A cousin put us in touch with the Red Crescent in Libya and early that Sunday two Libyan pilots called to say they have a plane in Italy ready to go. I would accompany my mother, Hanan, and her children to Zurich and put them on the flight to Benghazi. I would return to Pforzheim to help Majid fly my father home the next day, and head back to Texas as soon as possible. That was the plan.

Three cousins were visiting from London that weekend. They greeted my father, spoke to him and held his hand. He was placid and in no apparent pain. Perhaps recognizing others around him, he tried to talk. When I asked him to repeat what he said, he did not respond. The conversation went on without him. Seeing that things were calm, Majid and I took the visiting cousins to lunch at a nearby restaurant. When we bid them goodbye later, my brother and I were in a better mood. We were gone for about an hour.

3.

My father was not in his room when Majid and I returned. A pale-faced nurse told us that he'd had an accident. Apparently he attempted to get out of bed and in doing so fell and shattered his thighbone. Majid and I ran to the ICU and got there as they were wheeling my father out. There was no question of flying him to Libya right away, as he needed surgery to insert a platinum plate in his thigh the next day. It seemed ridiculous for my father to have such an operation when he was likely never to walk again, but something had to be done to alleviate the pain before he could be sent home. In his room, I caught my father looking at his propped up leg, seeming to have no idea what happened. The staff had anesthetized his leg and would do so during the operation—he would not survive full anesthesia. He was not going to survive his liver failure, but my father would have to stay in Germany until his leg healed well enough for him to travel. This could take a few weeks, the doctor said.

Once the news sank in, Majid broke down. The weight of being the one son taking care of the elderly parents had been difficult to bear, and at that moment it landed a powerful blow. He fell to his knees and began sobbing. "What have I done in my life to deserve this? Oh God, tell me what have I done!" he said. It was heartbreaking and pathetic at the same time. One of the nurses stood and looked at us not knowing what to do. I waved her away, and stood beside him. I felt sure that Majid's prayers were meant also for me to hear and I wanted to hear them.

I left the room to call the Red Crescent pilots to cancel the flight. I planned to call my department chair to cancel my teaching for the semester. I would stay with my father and Majid would join his family. I was not ready to go back to Libya. Even with my father dying that August, it did not occur to me that I would return to Libya. Then I began to imagine that things would improve with everyone gone. I would sit next to my father as his leg healed and I would read and translate as I'd done during his earlier ailments. A part of me saw my father's leap out of bed as a lunge back into life—perhaps there'd be time for a liver transplant—and I harbored a wish that my devotion to him would turn him around. Majid would return to take my father back, the two of them heading to Libya, leaving me to continue my exile.

In the meantime, my mother and Hanan and her children were to fly to Benghazi as planned. My mother had had two knee replacements and could have used more physical therapy in Germany. But she was overwhelmed and in need of the care of my three others sisters in Libya. In a few hours, they and I would fly to Zurich and I'd be with them until they boarded the flight to Benghazi.

4.

When my parents arrived in the Pforzheim hospital that August, we, their children, decided to place them in adjacent rooms to assure that Mother got all the rest she needed for her double knee replacement. A few days after her procedure, she began to have some physical therapy. A few days later she took her first steps, the following week she walked with the aid of a walker to my father's room. We'd go to my mother's room and she'd begin to tell stories, and soon there'd be smiles and laughter. In his room my father lived in semi-darkness—his eyes could not tolerate the overhead electric light—and he seemed visibly annoyed by the quiet banter of Hanan's two sons. He lay awake at night, tossed and turned in his bed. He woke me up often to readjust the many pillows that he'd been propped on, to turn him on his side or back, to help him to the bathroom, or to take his socks off or put them on. He and I would finally fall asleep at about dawn. At seven, the nurses woke us up. They took my father to the bathroom and bathed him. They served him breakfast too if he could eat. Otherwise he was fed with a drip. Cleaned and comforted by the nurses' care, he fell into a deep sleep until noon. I'd leave him and try to catch some sleep in Majid's room, or next to Hanan's children in their little apartment near the hospital.

Although I spent only four weeks with my father, I can break down those days into various stages. First, he could speak clearly and stand up to go to the bathroom. Then he could eat and speak, but not stand. Days later he seemed to be in no pain, but completely out of this world. Several times at night I put him in a wheelchair and took him for a stroll in the hospital garden. Out in the summer night, I hoped to evoke something in him, and though he never responded, he seemed at peace. The strangeness of those days was compounded by the polarity of our parents' situation: in one room my mother feeling healthier every day, and one door over my father looking morose when awake, or mentally absent, drifting towards death. We, their children, had made many difficult decisions about their lives. My mother, even as she was recovering, and wanting to be helpful, consented to all of them, including separating her from her husband in his last days and sending her home without him.

5.

At the Stuttgart and Zurich airports the airline staff did a superb job of getting my mother around to her flights. At the gate for the Benghazi flight, my mother told me repeatedly to go back; she was afraid Qaddafi's agents would report me. In the 1980s and 90s, when we used to meet up in Greece and later in Egypt, her fears of other Libyans were justified. I told her things have changed since then, but she was still worried some-one would report on her son who refused to go home.

The sight of my fellow Benghazians captivated me. Many faces looked familiar, and their chatter in that particular accent filled me with a strange sense of comfort. People in Benghazi attended so many weddings and even more funeral wakes that they knew each other *by face*, meaning that they can sort of tell which family or clan you came from by giving you a few hard looks.

Some of the men sat in the tiny bar right across from the gate. Unabashed before the denizens of their gossipy city, they sipped their last alcoholic beverages before heading home. I'd not seen that before, Libyans drinking publicly like that. Perhaps they were some of Qaddafi's high-ranking bureaucrats tormenting their people with brashness, or men who hated Qaddafi's prohibition of alcohol and wanted to show independence. Benghazi produced these kinds of men, a city of strangers who sought quick solidarity, but who missed no opportunity to upstage each other. A city of people who scrutinized each other, and who often rebelled against that scrutiny. I could not take my eyes off my fellow Benghazians, watching their gestures, listening to their patter, wondering if I could place them by face.

When the airline staff led Mother, Hanan, and her boys to the airplane, I followed to the edge of the entrance and watched as they rounded the curve of the gate corridor. I waited a few minutes in the gate, bending this way and that until I could see through the plane's windows. I waved to them, but they could not see me. The plane backed out of the gate and slowly made its way to the runway and disappeared.

At the airport train station, I took a train to the Zurich Central. There were no trains for Pforzheim until the following morning. With six hours to go, I walked around the train station, and after a long search found a bench in a quiet area and fell asleep immediately. An hour or so later two young policemen nudged me, startling me awake. Stepping back from me when I rose, they said I'd needed to leave the train station or go to a special room for people waiting overnight for trains. It was the only place I could be inside the station.

The only light in the overnight room came through the glass walls that separated it from the station. Inside stood several oblong nail-polish red plastic benches the size of caskets, giving the room the look of a futuristic funeral home. The benches were sturdy enough to serve as bunk beds, but were terribly unaccommodating. The room had other fidgety occupants lying on the benches, and smelled of a stench that had been covered with a powerful disinfectant.

I could not sleep. I should be with my father in his room in the hospital, I thought, or with my mother taking her back to Libya, or in Texas teaching my classes, or with Naima, my fiancée, who was in another country altogether. I got out of the strange room an hour later. I sat in a chair near the ticket stand and nodded for a few hours. At about four-thirty people began to show up at a kiosk serving coffee. I got a ticket to Pforzheim. On the train, I kept waking up every few minutes afraid that I'd miss my connection in Baden Baden.

6.

Back in the Pforzheim hospital, my father lay with his broken leg propped up. A feeder dripped painkillers into him. The staff planned to operate in a few hours. He looked peaceful, having been given a towel-bath in bed and dressed with a fresh gown. He was awake, but he did not seem capable of seeing, or if he saw, he certainly did not know whom or what he saw. I held his hand, and his grip responded firmly. I remember looking at the hand I was holding, and over to the other hand resting along his side. With his body bloated along the midriff, his chest and neck sunken, his face pulled tight against his head, and his calves thinned out to bone, he seemed misshapen and deformed. But the skin on his hand was healthy and still holding to its freckles. My father's hands were not an old man's hands. They were broad and strong, the palms soft and fleshy. I raised his hand up and for a minute ran it gently over my face, then put it down again beside him. I lay in the bed next to his. At some point I heard him cough or make a sound that sounded like a cough. When I turned around his eyes were still open.

I don't know how much time passed when all of a sudden I saw Majid standing by my father's bedside. He nudged my father's shoulder, then placed his head on his chest to listen for a heartbeat. Raising his head, Majid gave me a puzzled look. I got up and he ran to get the nurse. I moved toward my father's bed, but could not touch him again. The nurse came in, felt my father's pulse, then placed her two fingers on his throat listening intently. She then looked at me and said, in halting English, "I'm sorry. He has died."

Recalling that moment, I remember a burning in my eyes and a sense of numbness down to my fingers. My brother and I held each other in a strong, brief embrace. Neither of us could sit down, feeling beaten, but roused by the shock. There were arrangements to be made and phone calls to relatives in Libya and abroad. We also had to learn about Libyan regulations regarding the return of deceased citizens. To return home, my father would have to be taken to the Libyan embassy in Bonn to be prepared for burial. The embassy arranged for a hearse to fetch my father's body from Pforzheim to Bonn the following morning. They provided this service for free to all Libyan citizens, which seemed an honorable thing to do by the same embassy that not so long ago used to abduct and torture exiled dissidents in its basement.

I called the pilots of the Libyan Red Crescent plane to see if they were still available. They said that they'd decided to stay an additional day on our behalf, just in case. I had had a queasy feeling about that plane, a bird of omen flying around Europe hovering over my dying father to take him away. On the following day, Majid was to go to Bonn to process the death certificate. The embassy had hired a Muslim cleric to wash the body and prepare it for burial. My father's body would arrive in Benghazi in a wooden casket sealed with a wax stamp verifying correct Islamic ritual. It was in the middle of this confusion that I decided to return to Libya.

7.

But first I needed to retrieve my Libyan passport from the US and to deal with my American passport. My American passport was issued in Jerusalem a few months earlier, a replacement for one that got damaged while I was visiting Palestine. To return to Libya, I needed to get my Libyan passport, and to get rid of the American passport issued in Jerusalem. I called a new colleague in Texas to ask her to express-mail the Libyan passport. She said she was coming to London; I told her I will pick up my passport from her there. The other question was how to get to Benghazi. It was night in Germany, so I called a friend in the US and asked her to book a seat for me on the Swissair Benghazi flight scheduled on the night of September 14.

I made all these arrangements in my father's hospital room while he was lying dead in his bed. The hospital staff had not taken him away, only washed him again, wrapped him in a new gown, and removed the cast around the broken leg. Every time I saw it, I was certain that his leg continued to hurt him even in death. The nurse had also wrapped a gauzy strip around his face and head to keep his mouth from falling open. Neither Majid nor I ever mentioned to the people we called where my father's body was. Every time I faced my father I turned around and continued talking.

I spent the night in my father's room on the bed beside him as I'd done before. I called Naima, my fiancée, and let her know what happened.

She was kind and gentle as always, but I did not want to speak for so long that I'd get lost among my tangled feelings. I called a friend to contact the Libyan ambassador to the UN to provide a letter certifying that I was a university professor returning home in a family emergency. I was loath to do this, but felt compelled to have something to present to the Libyan authorities in case the interrogation I anticipated went badly.

Early the next morning I went to Majid's room to shower, then hurried back to take a last look at my father. When I got to the room, it was empty, my father not there, even his bed gone. A nurse told me the undertaker had come and fetched my father. I went to the hospital's main entrance to see if the undertaker was still there, but he'd gone. He had said he'd be at the hospital at eight, and it was not even seven and he'd already come and gone. Majid who hoped to ride with the body to Bonn also missed the driver. He now had to get there on his own. I had to arrange to get to the American consulate in Frankfurt. My father who was an early riser was ahead of us again, and we were now in a panic trying to catch up with him.

8.

Two months before coming to Germany in August 2000 I went to Ramallah to teach a creative writing workshop. I did not think twice about accepting the invitation even though Libyan nationals were prohibited from going to Palestine or Israel. According to Libyan law, a visit to Palestine or Israel is an act of treason. I had decided to go to Palestine because as of June of 2000 I still did not consider returning to Libya. I spent a great month in Palestine, met wonderful people, traveled to Jericho, Gaza, and Nablus. I carried my American passport on me every day and eventually it got damaged, frayed by my own sweat. On my last day in Palestine, I took the passport to the consulate in Jerusalem to make sure it was still useable. They decided to issue me a new one.

That was the American passport I had at the time of my father's death. Under normal circumstances possessing a foreign passport in Libya was dangerous, but having an American passport issued in Jerusalem was asking for serious trouble. Furthermore, I could not tell the American consulate why I needed a new one. They could simply refuse to allow me to go to Libya since American citizens were banned from traveling there at the time. There was no question that I had to get a new passport. On the way out of Pforzheim my driver dropped me at a photographer's and said he'd be back in ten minutes. I got the photo taken and xeroxed the passport and other documents needed to get a new passport. But I still had to lose the passport I had.

Holding my Jerusalem passport and waiting for the driver to return, I walked toward a garbage can to throw it away, but could not. I went back inside the building and looked for a place to hide it, but could not find one. I went outside again to a small garden across the street. All the garbage cans were open-faced and the passport could easily be seen. I saw my taxi approaching. I walked toward a thick bush on one corner of the little park and peered through it. It wasn't as thick as I'd hoped, but one would have to be looking for something to find anything there. I shoved the passport deep into the bush, turned around and walked toward the taxi as if I'd just killed someone.

9.

The photo in my bitaqa, my Libyan national identity card, that I started off talking about, is the one I took the day following my father's death. My eyes are reddened and my face more intense than I remember feeling. The arrangements that had to be made, the prospect of returning home, and getting rid of the Jerusalem passport, seemed to have pumped me full of adrenalin. It is the same photo in the passport that the US consulate in Frankfurt issued me within forty-five minutes.

I remember the flight to London later that day, but not at which airport I landed. I remember meeting two friends who lived there, but not where we met. I met my friend Barbara from Texas at Heathrow, but recall nothing about where I went on the way back, or even the hotel I stayed in. One of the London cousins arranged for a gathering of his Libyan acquaintances. It was just another social occasion for this group of Libyan expats who were dressed up to the hilt. They shook my hand, then sat in groups chatting and laughing. I could not stand being among them.

The next day, I discovered that Swissair had canceled my Benghazi reservation—due to regulations pertaining to the American sanctions on Libya. Now there were no seats available. I called the airlines several times, then went to their office and waited several hours until a seat became available. There were no other flights from Europe to Benghazi for days to come, and I wanted to go as soon as I could, perhaps afraid that my enthusiasm would wane the longer it took to get back.

On the plane, a large group of elderly Swiss tourists were heading to

Libya to see the great archeological sites. They cooed at their meal trays, read translations of John Grisham and fiddled with their crochet work. They made the flight seem like dozens of uneventful flights I'd taken. As we neared Libya, I could not take my eyes off the window, watching for the lights of Benghazi to appear.

At the airport in Benghazi, my friend Musbah stood behind the immigration processing area. I'd not seen him since we met up in Egypt nine years earlier. He waved and smiled while I stood in line. Not nervous or sad, I felt strangely empowered, deserving some happiness for coming home at last. The immigration officer who inspected my passport asked me to step aside from the queue. A young Internal Security officer in shabby civilian clothing came fifteen minutes later and led me to a brightly lit and extraordinarily messy office with a huge desk in the middle of it. He had a long list of questions and wanted to know my family tree in detail. Musbah, who came with me to the interview, told him that my last return to Libya was in 1992, which was not true of course.

"How do I know that?" said the Internal Security officer.

Musbah replied that a certain Mr. Faitouri, head of Internal Security for Benghazi, can confirm that information. Musbah had told me to not show the letter I got from the UN ambassador; it would only complicate things, he said. The young officer demurred then left the office. Instinctively, foolishly, I stood up to look at the huge ledger on the desk. It was open to a page from the letter خ (kh) section, filled with names inscribed in a rough hand. There were at least twenty-five Khaleds on the wanted listed, almost all of them accused of being zanadiq, or heretics, as the Qaddafi regime called Islamist militants. My name was not on the list.

The groggy, young officer returned and handed me back my Libyan passport stamped with entry on the date of September 14, 2000, twenty-one years, two months and four days after departure from Libya, ending this minor odyssey.

10.

I arrived in Benghazi on the third and last day of my father's wake and so did not attend the burial. At the wake, I shook hands with two thousand men. I saw relatives I'd not seen since childhood, and two boyhood football heroes who were distant relatives. Back with my family, I held and played with young nephews and nieces I'd not met. Dreamlike as it was, the return to Benghazi brought no surprises. I expected the city to be shabbier than I remembered, the people to be worse off. And it was as I predicted. When I visited my childhood house, the streets leading to it appeared narrower than I recalled. Scraped clean of asphalt, they'd become bumpy and almost impassable. I stared at every passerby and through every half-opened door, soaking up the strange familiarity, reintroducing my face to the old neighborhood.

Within a few days of coming home I began my repatriation. I brought copies of the photo that I took in Pforzheim to the Mukhtar al-Mahala, the neighborhood superintendent who stamped them on the back certifying that I'm indeed "Khaled Ahmad Mattawa." Filling the application for the national identity card, I submitted six of them along with the other documents. I retrieved my identity card receipt ten days later, and shortly thereafter made my way back to Texas.

Almost two years later, in June 2002, when I did in fact get the bitaqa, it carried the same photo as my American passport, a reminder of those strange days in September of 2000. Seeing my face on both documents together for the first time suggested that I was somehow able to outfox both nations, and that I had found a sense of autonomy that transcended exile and belonging.

Losing my father would not hit me until months after his death, harder than I imagined and in places within my being I did not know existed. He and I had managed our life as father and son through exile and with a bond of expectation and disappointment that no time or place could break. The photo to me now bears neither sadness nor nostalgia, but a sense of enervation, a mixture of guilt and self-justification that weighs heavily upon us when facing the myriad unfinished businesses of our lives.

⬜ ⬜ ⬜ ⬜ ⬜

19

IMAN MERSAL

The Displaced Voice

Let us suppose that the voice is a thread of light stretching between the mouth of the speaker and the ear of the listener, between intention and interpretation, and that an accent is colored oscillations vibrating around this thread but not congruent with it. At times, these oscillations may intensify the thread's light, adding, perhaps, to the original intention; at others, they may impede or disrupt it. A single word falling from a sentence threaded on a luminous cord suffices to make the thread strain and shake. The listener's eyes widen; his vision sharpens, hoping to catch the word dislodged by the accent before it hits the ground. The speaker's eyes may open wide as well. All his limbs and organs may rally to the cause, each in its own idiom, helping to convey the intention, gaps notwithstanding, to the ear of the person awaiting it. I am not referring to the individual voice here as a physiological product of vocal cords carried on the airwaves, nor as a vehicle of linguistic intent and its target, nor as a refutation of death, but as an energy born from the accent, in order to convey the individual voice, the language that voice utters and its intention.

The accent's energy follows a different tempo proper to the mother tongue, and when the voice carries it into a foreign language, the result is an illusion of an attempt to speak two languages at the same instant, one on the surface and the other concealed, one in motion and the other sidelined, up in arms at its neglect and abandonment. The accent is thus not necessarily a speech defect but rather the mother tongue's struggle against mortality. It is competing with the foreign language via sabotage, sabotage of the bond between voice and rhythm. A syllable is amputated here or there, an unfamiliar letter rushes forth when it should have bided its time, a sound leaps onto the head of another and chomps off a part of its allotted space. The sabotage may also come from the generosity of the mother tongue in its dealings with time, adding a few split seconds with its vowels where the foreign language permits none. Thus, *street* becomes *es-treet*, and *clothes* becomes *cloz-ez*.

If we imagine the person with the accent as, in the act of enunciation, a displaced individual, then let us together imagine the accent as a displaced voice. This person with an accent may practice long and hard in order to fit into his new place, and he may succeed in hiding his accent or in suppressing it for a long time. But, sooner or later, along comes the fatal moment when practice fails him. It is no accident that moments of anger are those where the accent, in all its glory, is most likely to rear its head. Perhaps this is because anger sticks better to swollen vocal cords than satisfaction does, and is better at agitating the memory and calling forth the first language to exact revenge, applying its phonology and stirring up chaos. Someone with an accent need not be an emigrant from one language to another. He may well be internally displaced, an emigrant from one dialect of a language to another. Awad, the doorman of the building in which I live in Cairo, speaks to its residents with unimpeachable decorum, and in faultless Cairene. But his Upper Egyptian accent leaps out the moment he yells at one of his children or becomes embroiled in an argument with one of the doormen of the neighboring buildings.

ıΙıΙı

A person's voice can be more individual in his mother tongue, recognizable by its particular timbre, its grain, should I quote Roland Barthes. When the voice takes on another language, the accent is muddled in its individuality, tirelessly pointing back to the concealed collective phonology of its mother tongue. For example, the English *H* is more akin to an Arabic *Kh* when my colleague Natalie pronounces it. This is not just Natalie's voice, but the voice of the Russian language asserting itself. In my first year in America the sound of the letter *P* seemed capable of dislodging any word that contained it from the thread of light behind which I stood. This is the letter that we often refer to as *heavy B* in Arabic, a letter that doesn't exist in our language; a failure to pronounce it is enough to suggest to the listener that Arabic lies dormant inside you.

ıΙıΙı

When I applied for a position as professor at the University of Alberta, I had to jump through all the hoops that the academic marketplace requires: teaching a class in front of an academic committee, individual meetings with professors, students and the dean. But the severest trial of all was to deliver a forty-five minute lecture to a packed academic audience. It wasn't the content of what I wanted to say that terrified me but rather how I could deliver it smoothly. How could I manage to do so without colliding with the bumps in the long words, words with their dread consonant clusters, pivotal words whose fall out of sequence would mean my fall from contention for the job. The accent at that moment had to be considered as no less than a speech defect whose repercussions must be minimized.

Wāṣil ibn ʿAṭāʾ, who lived in the eighth century, was an eloquent and provocative Muʿtazalite theologian from Basra who preached in Arabic, his mother tongue, and whose enemies bullied him because of his inability to properly pronounce the trilled *R*. But his linguistic genius inspired him to hide his defect by avoiding words that contained this letter, replacing them with synonyms: *dunuw* for *qurb* (proximity), *ʿala* for *ʿanwar* (lights), *yaʾfu* for *yaghfir* (forgive), *madjaʾ* for *firash* (bed), and *ghayth* for *matar* (rain). He even crafted an entire sermon without one single *r*. That is what I had to do—circumvent the sounds the accent might muddle. I no longer remember how many words I had to substitute, but I do remember my ideas flourishing in this substitution game. Some words, however, could not be replaced and I remember one: architecture. My solution was to rewrite it in Arabic script, trying to visualize it that way, in the shape of a reassuringly familiar language, so that I might remember how it sounded. But at the critical moment, I tripped over the word, and a mosque, an Omayyad mosque, specifically, seemed to be collapsing somewhere, the sound of its broken glass windows issuing on the thread of my voice.

ı|ı|ı

When speaking a foreign language, the accented speaker does not choose the most precise words to convey what he means, as he presumably does in his mother tongue. Instead, he must avoid those words, despite their precision, that might undercut his voice, the oscillations of the accent short-circuiting them one way or another. We can imagine that this lack of precision may perturb the content of the spoken message. It may even prevent the message from arriving. But what is more intriguing is to imagine the accent changing the content of the message, or setting it on a different path, substituting a cooler message for one more sympathetic, a cautious phrase for one more daring. After the arrival of a message which the accented speaker did not intend, he may be startled by its beauty, however unintentional. The message has, as it were, been born, and a correction made to match an intention that only its author knows might well be disappointing to an ear that has already received it. And so the speaker may continue with the error, pursued by a feeling of having veered off course. It is not only language that may be inadequate, but the voice itself. An accent sets you to quarreling with the words as you struggle to overcome the inadequacy of your voice, and leads you, like a Sufi mystic, down paths and through messages into states of spiritual enlightenment the existence of which you would never have suspected were it not for this interminable game of choice and avoidance.

The body is a visual support upon which the thread of the voice depends for its safe arrival. The absence of the body weakens the thread, rendering it vulnerable to breakage and loss. I can often easily understand someone with an accent when we speak face to face. On the telephone, however, the gaps in the message swell and I may pretend I have an old receiver of poor quality so that the speaker will repeat his sentence. The comfort of the listener's body calms the anxiety to which the voice is prone, aiding it not in overcoming its disability but rather in ignoring it. When you expect that the ear you are speaking to will not understand you, you may raise your voice to confirm your presence, to become visible, to occupy as much space as a voice can occupy. Or you may lower your voice, as if you hoped to disappear from a scene in which you are condemned to failure. In both cases, the accent holds sway over the voice and controls its volume.

When I would accompany my grandmother from the village to the city of Mansura or to Cairo—on a visit to someone in the hospital or to citified relatives—she seemed like a different person to me. Her clothes looked tight; they were part of her formal wardrobe, reserved for outings, and had languished in the closet for quite some time. The gold she never wore in her day-to-day life of baking bread and cooking changed the look of her face and her neck. The roughness of her fingers, decorated with rings, attracted my attention. Certainly, seeing her leave the house where she had the luxury of exercising control over all the members of a big family and becoming a mere visitor in the big city had something to do with my feeling that she was not quite the person I knew. But her accent also played its part in the transformation. I imagine her now saying something on the order of *Mohammed Abu Isma'iin married Noohaa.* The sound of *Isma'iin* for *Isma'il* and *Noohaa* for *Noha* led me to doubt her absolute authority and made me nervous for reasons I couldn't pinpoint.

An accent only becomes a source of shame or anxiety when it signifies the lower status of the voice speaking to the ear listening. What determines status usually amounts to more than just the voice and its intention. It may be any of a number of relationships: that of the center to its periphery, of the colonizer to the colonized speaking his language, of the urban to the rural, or of the fortunate classes to those less privileged. I can't imagine someone with an Oxford accent feeling ashamed when speaking to someone with one of England's working class accents. Nor would a Parisian feel anxious listening to his accent side by side with that of an immigrant from Senegal. An accent is thus a transparent metaphor for relationships of power.

Sometimes the lower status accent in these relationships of power tries to get rid of its shame by seeking shelter in its foreignness and strangeness, by choosing to be exotic. I suspect I may do this upon occasion. But I only recognized it as a strategy after seeing it in the performance of women intellectuals as they deliver their lectures at academic conferences, or of authors discussing their work with an audience that speaks the power language, the language of the center. I have an Egyptian friend who was lucky enough to be educated in English from nursery school on and who did his degrees at a university in England. This friend once said to me, in flirtation or as a compliment, "I love your English." My angry reaction to his sentence surprised me; but nobody likes to be exotic at home. My friend's backhanded compliment carried a whiff of condescension, as if he were conversing in his own language, with an accent that made him closer to the real Englishman, able to recognize and even love the exotic.

After all these years of speaking and teaching in a foreign language, years of wrestling with an accent, I am startled by a feeling that my voice in Arabic is different from my voice in English. Not better or worse, just different. I remember my astonishment once upon hearing, by chance, a recorded message I had left on the answering machine at a friend's house. I was asking her to clarify directions to her address that I had, as usual, gotten lost trying to find. In it, inadvertently, I found a poignant illustration of Agamben's assertion that the essence of a message is inseparable from the voice that speaks it. For this was a lost, anxious voice, a voice with an accent. And this could be nothing but a message of longing for a destination, longing distilled syllable by syllable, step by step, on this journey of stuttering and wrong turns.

◻ ◻ ◻ ◻ ◻

20

PHILIP METRES

The Paperless "Palestinian" and the Russian P'liceman

"When I tell people about you," Sergey Gandlevsky said, pulling out the last cigarette and crushing his empty cigarette box, "I say that you're from Ramallah."

Gandlevsky was visiting from Russia, and we'd been on the road for weeks doing readings, part of a coast-to-coast bilingual poetry barnstorming that we'd concocted, to fill his pockets with American bucks. I'd been translating him for over ten years, ever since we met in 1993, and he knew me well enough to know I wasn't Palestinian. In fact, I'd just told him that I discovered that the owner of this local Amherst Starbucks was Lebanese. It's a trait I've inherited from my father, always inquiring where people are from, particularly if they may hail from the Middle East. Dad always made a point of it to claim people—Ralph Nader, Tony Shalhoub, Diane Rehm, Paul Anka, Dick Dale, Salma Hayek, even the slightly-embarrassing ones like Jamie Farr and Sammy Hagar and Paula Abdul—as cousins from the Old Country.

"Why from Ramallah?"

"Just a bit of black humor, he said, pausing to let the nicotine surge into his alveoli before exhaling his tobacco into the air. "They think that Ramallah is the world center of terrorism."

When Amy and I traveled in Greece for our honeymoon, locals would come up to me and begin speaking the language of Homer and Ritsos, but I was as lost as Odysseus after Troy. In France, they thought I was Moroccan or Algerian. When I was quite young, biking in my new neighborhood in the suburbs of Chicago, some boys looked up and started calling me a spic, hurling a stony rain of crabapples after my Latino bike, pedaled frantically out of range.

I think of avant-garde poet Dmitry Prigov's lines:

I'd be Catullus in Japan
And in Rome, Hokusai
And in Russia, I'm the same guy
Who would have been
Catullus in Japan
And in Rome, Hokusai.

Misrecognition is an unexpected, unasked-for gift. In misnaming, in the ill-fitted confusion of word and world, poetry begins.

At Ben Gurion airport, I was—without question—Arab. Traveling with my family in 2003 to Palestine, where my sister was due to be married to a Palestinian man from the little village of Toura, we'd been told by my sister to say that we had come to The Holy Land as tourists to see the Holy Sites. This strategy might, she'd told us, spare us the special interrogation, which involves hours of luggage plundering, incessant cross-examination, and humiliation.

Despite my pose as a tourist, from her high perch, like a judge before the accused, the passport control guard stared at me the way the sun glares through a magnifying glass. The way acid eats through glass. She inquired about my grandparents and great-grandparents, as if to determine the potential layers of criminality that might exist in my DNA. Yes, my father's side is from Lebanon. Bsharri. Dayr al-Qamar. Yes, that makes them—and me—Arab. Though probably many of them would have thought of themselves as Phoenician, or Christian, or Lebanese. Such distinctions melt before the rational paranoia of the great-grandchildren of pogroms and the grandchildren of the Shoah.

Somehow, as if against her better judgment, she let me pass.

The truth is, I don't even know what it might mean to feel Arab, even if my father, his family, and the Arabs we met, always pronounced me Lebanese or Arab. The black hair, zaitun (olive) eyes and skin, and the generous nose—certainly the generous aquiline nose—seem evidence, to the eyes of my people, evidence that I was part of the tribe. The feeling of being claimed is halfway to feeling home, even if on the inside I felt like I didn't quite belong. My tongue was utterly dumb whenever my interlocutors would switch to Arabic. But as I've aged past the adolescent need to differentiate oneself from one's parents, I've found myself looking backward as much as forward, trying to understand what might be coiled in my DNA, what ancestral spirits reside in me. A recent publication mistake—in which the Arabic text I'd included in my poem, *A Concordance of Leaves*, got reversed in an anthology for Palestine, so that it read backward—instigated my diving into learning to read Arabic for the first time.

On the subject of Ramallah, my fictional hometown, I can say, having visited it just after the Israeli siege in 2002, I can report that it was robust, full of people pursuing life in its sundry material guises. Not that I expected to see bandolier-wearing guerrillas sauntering the street, or men with bomb belts showing beneath their button-downs. But I don't think I could have imagined the pulsing life in the streets; huge sacks of grain lifted out of flatbed trucks in front of internet cafés; bustling banks and corner shops; women in hijab and no hijab; banner ads splashed across buildings for Marlboro and Milano shoes; the merry-go-round of cars at Manarah Square—just modern city life and all its eros and contradictions. I half-expected to see Mahmoud Darwish in a café drinking coffee, having just published *State of Siege*, his intense and fragmented long poem about surviving life during the Israeli invasion of the West Bank. At one point in the poem, he invites Israeli soldiers prowling outside to come in and have coffee—"so we can be reminded we're human like you."

Yes, in Ramallah we passed the occasional detonated remains of a car, dissected by an Israeli missile, left on the side of a main road as if to remind people of what they won't forget anyway—that over their lives hovers the constant presence of a military occupation, even in the heart of Palestine. In Ramallah, despite gnashing their teeth on the bitter fruit of domination, people just go about the business of daily life, trying to put khubz on the table, facing daily checkpoints and other unimaginable obstacles that would make even a Russian, born and bred on the sadism of the Soviet State, blush.

But Gandlevsky's joke wasn't the first time I was mistaken for an enemy to the civilized world. To be brown in much of the Western world is to be mistaken for being dangerous. Once in Russia, on my way to interview the poet Stella Morotskaya in 1996, I was stopped in the metro by the local *militsiya*, the police, who were executing a flying checkpoint, scoping out anyone who looked foreign.

When they found that I hadn't registered my visa at the local police station, they detained me. Apparently, it was required to register with the local police to let them know that you were visiting from elsewhere, a requirement that I'd overlooked amidst the rest of the bureaucracy of getting into the country. So they directed me to stand at the entrance of the metro with the others. I was in the line of shame, with three Vietnamese, a couple Georgians, a Caucasian, and a handful of homegrown Russian derelicts too drunk to stand up straight. If my eyes could see straight, I'd say that it looked like, off to the side, the Georgians rapidly conducted a business deal with the porcine officer that went in their favor—some thousands of rubles for breathing fresh air and freedom. I was worried, but too afraid to offer a bribe. What I really wanted, most of all, was to get my visa registered so that this wouldn't happen again. The only way was to go to the station.

The day was ceding to evening, and the air became chilly. I was in a light jacket, standing still, unprepared for this Moscow fall. A half hour passed, with more others joining the line. My anxiety was rising in proportion to the general chill. An hour. To be unregistered is Russia is to be paperless, utterly vulnerable. I felt naked, stripped of rights that I'd felt were as natural as my own skin. I began to shiver, like a rabbit in a hunter's hands.

"What do you want?" I called out to a passing officer, his fur hat's badge gleaming in the metro fluorescence. "Let's go to the station and pay the fine so that I can get my visa registered."

"Just a minute," he said. He pulled me aside, whispering, "Why go to the station? You can take care of it here." His fat cheeks were pink from the cold, but this was no time for pig jokes. He was more of a wild boar, a shaven wild boar. He had me by the stones, and he wasn't letting go.

"How much?"

"Five thousand rubles, and place it in my pocket." He didn't want to be seen reaching for a bribe.

Is it a greater crime to *reach* for the bribe? Either that or he enjoys having another man's hand in his pants.

"No, I'm not putting it in your pocket."

He handed me an empty cigarette box.

"Place the money in here, and put it in my chest pocket."

It was the equivalent of about ten dollars. I did what he asked, sliding the box into his chest pocket, right above his heart. I hustled out of there, and didn't look back.

For the rest of my month in Moscow, every time I saw a police officer, I ducked behind a tree or a *dedushka* and headed another direction.

I'd recently translated a series of poems by the aforementioned

Prigov about the P'liceman, the Soviet version of Officer Friendly—if Officer Friendly had served in the Red Army and liberated Europe from the Fascist Scum, and then returned home to serve to protect the peace of his homeland, albeit with a beer in his hand. I found the poems absolutely hilarious, but also haunting, the way great poems seem to cut in all directions, like flung Swiss Army knives, with all the knives open:

> In the café of Literary Workers
> Mr. P'liceman drinks his beer
> Downing them in his usual manner
> Not even seeing the literary workers
>
> But they all keep looking at him.
> Around him it's light and empty
> And all their different art forms
> In his presence mean nothing
>
> He represents Life
> Manifested as Duty.
> Life is short, but Art is long.
> And in the battle, Life wins.

The final stanza—with its quotation of the classic aphorism in the penultimate stanza (*vita brevis, ars longa*)—utterly flips the script. Poets write out of the hope that their art will give them a second life, to outlast this mortal flesh, this transient existence, ever speeding into nothingness. But Prigov's poem proposes that life, realized in the form of this brute, beer-swilling protector of the social orders, always triumphs. Art may be long, but it is a frank testament to its failure. The proposition is both consoling—in the sense that all our conceptions of the world cannot capture the world—and terrifying—in that nothing we make will ever promise us eternity.

And now I'd met with what it means for life to win, life in the form of brute force, the brute force of an extralegal officer of the law.

At her office, just after my encounter with the p'liceman in the metro, Stella Morotskaya tried to soothe me with cooing sympathy and hot black tea. I closed my cold hands around the thin porcelain cup, waiting for its warmth to translate to my fingers. And, after my fingers lost their frost, I lifted the cup to my cold mouth—so that I could speak again, in the language of the country in which I kept finding and losing myself.

□ ▯ ▯ ▯ ▯

21

SUSAN MUADDI DARRAJ

Bint al-Halal

Mosaic of an Arab American Girlhood

Fragment: Blue

You are born. As a child, you assume this had been a good day.

How your parents must have rejoiced, you believe, in the birth of their first child. However, you start to doubt this at some point—you're not sure exactly when—because you notice extra wide smiles, enthusiastic handshakes whenever someone drops the news that a baby is expected, that another child will enter the family, the world, and that it will be a boy.

Much later, in your teens, you attend your cousin's baby shower and enter a magical world of blue: blue tablecloth, blue balloons, blue baby rattle party favors attached to gauzy bags of blue and white Jordan almonds. There is so much homemade food that the entire population of occupied Palestine could attend and there would be leftovers. The chatter is all about boys. They will wear you out. You have to watch them every second. Oh, you enjoy sleeping? Well, forget about sleeping soundly for the next ten years. All complaints, but delivered with a light touch and a laugh. A sense of relief.

You listen to the chatter as you help out the hostess. You refill empty pans, make sure elderly aunties are served first, and help wash pots at the sink. This is what the women in your large family do—they join forces to make sure that every gathering is a success, by which you mean that the rice is piled high and the grape leaves don't unravel.

While wiping down the drinks table, you overhear one of your three hundred aunties talking to the mother-to-be. She openly tells your pregnant cousin: "Thank God it's a boy. Your husband must be so happy."

"He is," says the star of the show, rubbing her belly like a trophy.
"Such a blessing."

"Alhamdul-ilah."

"Alhamdul-ilah."

You stand there, by the stack of blue cups, holding a sponge, wondering for the first time how your own mother must have felt or what people said to her when you were born. Did she feel like she'd somehow failed? Did people make thoughtless comments to her? Did people congratulate her more heartily later, after your three brothers were born?

Should you say something to your aunt? To your cousin? And what would you say? *If it were a girl, would your husband actually be pissed?* You decide to remain quiet. It's your cousin's shower, and you don't want to cause a problem. This auntie is an old woman, one you rarely see, and you will seem rude for confronting her.

You are *bint al-halal*, a nice girl, and one of the rules is that you not upset anyone.

But someone has to know. And since you don't have a sister, you turn to your mother. Even while your American high school friends are resenting their mothers, yours is still your closest confidante. You want to hear her thoughts about the incident, which has stuck to you the way that the plastic that covers her good sofa sticks to you on a summer day.

During a quick lunch together, as the appetizers between you disappear, you relate what you heard and ask, "Were you and Baba disappointed that I was a girl?"

She's startled, which makes you feel guilty for even asking. She asks, "What's *wrong* with you?"

"It's OK. You can tell me."

"Baba loves you. And I love you."

"I know you do," you start to say, "but what was your first reaction? Deep down. And his first reaction? Was he even a little bit annoyed?"

She brushes off your question and says, in Arabic, *b'tfalsafee*—you are philosophizing, that is, making a big deal out of nothing.

Fragment: March

One August day, you get ready to attend a walk-a-thon in support of Palestinian human rights. Members of your community are going to take over the streets of Philadelphia, at least for a couple of hours.

Along with your brothers, you have spent much of your childhood being taken to pro-Palestinian events around the region. You fall asleep on the two-hour ride home from New York after a fundraising dinner to support schools in Palestine, and you wake up early every Sunday morning to attend Arabic classes that the community has organized. You write letter after letter to Kmart and Woolworth's, asking them to remove a mask called *The Sheikh* from its Halloween merchandise. You are the only student in your school who knows the names of her senators and representative instead of the names and stats of baseball and football players. You can practically recite from memory parts of the texts of UN resolutions 242 and 338.

Today, you are marching for Palestine.

It's going to be a hot day, so you put on a pair of shorts.

When your family reaches the city intersection that is the meeting spot, you hurriedly unfold your Palestinian flag so you can wave it during the walk. The planned route is not long, but it winds through the down-town streets, ensuring that your flags and signs— *Peace with Justice for Palestine*—will capture attention. Your friends and cousins arrive steadily, and you're excited that there will be a strong presence today.

A group of young men show up, and they're obviously Arab—they have the dark skin and black hair like the rest of you. But they glance at your group, then cross the street and remain there. Far away. One of the other parents knows them and approaches them to ask what is wrong, then returns to deliver the message: they won't walk with your group because some of the girls are wearing shorts.

Slowly it registers: They are ashamed of you for walking and showing your bare legs. It would be their preference, this parent explains, that you change your clothes. Only then would they be willing to join the march and be seen with you.

A lot of the adults, including your parents, are angry. "Let them go home," you hear people say. "How dare they speak about *banaat al-halal*, nice girls, like this?"

The back and forth grows angrier and more testy, and eventually, your group begins walking without them. You cover at least one city block scoffing at their rudeness.

Nevertheless, you feel like you've done something wrong.

Your parents have always been strict about how you dress. Once, you tried leaving the house in a tank top and ripped jeans, and they forbade it. In your anger, you shouted that you had a right to express yourself any way you wanted. You were calmly informed that you were mistaken.

Your lipstick couldn't be too red, your hair couldn't be too high, clothes couldn't be too tight.

But in this moment, during the march, they are furious at the idea that wearing a pair of shorts is somehow wrong, that their parental judgement has been questioned. And really, if they thought your shorts were fine, why are you worried about these guys, who simply shook their heads and walked the opposite way?

Why does that look of disgust in the eyes of those young men bother you so much? It's *that look*—it says you are *bint al-haram*, someone who is shameful, a whore—that astounds you.

Fragment: Exotic

After high school, the only real option for you (besides getting married) is to attend the local campus of the state university. No dorm rooms for you. Bint al-halal shouldn't live away from her parents' home, so you officially become a commuter. You buy an old Toyota for $3,000 and you work two jobs to pay for gas and college textbooks. You have a small scholarship, and your parents help with the rest of your tuition because, while they don't want you to move away, they also don't want you to graduate with debt.

Friends who have known you since middle school express surprise that your strict Arab parents believe a girl should get an education. Your parents express surprise that your friends, who have known them since middle school, are surprised.

One of your jobs is working at a B. Dalton Bookseller, a now-dead mall version of Barnes & Noble that carries three types of items: James Patterson-ish thrillers, blank journals embossed with words like *Dreams* and *Inspirations*, and a toy section in the back that is deceptively labeled *Children's Books*.

There is a customer—a thirty-ish man, white, glasses—who comes in every week. He is a Michael Crichton fan, but you don't hold that against him while he flirts earnestly. You find him to be sweet and look forward to his visits, when he talks about music, the Jersey weather, the dying mall itself ("If Sears goes, that's it").

One day, he asks if you are Italian.

"No."

"Mexican?"

"No, I'm Arab," you say, suddenly sad because you know where this is going, and embarrassed for what he is surely about to say.

He says it.

"Wow. Awesome. You just look so exotic."

Cars are exotic, you want to say. Maybe fruit. Not people. Not you.

Fragment: Summer Abroad

You are in your early twenties and not married yet, and some people in the family fear your father has allowed you too much education. You decide to spend a summer studying Arabic at Birzeit University in the West Bank. The news spreads that you are going back home, and family and friends in the community openly speculate that you'll come back with a fiancée. Nothing better, after all, than going home to Palestine and marrying a boy from one's own town. They smile indulgently when you insist that you are going to study, to improve your Arabic. They don't believe you, and you are too polite to tell them you dislike their insinuations.

The university is a half-hour ride by taxi from your parents' village, where you have a huge family. It is an international program, and your fellow students arrive from France, Italy, Canada, North Africa, and other nations. You decide to live as close to campus as possible, because sometimes the military closes the roads, turning thirty minutes into a day-long ordeal. There is a choice between living in an apartment in downtown Birzeit, or in the girls-only dorm in Ramallah, which is protected by a tall, wrought-iron gate and monitored by a security guard.

There is really only one choice for bint al-halal.

The dorm was formerly the Red Palace Hotel, which the university purchased, and you can tell it was luxurious from the exquisite mosaics on the floors and the beautiful, wooden furniture in some of the rooms. You bunk with an American girl who has short, reddish hair and smokes eighteen hours a day. The Palestinian girls who live in the Red Palace are pleasant and curious: *What's it like for an Arab girl to grow up in America?* You feel good about belonging with them, about how they want to sit with you, how they invite you into their rooms for tea and chats.

On one of your first weekends in the Red Palace, however, you go out to dinner with your roommate and another American girl; the other girl is from Kansas and has long, light brown hair and a wide, genuine smile. The three of you find a falafel place in Ramallah, and all you can talk about missing home, the Red Palace's grim dorm mother, and your classmates, especially the cute guy from Germany. After you eat, because the conversation is so good, you decide to get some coffee too.

By the time you head back to the Red Palace, it is getting dark. When you arrive at the dorm, you feel sick when you realize the iron gates are locked.

You've forgotten the curfew.

Your roommate starts to climb the gate, but it is no use. She slips back down every time. The Kansas girl shouts at the guard, who is stationed at his post further up, closer to the building, but he cannot hear her.

"What are we going to do?" you ask each other, and finally, your roommate lights a cigarette and says confidently, "We'll just walk back downtown and find somewhere to sleep."

"Like where?" you ask in a panic. You imagine yourself sleeping in an alleyway, of being picked up by the Ramallah police who may recognize your last name and call your aunt, who lives in the village ten miles away. An image of your father and mother waking up in New Jersey to a phone call, informing them that their daughter has ruined their reputation, plays itself like a horror movie in your mind.

"A hostel or something," she says, looking at you like, *Of course, what's the big deal?*

Of course. Of course.

The streets of Ramallah look different now. It is dark and everyone stares openly at the three girls who should obviously be back in the Red Palace. Your roommate's cigarette is like a flag, waving and calling for attention. You walk with your head down, because there are many people from the village who come to Ramallah. There is a danger of being found out.

You simultaneously hate yourself for worrying. American girls do not fret about who might see them, who might head back to the village and start whispering. Kansas asks you if you are OK, but you cannot tell her what's troubling you. They will not understand you if you say, *Oh well, actually, if someone from my parents' village sees me out here and starts telling people, then I will basically have my reputation ruined, which is kind of a big deal. And by the way, can you please put out that cigarette?*

Your roommate finds a hostel by a coffee shop, near the vegetable market, remembering that one of her classmates spent the night here when he first arrived in the city. It is small and cramped, but there is nowhere else to go. The young man behind the desk zeroes in on you, and he tries to speak to you in Arabic. Does he know you? You think of the baker, who told you a few days earlier, "You must be related to Yassir. I heard his American cousin was studying here and staying at the Red Palace." Ramallah is a city, but it is small.

You respond only in English. "Just one room," you say over and over, and hand over the money you, your roommate, and Kansas have pooled. He shrugs and hands you a key.

The room is beige—everything beige. That makes it easier to see the lone, long black hair on the sheets. You sleep on top of the covers, your heads on your purses.

A rooster's crowing wakes you at dawn, a reminder that you are close to the vegetable market. The three of you wake, wash your faces and clean your teeth as best as you can, then hurry downstairs. The man behind the desk is there, along with a second man. When you return the key, he tries to hand you a card to complete, which he never gave you the night before. You wave it away, again resorting to English.

"Al ism?" he asks politely, but firmly. *Your name?*

You pretend not to understand. He knows you're faking, but you don't care.

The three of you practically run to the Red Palace, where you find the gates unlocked. Inside, your dorm mother is freaking out and sharply reprimands you all, and your Palestinian dormmates stay stonily silent around you for the rest of the week. Living in the Red Palace, in a secure place, is the only way they can attend university, and you're jeopardizing that dream.

"See?" says your roommate, who has laughed off the reprimand. "You were worried for nothing. You need to relax a little."

Fragment: Michelle

At one point, midsummer, you cross the Allenby Bridge from the West Bank into Amman, Jordan, where you have scores of relatives, as well as family friends. One particular family, an auntie and uncle of sorts, are on the list of people you are expected to visit, since you are in town, to show your respect.

It is appropriate to bring a gift, but you've crossed the bridge with nothing but an overnight bag and your purse. You stop at a chocolatier and pick up a box, then take a cab to their apartment. Located on one of Amman's seven hills, it's not a new neighborhood. It looks like it used to be quite posh. But now, the residents of this hill are just middle class as fancier, larger, and buildings made with whiter stones—small palaces—are erected on other hills.

You walk up a plain stairwell and knock on their medical-green metal door. A woman you don't recognize opens it. She is petite, South Asian, with shiny black hair tied up in a neat bun. She does not shake the hand you put out, and does not seem to understand your Arabic very well as you introduce yourself. Instead, she smiles at you in confusion, ushers you in, and calls for *Madame* (not the Arabic equivalent, *sitt*, but *Madame*).

This small-boned woman is not a family friend, you find out soon enough, but the live-in maid, who sleeps in a room off the kitchen that is the size of a pantry. You also find out that nobody in the family seems to know her real name. Instead, they call her Michelle, a European name that fits in well with the environment they're trying to create for themselves.

Their apartment is small: three bedrooms, a small living room, and one bathroom that they all share. But it sparkles. Everything is framed in or accented by gold: mirrors, table legs, photographs, even their Bible. Vases of plastic flowers sit on every available surface, while embroidered pillows decorate every chair and couch.

You are treated to a traditional Arab family visit: a cold lemonade, then some cake, fruit, and tea, and finally some coffee in tiny demitasse cups. At your own home, in New Jersey, you've witnessed the art of hospitality hundreds of times. Your mother serves cold iced tea and ginger ale in glass carafes, then spreads a buffet of hummus, cheeses, crackers, olives, raw vegetable platters on the coffee table before guests who had insisted they'd just had dinner but are now eating nonstop. Your father eventually opens a bottle of Johnnie Walker, and he is attentive to topping off the glasses. The coffee comes last, usually carried in by your brothers or yourself, on a tray, along with plates of baklawa. In your home, hospitality is a family affair.

But here in Amman, She Who Has Been Renamed Michelle, who arrived from Sri Lanka to sleep in a closet and clean and dust and babysit and fetch groceries and massage Madame's feet—here, Michelle does everything. Even the family's young children give her orders, and when I stand to throw out a tissue, She Who Has Been Renamed Michelle hurries over to take it from me.

"She loves to help," says uncle.

Later, when you try to return your cup and plate to the kitchen, they stop you; they are looking at you now like you are some silly, and possibly dull-witted, American. They resent you for not enjoying their hospitality.

You try to look She Who Has Been Renamed Michelle in the eyes when you leave, and say thank you, but she is busy cleaning up. And what would you say? And how would it help her?

No, if you said something to her, something to separate yourself from them, it would only be a way to feel better about yourself.

You feel like you are witness to a crime.

This universe—where one woman must work tirelessly so another can be referred to as *Madame*—is unfamiliar, even though you thought you were back home.

Fragment: Fertility

It is a May morning, back in the US. Final exams start tomorrow. It is not anxiety that is waking you up early, but something else. A strange pain in your pelvis. You try to go back to sleep. A few minutes later, the pain that has been fluttering for a while suddenly stabs you right in the gut. Your body, in spasms, writhes on your bed, and you scream.

Your father rushes up to your room and helps you stumble to the bathroom. He holds your hair and rubs your back while you vomit into the toilet, as you gasp through the pain that is seizing your whole body.

You are frightened.

So is he.

The next morning, you are in surgery, having an ovarian cyst removed—or rather, what's left of it, since it has ruptured. When you wake up in the recovery room, your relieved parents burst into tears. Your friends and cousins and coworkers come to visit, call you on the phone, and deliver small gifts: comic books, flowers, chocolate.

Over the next few days, in your morphine-induced phase, you are aware that some people are concerned about your fertility. "Are the ovaries ok?" and "Did they have to remove part of the tube?" and "Will she be able to have children?"

You don't care one bit. You're offended that this is an issue. Below the surface of the whispers, you grasp at something subtle floating there: a problem might affect your marriage prospects.

But it doesn't matter. Because the pain is back now, and there is a beautiful, miraculous button at your fingertips—a button that releases morphine right into your IV. You push it, and soon you slide, carefree, back into sleep.

Fragment: The Player

You have a friend in college whose life seems perfect. At least, it's a lot better than yours. She's beautiful, her parents are rich, and she drives a nice car. You like to have lunch with her between classes. During your chats, you feel deeply connected to her. For once, you have a real friend, something that was rare in high school.

For a few weeks now, she's been dating a guy on the school's baseball team, who walks around campus like a demigod. He's cocky, for sure, but he likes your friend and she says he's adorable. They go out on dates. She invites you on a double-date with another member of the team, but she understands when you say no. It's hard for you to get out, because your parents are so strict. She understands, and she never makes you feel bad.

Then, one Monday, she's not in class. She doesn't come to campus for a week. You call and call, but she won't pick up. Finally, she answers. "Where have you been?" you want to know.

In a hushed, trembling voice, she tells you that the baseball player forced himself on her.

"What do you mean?"

"He wanted to have sex. And I didn't. And he did it anyway."

Later, you learn that he's been bragging to the other guys about it. She returns to campus eventually, but she attends her classes and then heads home immediately after. No more lunches. No more deep talks.

"Why don't you report him?" you suggest one day over the phone. She doesn't like to talk about it, doesn't want anyone else to know, because she's certain she'll be called a slut. But surely, he should be kicked off the team, thrown out of school, punished in some way? Something bad should happen to him for what he has done to your sweet, kind friend.

You can hear her condescension, her fatigue, through the phone line. "It doesn't work that way."

Fragment: Jasmine

As an undergraduate, you have a semester-long flirtation with a prelaw major who finds it weird that your family doesn't approve of dating.

"Why can't I pick you up?" he asks. "I mean, I don't mind coming to meet your parents."

"It's not that simple."

You hate your parents' rules and fears. You hate feeling deceitful.

This is not new for you. Since you were little, it seems like everything is haram. Your sixth grade field trip was an overnight campout, but you were the only sixth grader who did not go. High school dances would have allegedly ruined your reputation, so you never attended homecoming. Never went to prom. Likewise, you did not go along with the other hundred-and-fifty kids in the weeks before graduation for the senior class trip, because it was an overnight stay. You'd entered high school with alien status, mostly due to the fact that you were a kinky, curly black head in a sea of smooth blondes, and as the years progressed, your absence at major school events cemented your position as an invisible girl, someone who was never noticed (and when you were, people always said the same thing: *Oh yeah. She's nice. I don't think she hangs out much.*)

But you're in college now. And you will do what you please, go wherever your little Toyota will take you.

The pre-law major is a serious Disney fan, you find out. You decide to date him anyway. He and his parents drive down to Orlando every summer to spend a week in their Mecca. He knows all the parks, all the rides, gets a newsletter in the mail to update him about park events and upcoming attractions. That summer, Disney releases *Pocahontas*, and he takes you to see it. You meet him at the theater, of course, and you watch the film together while holding hands and eating popcorn.

Now, as you look back, you remember how your nineteen-year-old self thought something was odd about this film. You couldn't immediately place it, though. After the credits roll, your date cannot stop talking about the big drama: there is a murder in the Disney movie, and a death has never before been shown in a Disney film. He knows this because he is a Disney fact collector.

He takes you out for ice cream at Haagen-Dazs afterwards. "That movie was so great," he keeps saying. At one point, he adds, "Disney is really getting into the diversity thing now."

You remain quiet, unsure of what to say. It has struck you now, what was so odd: the movie was not accurate. Disney, you want to tell him, took a kidnapping and rape out of history's pages and turned it into a love story, complete with songs. As you ponder how you might—politely—express your thoughts, he starts talking again.

"You know who the hottest Disney character is, though?"

"Who's that?"

"Definitely Jasmine."

"Oh. Actually—." You tell him that you and your Arab youth community group spent a day writing letters in protest of the movie's opening song, where the bandit sings about coming from "a faraway place/ Where the caravan camels roam/ Where they cut off your ear/ If they don't like your face."

"You remember that song?" you ask him.

Of course he does, and he quotes the rest of the lyrics for you to prove it: "It's barbaric, but hey, it's home."

"Oh, wow. You really do know all the Disney songs."

"You look like her."

"Jasmine?"

"Your hair. Your skin."

"Ok."

"You're really sensual looking." He's looking at you in a way that creeps you out.

"Oh," you say. You change the subject but here is what you think to yourself: if you needed to, you could actually, if it came down to it, break his nose. Your brothers taught you how. But right now, you're relieved that you drove here tonight in your own car.

Fragment: A Story

One day, when you're close to college graduation, your mother takes you on a shopping trip. Your parents are having a party at home for you, with one hundred relatives and friends. She's ordered a full sheet cake and a large tent for the back yard.

She's also decided that you need something new to wear.

"We're very proud of you," she says, looking pensive and thoughtful, as you walk through the mall's hallways.

"I couldn't have done it without you," you tell your mother. You mean it. You know there has been a general expectation that you should be married, that your parents have turned down inquiries by families with bachelor sons, telling them, "Our daughter plans to finish her studies." It has not always been easy for them in your small, proud, working-class community, to be the parents of someone who wants choices.

"I want to tell you a story," she says suddenly, and it's the tone she uses, that reflective voice, that tells you to be quiet and listen carefully.

When I finished high school, even though my English wasn't great yet, I didn't think I could go to college. We didn't have money, there were so many of us and your grandparents couldn't afford it. I'm the oldest girl. How could I ask them for money when there were six more after me? So I got a job, working in an optical warehouse. All I did for the whole day was take the order form, match it to a box on the shelf, and bundle them together. For eight or nine hours. I knew within a week that I would go crazy if this is what I had to do for the rest of my life.

I decided to see if I could go to school. I found out what it cost to go to the community college for a year. I could get a certificate, even a degree, and work in an office, doing bookkeeping or something. I was good at math. It was so much money, but there was a union where your grandfather worked, and they offered a scholarship to children of members. I tried to get the papers but the deadline had already passed. I would have to wait another year to apply.

I went back to that job, worked another day or two, and then something got into me. I never felt anything like it. I told myself, You have to figure out a way to go to college this year, not next year. Now. *I had to do it now*, because I felt so scared that it would never happen.

Someone at work told me to get a student loan, so I went to the bank near my house. They said no, because—well, of course they did. I was a risk for them. Fine. I went to another bank. No. Another bank. No.

I must have gone to a dozen banks. I was determined not to go home until I had the money. At the last place, the lady said no, and I said, Please, I really need it. I need to find a way to get a loan. I spoke in a way I've never spoken before—I was so firm, really tough. I know I made her uncomfortable, but I guess she felt sorry for me, because she found a card with the name of another bank on it, and said to try there.

That bank was far away. I had to take a few different subways to get there, and it was in a neighborhood I didn't know at all. But I found it. And I got the loan.

I went to school that year, and the next year, I got that

scholarship. That was how I finished my Associates' degree. And I never felt better about myself because I didn't accept no.

You know something . . . I've wanted to tell you this story for a long time. I want you to know this about me.

I'm quiet when she finishes, and a few minutes go by before she adds, "It's really important that you know that, you know. Don't accept no. From anyone. You understand?"

"Yes."

"I bet that is something they didn't teach you in college, did they?"

Fragment: Arab Fragility

After graduate school, you get married and move two states away from your parents. It takes you a while to acclimate, to find a job, to make friends. Eventually, you and your husband, who is also Arab, fall in with the local Arab community in your new town.

One day, you invite two friends over, both of whom grew up in Amman. Bemoaning the lack of good help, they talk nostalgically about their live-in servants back in Amman in ways that make you cringe.

"Our maid was so wonderful," says number one in Arabic. "She was with us forever, since I was a baby. She used to sit with me at night when I was little and comb my hair before I went to bed."

Number two claimed fondly, "Mine used to warm my towel on the heater so it was warm when I got out of the bath. When I take my own kids now to visit, she does that for them."

"She's still with your family?" you ask, quickly doing the math in your head.

"Oh, she's young," she says. "She was about sixteen when she came to work for us."

You imagine a young girl—in your mind, she resembles She Who Has Been Renamed Michelle—arriving in Amman at sixteen, forced into a job far away from her family. You wonder when she first understood that she was essentially a slave in this new country. How long until she accepted it.

You wonder if she has been raped. Slapped. Beaten.

The guests in your home are still complaining about finding people who will scrub floors and wash and fold laundry the way these women used to do. You ask your two guests what their families paid the women. The number shocks you—you don't remember it exactly, but you remember thinking it's the price of dinner in a nice restaurant—and what's more, the money is not paid to the women, but to their agents—the companies that hire them, handle their work visas.

"But they loved living with us," says number one primly, and you can see that you're being rude, you're needling her, you're making a guest uncomfortable in your own home.

"How do you know?"

"Of course they did."

"Maybe they were scared. Maybe they were pretending."

Arab fragility is in full effect now.

"*Ya bint al-halal*, we treated her so well!" they say defensively. "So nice of you, living here in America, to understand back home better than we do."

You register the passive-aggressive attack on your not-Arab-enough status. Fine. But then you also tell her that this is the equivalent of modern slavery, and that you've been reading—since the time you met She Who Has Been Renamed Michelle—about the way this industry works in Amman and other Arab countries. That many of these women are sexually and physically abused. That if they get pregnant, they are returned to their country, lest this bint al-haram taint the rest of the household. That they're paid so little it should make people ashamed.

That some of them never see their families again because they cannot afford the trip home.

You tell these polite ladies exactly what you think, even though it's not very nice of you. You tell them that some women are suffering so that others can create a bubble of elitism around them. Women are exploited to suit someone else's princess fantasy. And this is not okay. This shouldn't be romanticized. It shouldn't be normalized. And you're not surprised when they don't visit you again.

Fragment: A Birth

You will be having a daughter.

You have been waiting for her for almost four years, wishing more than anything for a chance to be a mother. Honestly, you were sure at one point it would never happen. You spent many mornings plunging needles filled with fertility medicines into your abdomen, into your thighs, many evenings in which you carefully lined up an assortment of pills. Many late mornings spent, anxiously waiting for the call from the clinic, your inner elbow still sore from that six a.m. blood draw. Every time, you cried when the nurse rushed through her scripted lines on the telephone: "Unfortunately, this time we did not have success, but we have learned something new to apply to our next cycle of treatment. . . ."

And when you finally did become pregnant, you spent many weeks lying down, on a strict regime of bed rest, because the pregnancy was high risk and you could lose this child before you even met her.

You resist the idea of a baby shower, worrying that you are jinxing yourself.

You don't really want to tell people, but soon the news trickles out anyway. One older lady, during the church's coffee hour, asks what you're having.

"Bint."

She smiles and grasps your hand thoughtfully. "It's okay," she comforts you. "Next time it will be a boy, inshallah."

You excuse yourself and walk away. Sometimes, there is too much anger to be swallowed. If you tried, you would choke on it.

At some point, when you are eight months pregnant, when she is kicking regularly to remind you she is alive and well, you finally surrender a little bit. You allow yourself to be happy. You allow yourself to consider names.

The only name you want is Mariam, the name held by so many Arab women, including your own grandmother.

The baby name dictionary tells you that the meaning of Mariam is debated: some sources say it means *wished-for child*, which is certainly applicable. Other sources, however, say it means *sea of bitterness*. This is also applicable, if she will grow up as an Arab American girl: there will be an abundance of frustrating, sad moments.

You hope she will be more successful than you, that she will not feel pulled between the binary choices of halal or haram. Hopefully, she will reject the split between Arab and American, East and West, good and bad, of anything that threatens to divide her.

She will have to define herself against everyone's expectations and create an identity that is her own. She will have to reassemble the pieces offered to her by life to form any self-image she desires.

To fit the mold she has created, she may have to shatter some of those pieces.

One day, she goes quiet inside you. She has stopped kicking. Just as you begin to worry, your contractions fold your body in half, stunning you with their ferocity. The hospital bag has been packed for weeks, and you head to the hospital. Before you leave the house, your husband, who's as excited as you are, tells you to pause while he snaps a picture. The before picture—before a child, before a birth, before the change in both of your lives.

She arrives, two weeks early. After twenty-four hours of labor, she slips into the world, quietly, watching us, hardly crying at all.

Mariam.

Your daughter is born.

She grips your finger, clutching it to her with surprising strength.

Your daughter is born.

It is a good day.

❑ ❑ ❑ ❑ ❑

22

NAOMI SHIHAB NYE

One Village

It is fifteen years since I have seen my grandmother. I feel some guilt about this, but her face, when we meet in the village, betrays no slant of blame. She is glad to see me. She blesses me with whispered phrases, in the old way, Mohammad this, Mohammad that, encircling my head with her silver ring. Later she will ask, "Why didn't you ever write a letter?" and the guilt will return, unabsolved by fact: *she can't read. Who would have thought she'd want a letter?* I had forgotten she is so small, barely reaching my shoulder as I hug her tightly, kissing both cheeks. I am stunned with luckiness; so much can happen in fifteen years.

The village smells familiar—a potent soup of smoke, sheep wool, water on stone. Again it is the nose retrieving memory as much as eyes or ears. I poke into courtyards, filled suddenly with lentil broth, orange blossom, olive oil soap. Whole scenes unfold like recent landscapes: a donkey who once entered the room where we were eating, a dusty boy weeping after a wayward kickball knocked him on the head. I was a teenager when last here, naïve in the way only teenagers can be naïve. I wanted the world to be like me. Now there is nothing I would like less. I enter the world hoping for a journey out of self as much as in. I come back to this village remembering, but it is more like I have never been here before. This time I am awake.

"What do you do every day?" I ask my grandmother.

She replies in Arabic, "*Cod.* Sit. Every day I sit. What else would you want me to do?"

But I will find this is not quite true. Each morning she prays, rising at 4:30 to the first muezzin's call. It seems strange that the sun also rises this early. The days stretch out like gauze. We are pulled up from sleep by too much brightness.

Each morning my grandmother walks across the road to *the cow,* singular, to carry home a tea-kettle of fresh warm milk. Take me with you, I say. And she will take me, laughing because I like this black and white cow enough to touch it on the head and thank it, *Shookran, haleeb.* She speaks to cows, my grandmother will say later, pointing at me. This is a girl who speaks to cows.

Every day she lights the oven, fat stone mound heated by dung, *taboon* for bread cooked on the black rocks, she enters barefooted, her headdress drifting about her. "Could be dangerous," says my father, "I don't think she should light it anymore," but it is one of the ways she remains a part of this village, one of the things she does better than anyone else.

Her face is deeply mapped, her back is slightly bent. Three years ago she made a pilgrimage to Mecca, became a Hajji. For a year afterward, she only wore white. Today she alters this a little, wearing a long white dress embroidered with green over black-and-white pajamas. It is cool here in the West Bank in late May; people think of the Middle East as a great desert, heat rising in waves off sand, but that is not quite true. Perhaps it is true near Jericho or in the Gaza Strip, but here in this village the days are light and breezy, the land is a music of terraced hills.

No one had to make the desert bloom; it was already blooming. Feelings crowd in on me. Maybe this is what it means to be in your genetic home. That you will feel on fifty levels at once, the immediate level as well as the level of blood, the level of your uncles, of the weeping in the pillow at night, weddings and graves, the babies who didn't make it, level of the secret and the unseen. Maybe this is heritage, that root that gives you more than you deserve. Staring at my grandmother, my *Sitti,* as she sits on the low bed, rocking back and forth in time with conversation, tapping her fingertips on her knees, this is the food off which I will feed.

"Does he beat you?" she asks of my husband. "No? Ah, good. Then he is a good man." It is simple to define things here. If God wills it, it happens. A bird shits on my head in the courtyard. "That means you will soon have a boy." Looking up, Sitti says, "It's an impolite mother who didn't put underpants on her baby." Conversation stops. My uncle slaps his head and laughs. "She's always saying things like that."

It's amazing what facts we have about each other. She knows I write. What does that mean to someone who never did? I know her husband had three simultaneous wives, but my Sitti was the one he thought of as the real one. Her husband, my grandfather, died when I was five. We were living in St. Louis; the news came on a thin blue air-letter sheet, my father lay in silence across his bed for a whole day. "Be kind to him," my mother whispered. It was the first time I ever heard the phrase, "Be kind." My grandmother had a daughter, Naomi, *Naimeh* in Arabic, then five babies who died, followed by two sons, of which my father was the last. Naimeh had two children, then died suddenly. My grandmother was having my father at the same time Naimeh birthed her second boy. My grandmother suckled her son and grandson together, one at each breast. I know these things, I grew up on them. But this trip I want to find out more: the large birdlike tattoo on her right hand, for example, from where?

"Many years ago, a gypsy passed through. She was hungry and offered to tattoo someone in exchange for food. She poked pins in me and the blood poured out like water from a spring. Later the skin came off five times and I was left with this. Beautiful, no?" She turns her hand over and over, staring at it. It is beautiful. It is a hand ready to fly away. I want to hold on to it.

Across the valley, a new Jewish settlement sits like white building blocks stacked up on the green hills. At night the lights are a bright outline, the shape of the Big Dipper on the ground. No people are visible —just buildings, and lights. "What do you feel when you look at that?" I ask my grandmother. "Do you feel like those are your enemies?" In 1948 she lost her home outside the Old City of Jerusalem to the Israeli occupiers. She moved with her husband and sons back to this village. She is a refugee, but never went to a camp. My father is a refugee who went to America and married an American. What does Sitti think about, now that the village itself sits in occupied territory, in a region the Arabs will only refer to as The West Bank *via* Israel? Does she feel scared?

She waves at the ugly cats lurking in every corner of the courtyard. Most have terrible fur and bitten-off ears. She throws a loquat pit at a cat with one eye, and it runs. "See those cats? One night last year an Israeli jeep drove into this village and let them all out. Everyone saw it. What could we do? I think about that. And I think about the good ghosts we used to have in the big room, who floated in the corners up by the ceiling and sang songs late at night after we were asleep. I used to wake and hear them. Happy friendly ghosts, with warm honey voices, the ghosts of the ones under the ground who used to live here, you know? I tell you, they had parties every night. They were a soft yellow light that glowed. Then the Jews built that settlement across the valley and the ghosts were scared. They all went away. Now you wake up, you hear no singing. And I miss them."

My uncle, a stately Arab in white headdress, functions as *mukhtar*, or mayor, of the village. He is proud of his new bathroom of yellow tiles. It has a toilet, sink, bathtub, shower. He is planning a kitchen under the stairs.

His wife is a good-humored woman who bore him twenty-two children; twelve survived. Her dresses are a rich swirl of Palestinian embroidery, blue birds and twining leaves, up one side and down the other. Her two daughters remaining at home, Janan and Hanan, are the ones who can sew. Of herself she says, "I never learned how."

Sitti lives with this family, her family, in one of the oldest homes in the village. Stone walls and huge arched ceilings grace the main room, where most of the visiting and eating takes place. The family sleeps communally, parents on foam mattresses on the floor, Sitti and guests on beds. Everyone gets covered with fat sheep-wool comforters. I like how these are fixed with button-on sheets; a sheet gets dirty, you unbutton it and start again. I swear I have come back to something essential here, the immediate life, the life without refrigerator. Each day, you gather up what you need.

"How did this rice pudding get so cool?" I ask dumbly one morning, and Hanan leads me to the stone cupboard where food is kept. It is sleek and dark like the inside of a cave. She places my hand against the face of the stone, smiles at me, and shrugs. This is where the olives live, where the goat-cheese floats in olive oil in a huge glass jar. A honeydew melon tastes almost icy.

If you want meat, you go buy it right before you are ready to cook it.

One afternoon a plump red-faced woman appears in the doorway with a stack of grape leaves. She trades them with my aunt for a sack of *marimea* leaves, good for stomach ailments, brewed in tea. I can see by their easy joking this is something they do often. The woman motions to me that I am to walk home with her, why? This Arabic of hers is too jazzy for my slow ear.

Down alleyways, between houses where children spin tops on the flattest stone (as a child my father taught me how to pare the top off an acorn to make a quick spinner). Up ancient stairs, past a mosque with its prayer rugs and mats spread out, waiting. Where is this woman taking me?

I stand in the courtyard of her home where pigeons are nesting in rusted olive oil tins nailed to the wall. Their soft songs curl on the air. The woman comes to me with her hands full of square homemade soap. She presses it upon me, saying, "Take this back to America, you need this in America." She says other things I can't understand. Then she reaches into a nest and pulls out a small bird. She makes the motion of chopping off its head and I protest, "Oh no, please! I am not hungry!" She wants me to eat this teenaged pigeon, if not today, then save it for tomorrow. I tell her I can't eat it tomorrow either. She looks sad. It was a big gift she was offering. "I will take the soap to America," I say. We kiss and stare at one another shyly. A line of children crouches on the next roof, watching us; they giggle behind their hands.

What is this need to give? It embarrasses me. I feel I have never learned how to be generous. In a Jordanian refugee camp last week, I was overwhelmed by all the offers of coffee and Pepsi which were showered on me by strangers. Would I ever do that in America? Invite a stranger in off the street for coffee, simply because she passed my house? Here in the village, the gifts I have brought seem foolish when I unpack them. Panty hose in rainbow colors, two long seersucker nightgowns for the older women, potholders, perfume. What else could I have brought that would have fit this occasion? A lawn of grass? A kitchen table, swoop of formica, so the girls might pare their potatoes sitting up at something, rather than crouched on the floor? Bicycles with sizzling thin wheels, so we might coast together down past the shepherd's field, past the trees of unripe plums? But I unpack a tube of Bengay for Sitti (someone told me she needed this), a plastic bottle of Ecotrin, and give her instructions, like a doctor. I want to make it very clear she should never take more than two pills at once. She nods gravely. She tucks these into her bodice, the front panel of the dress left open like a giant pocket.

"Is there anything else?" she asks. And I run back to my suitcase, unfold a gauzy white scarf bordered with yellow flowers—someone gave me this ten days ago in Pakistan—I carry it towards her like a child carries a weed flower tentatively home to mother.

Now she smiles, rocks back on her heels. This strange slash of cloth is a pleaser. She lifts her loot onto the floor, where she will unfold it all again with my aunt, murmuring and touching one another's presents. This is the worst moment of all. I didn't bring enough, I think. I gaze nervously toward my father, who is smiling shyly. He unpacked his presents a few days ago, he's already been through this. "It's fine," he whispers to me. "We'll go buy them chocolates too. They like chocolates."

In the corner of the room is a large old wooden box painted green. It has a padlock on it, like the locks we use on bicycle chains in the States. This is where Sitti stores all her gifts, unlocking the trunk with a key from between her breasts. She places them carefully on top of whatever else is there, and pats it all down. Janan teases her, "Can we see your treasures?" Sitti protests, locking the trunk hurriedly. "Not now," she says. "Not this minute." I think of the burglar alarms in America, the homes of furniture, silver, appliances, the way I complain when somebody steals my trash-can at night. And it seems very right that a Palestinian would have a trunk in the corner of the room, and lock it, and look at it often, just to make sure it is there.

In the village which used to be famous for grapes, most of the grapes have died. A scourge came ten years ago, they say, and withered the crop on the vines. They have never recovered. A few fields show traces of them: arbors where grapes once flourished, small rock shelters built so the people who came to gather the grapes could rest. I want an agricultural expert like the ones we have in Texas to come analyze this soil. I want a miracle in farming, right here, now, to give this village back its favorite food.

The loquats in my uncle's patio are yellow-ripe and ready. Sitti won't leave the house unattended, for fear someone will steal them. One day we almost get her to go to the Turkish baths in Nablus, but she remembers the tree. "I can't leave a ripe tree," she insists. We peel the loquats with tiny knives; the slick seeds collect in an ashtray.

We go for luncheon at the home of Abu Mahmoud, an elderly man known for his militant discussions. "I'm bored with him," confides my uncle. But when we get there, he's only interested in gardening. He gives us a guided tour of his fields: eggplant, peppers, apricots, squash. Proudly he shows us the apple trees which will produce for the first time this year. He stuffs my pockets with unripe fruit; I tell him, "Wait, wait, please wait." He stands me on the balcony and gives me binoculars, so I can stare at the Jewish settlement which happens to be in a direct line from his window.

"There are no people there," he says. "Just buildings. Maybe there are guns in the buildings. I'm sure there are guns."

"Are you scared?"

"I'm tired of fighting," he says. "All my life, we've been fighting. I just want to be sure of one thing, that when I wake up in the morning, my fig trees will still be *my* fig trees. That's all."

This sounds reasonable enough.

A few days later I'm driving with an American diplomat through this village. I tell him about Abu Mahmoud. I tell him how furious I was two days ago when an Israeli jeep pulled up and trained its machine-gun on a group of elderly men who were greeting my father. What right had they to do this? I demand. The men were talking pleasantries, *how is your wife, how is the journey from America these days*, no politics. I tell my friend I know now why little boys throw rocks.

He pulls over. "Look at this!" He sweeps his hand. Women are parading back from the spring with huge pails of water on their heads. A boy leads a donkey laden with giant bundles of twigs. Beside a store, a man unpacks a crate of radiant tomatoes. He stares curiously at our diplomatic license plate.

"Look at a village like this," says my friend, "and the presence of the Israelis seems more inappropriate than ever. Zionist women arriving from Brooklyn, heading straight to air-conditioned condominiums, calling this their homeland; sometimes it makes absolutely no sense."

The wedding picture of my parents hangs high on my uncle's wall. It is slightly crooked; I keep scouting for a ladder, so I might straighten it. One day it hits me—how long it has been hanging there. "Did you put that up in 1951?" I ask my grandmother, a woman who doesn't even know her own age. She says, "I put it up when I got it." There is my father, thin, darkly intense, in a white linen jacket hanging nearly to his knees. My mother, fair and hopeful, already learning about pine nuts and tabooleh. In how many houses have they lived? And I suddenly want to leave the picture crooked, because it may be the single icon of our lives that has stayed in one place.

My father and I hike to the tomb of Sheikh Omar. It is high on a hill. We must overstep the lentil fields to get there. My father stoops to pluck a handful of lentils. He says, "Once you eat them raw, you never forget the taste." I ask about Omar, who was he, when did he live? My father says he was a disciple of Mohammad. Dates escape us. He lived a long time ago. The villagers know this is his tomb, so they have built a mound of a mosque to honor him.

Inside the floor is covered with faded prayer rugs. Silence. A ring of half burnt candles in one corner. We take off our shoes and kneel down. I don't really know how to pray in the Muslim way, but I know there is something very affecting about people putting down shovels and brooms five times a day to do it. I like how life goes on in the rooms where someone is praying. No one stops talking or stares; it is a part of life, the denominator. Everything else is a dancing away.

My father wants to show me his land. He bought it in the 1960s, before we came to Jerusalem to live for a year. Now he doesn't know what to do with it. Who can build here, knowing the shakiness that sleeps in the ground? And yet people do. They do it every day. The diplomat tells us the latest tactic is to surround a village with wire, call it *our new military outpost*, and oust the villagers. Who can be sure? The village of Latroun, where the wine comes from, is flattened and gone. No sign remains that there was ever a village. I remember it fifteen years ago as a regular, daily, bustling place. Its complete disappearance strikes me as horrendous, impossible, bizarre. This is only one of the new absences. In which camp or distant city do those villagers now reside?

My father's land is steep and terraced, planted with olive trees—five big ones, five small. When my aunt notices a broken branch, she stoops to stroke it, says "Why? Why?" She tries to tie it up again with a stalk of wheat.

"I could make a good house here," my father says wistfully. "It would make my mother very happy. Do you know, that is her one great hope? That her American son will make a big house and come back here to live? How could I ever do that?" There is a sadness in my father I have not felt so clearly until now. Something about this land brings it out, lays it clean before us.

He asks me why he is obsessed with land. In Dallas, Texas, he scouts for condominiums, buys whole blocks of duplexes, renovates them for resale. "Everyone is that way these days," I say. "It's the American trend, real estate, buy and sell, you're not alone."

"But you don't feel like that?"

The idea of land is an alien one to me. My husband and I own our home and a swatch of Texas hillside. I think it's a boring subject. "No, I don't feel like that."

Then again, I'm not a refugee. I've been robbed twice in my life and felt the closest to imagining what a refugee might feel. But we had insurance. A refugee has no insurance. A refugee feels violated in a way he may try the rest of his life to understand.

I tell my father I like his land.

We walk to a place called The Museum of Curiosity to see a woman who sells souvenirs. She's big and ruddy, a recent widow, and welcomes us with all kinds of exclamations and flourishes. Her shop is a jumble of Bedouin coffeepots and amber beads.

I am intrigued by the massive clay pots lining her porch. At my grandmother's house, there are two of these in the courtyard, holding water. I know they were made in this village; at one time this place was a well-known center for pottery. Why not today? My grandmother told me, "The clay went away."

I ask the lady about her pots. Does she keep them as a collection or mark them for sale?

She throws up her hands. "Oh, the Israelis love to buy these. Just today a man came and will return later with a truck to pick up a hundred of them. They like them in Gaza. Maybe they use them for flowers, I don't k now."

"Show me the hundred," I say.

She leads me up the hill to a small stone house and motions me inside.

I see a whole congregation of giant hundred-year-old pots, some natural pink clay color, some marked with a blurred zigzag border or iron oxide lines, propped against one another, holding one another up. Their fat-lipped mouths are all wide open. I want to fall down into their darkness, hide there until I learn some secret perpetually eluding me. I want to belong to a quieter time, when these pots stayed living with the hands that had made them. I am very sad these pots are going away.

She'll get more, she tells my father. She'll go to other villages and buy them up. It's hard times, she says, and people will sell what they have, to keep going.

We eat dinner with Abu Akram, my first cousin, aged fifty-five. This trip I have tried to clarify relationships. For the first time I meet a beautiful olive-skinned second cousin named Sabah, morning, and we tease each other like sisters.

Abu Akram is at this moment a subject of controversy. He is building a three-story house that will be the tallest one in the village. Why is he doing this? No one likes it, they claim it blocks the sky. But he believes in the tradition of the extended family living under one roof, he says. His sons are marrying and their wives are having children and this way there will be room for everybody.

We eat grape-leaves stuffed with lamb and rice, hummos, and frikke soup, a delicate broth thickened with wheat.

Over the table hangs a hand-colored portrait of a young man. I ask if this is another cousin.

Abu Akram says no, this is a boy who was in school when he was still principal. The boy was shot down last year by an Israeli soldier, near the post office, after someone threw a stone at the tires of the soldier's jeep.

"*Someone* threw a rock? Did this boy throw the rock?"

Abu Akram shrugs. "It was never clear. He used to be very good in math. I put the picture up because we all liked him."

I ask my grandmother why things happen as they do, and she says God wants them to. I think of a poem by a Vietnamese refugee girl that ended, "God cannot be mean to me forever." I ask my grandmother if God can be mean. She looks at me for a long, long time. I don't think she ever answers.

I ask my grandmother if I can see her hair, and she shakes with laughter. "It is only as long as a finger," she says, holding up a finger.

"I don't care. I want to see it." She keeps it so well-hidden under her scarves, it is hard to imagine.

"Then get up tomorrow at four o'clock before prayers," she says. "My hair will be visible at four in the morning."

I set my clock.

At four she is still asleep, on top of her covers. I poke her shoulder.

"Where hair?" I say. At four in the morning I have no verbs.

She bounds up laughing. "Here, here, here." She unpins her white over-scarf and the satiny green and yellow one beneath. She unknots a quilted maroon cap that lives under the scarves, and shakes out long strands of multi-colored hair-gray, white, henna-red. I touch its waves.

Nice hair," I say.

It is longer than she said it was.

And then she goes to pray.

Small things irritate me—why the Hebrew is larger than the Arabic on road signs, even in the West Bank. My cousin Mary refuses to eat the packaged lehe yogurt, because the label is in Hebrew. And why do these box-like Israeli settlements have to shave off the tops of hills?

It also bothers me to see halter-tops and short-shorts in the streets of Jerusalem. My grandmother would be amazed. An American friend says, "You know why I moved here? I thought I was going back to some old world. Last week there was an article in the paper saying Rod Stewart is coming to perform here, hooray, hooray. And I decided it's about time I went home."

My father offers to take me to the Sea of Galilee, to Nazareth. He's described Galilee's crisp little fish to me since I was a child, surely I must want to go taste them. But I don't want to go, not now. For now I feel very committed to staying in this village as long as I can, soaking up my grandmother 's gravelly voice, her inflections, it's the way I make my own tattoo.

In the mornings Hanan and Janan wash clothes in a big pan in the courtyard. Piece by piece. We hang them on the roof like flags. Our breakfast is fried white cheese, flat bread, rich yellow eggs. My grandmother wants everyone to eat cucumbers which she peels slowly with a knife.

After noon, I read and nap. I walk up and down the road. I follow the hillside path to the abandoned home of my uncle Mohammad and stand on his porch, realizing how the poem I once wrote about him accurately imagined his view into the valley. It's strange to live lines you have already written. I could stay here. There are even shelves, for books. He went to Mecca on pilgrimage and was struck down, hit-and-run, by a passing car. We never met.

In the afternoons I prepare the dinner with my cousins. We stuff squash, cube meat. One evening, I show them how to make mashed potatoes, which inspire my grandmother to say, "Stay here, we'll let you cook all the time."

In the evenings we sit, visit. The generator comes on for three hours, pumps the houses full of light. A television emerges from a cabinet. We are watching an Egyptian soap opera in which each character does nothing but cry. By the third evening's installment, I call this a comedy.

My father switches the channel; there is *Dallas*, big and clear. He says the Arabic subtitles don't fit the dialogue at all. When J. R. says, "What a bitch," the Arabic says, "I am displeased at this moment."

All low-cut segments are deleted.

Do they like this show? They shrug. Television doesn't seem to interest them much. Maybe they liked it last year, when it was new. The point is, what does it have to do with this life?

I am sleeping upstairs, in a room by myself. One set of stairs leads directly into the courtyard; another leads outside, to the front of the house.

At two one night there is a wild knocking on the outer door. It takes a while for it to filter through my dreams and arouse me; I am conscious, nonetheless, that it has been going on a long time.

Men's voices are shouting *open up!* in Arabic. I think, *fire?* Trouble in the streets? This is a quiet village. I peek out a side window and see a group of Israeli soldiers, perhaps thirty, with machine guns. I'll be damned if I'm going to open this door.

An old story flashes up from the past; my father, as a young man in Jerusalem, working for the BBC, was awakened by a similar knocking at his door.

"What shall we do?" asked his terrified mother.

He said, "Just cover my head."

Tonight I do exactly that, cover my head, and the knocking goes on, perhaps another five minutes. I am thankful for these huge iron locks.

Then I hear the men jogging around back to try the ground-floor entrance. My uncle is roused and steps out, groggy, in white night-shirt. He tells us they want him to come *show them a house* and pulls his suit-coat over his pajamas. They all leave. As *mukhtar*, he is obliged to act as counselor, mediator, guide.

We wake up, all nerves, and huddle downstairs together in the big room. Janan serves tea like a sleepwalker. I wonder how many times a day she makes coffee and tea. For every guest, for every meal, between meals, before bed, upon rising; it seems endless. I worry about my uncle. When do you know what stories to believe?

Sitti sings to me, a marriage song. "What's this?" I say. "I've been married four years."

"I know, but I missed it."

My uncle returns after an hour. He says he pointed out the house they wanted, they woke up the family within, searched the rooms, dumping out everything, and arrested the twenty-year-old son.

For what?

He says, "You think they told me?"

The next day the story will circulate in the village: this boy has been in Syria recently, he is connected with people there. And why not? You visit a country, you usually see people. I think of the American nurse I met in Amman, she was furious with the Israelis. She said, "The last time I crossed the border, they took me into a room, stripped me, shone an X-ray device up my vagina to see if I was carrying a bomb inside my Tampax, and asked me if I had any Arab friends. I said, 'Hundreds! I work with Arabs every day!' And they asked me to list all their names."

We will not hear of this arrested boy again before we leave. He's been sucked up by silence. For the rest of our stay, I sleep downstairs.

One day my father and I catch a bus into Jerusalem. He is going to try, once again, to rediscover his old home, the one he has not seen since 1948. He saw it once from the rooftop of my school in the Old City in 1967, and he wept. I'm a little worried about trying to see it face-to-face today, especially after my father stops to uncork a nitroglycerin tablet from his pocket and pop it down without water. He says he hasn't taken a heart pill in two years, but he's "having pain."

The Old City's hodge-podge self is a comfort, though punctuated by new phenomena: a bevy of fifteen-year-old Israeli girls in military formation, with M-22s. The shopkeepers seem more full of jive than I remember. They used to be serious, preoccupied, poking in their shelves. Now they've come up with catchy phrases designed to hook us in: "How ya doing, stop here, I have Holy Land wood, every kind . . ." I buy one broom for fifty cents from a toothless old man who sits weaving them, straw between straw. He knows no jive. My father leads the way.

We pass a bright bouquet of T-shirts: Jewish schoolchildren with canteens and lunch-pails, listening to their teacher. We pass a new museum which has collected "Samples of Jew-Hatred" from around the world.

A difficult part of my feeling for Israel is this: I have always been particularly attracted to Jews, as if we were Semitic cousins, which indeed we are, sharing similar tastes in landscape, literature, food. Many of my best comrades, ex-boyfriends, and local heroes have been Jewish, and just to hear my New York Jewish writer friends *talk* can put me in a swoon for hours.

But this other thing, this Israel, lacks sense to me in a way that is profound. I understand the business about wanting a home—having once participated in an Armenian community for a year, I realize the desperate shapes this yearning can take-and I know, as everyone knows, the Jews were a people brutally wronged.

But then to make a home at the expense of others, to concoct a racist state, by God, for that's exactly what Israel is, seems stranger than ever.

My father says he walked this road to school. We circle between massive stone walls, balconies, teenaged vendors with towers of bread.

Once we cut through someone's private garden. "It didn't used to be here," he says. "This used to be a street." We pull back wires, and step between.

In front of us, a flight of iron stairs ascends. "I cannot tell you," he says, hand on the railing, "how many times I traveled up and down."

There is construction going on, a pile of stones, somebody 's tools.

I stare at the house where my father grew up, realizing it is nothing like I have pictured it. This is larger, higher up, with a view. It is an old-world, stone, connected-to-other -houses house. I never pictured it connected.

A young Jew in skull-cap approaches us.

"May I help you?" He picks up a hammer.

"We're just looking," whispers my father. "We just wanted to see something."

The man speaks cheerily. "We're renovating here. This will be one of the new dorms for rabbinical students. Ha—'new'—but can you believe it? This building is 700 years old."

He talks so Brooklynish I have to ask, "Are you from New York?"

Proud. "I am. But I've decided to be an Israeli. I'm what's called a New Immigrant, under the new plan, have you heard of it? I'm working for the Rabbi here, do you know him? It's really fantastic, this feeling of being a settler, now I know how the pilgrims felt."

He's so enthusiastic, I can't help liking him. Anyone would. He's staring at my father, who's still staring at the house. "If you know the Rabbi," he repeats, "maybe you could go inside."

Now my father looks at him. The refugee and the settler. "I'm an Arab," whispers my father. His voice is strange. "I used to live here. This used to be my house."

The man looks puzzled. "You mean, you sold it to the Rabbi?"

My father shakes his head, slow-motion. "I didn't sell it. We never sold it."

There is a stretched-out silence in which the settler stares at us, shuffles his feet, and half-opens his mouth, but the Arab man is taking his daughter's arm and backing away.

"I'm sorry," the young man blurts. He looks shook up. "I'm really sorry."

And I really think he is.

Back in the village, my father reports, "We saw the house," and my grandmother sits up, interested.

"What did it look like?"

"It looked—nice."

I heard about the time my father found my grandmother in a funeral procession, weeping and wailing for the deceased. He'd just arrived, and asked her, "Who died?"

"I don't know," she confided, real tears on her face. "I just wanted to help them out."

No one will build a house west of the cemetery. It's bad luck. Marriages are still arranged. Folktales abound, in real life. My grandmother advises us that we are to give thirty pounds to the poor right before she dies, and thirty pounds immediately afterwards. We're to bury her with a pocket of air above her in the ground. She says she doesn't like to talk to people lying down. If someone reports the birth of a girl baby, she shakes her fist. I ask her, "Why are you happier over boy babies?"

"It's obvious," she says. "A girl goes away with her husband and belongs to someone else. A boy sends money home and continues to belong to his own family."

"What about belonging to yourself?" I say. "I'm married, I work, I'd give my father money if he needed it. What about belonging to the *world*?"

She tilts her head at me. "You're odd."

Three days before we leave, I ask my grandmother, who's been mooning around the courtyard, "What's wrong? Are you tired?"

Her face trembles and falls into tears. "I'm only going to be tired after you go. Then I'm going to be very, very tired."

When she cries, I cry.

We too are houses connected.

Two days before we leave, the gifts come showering down. My aunt gives me a red velvet prayer rug from Saudi Arabia. My uncle hands over worry beads. "From me," he says in English. He worked in the States once, for two years, in a produce house where everyone only spoke Spanish. The souvenir woman delivers a necklace of orange stones. Janan is stitching me a small purse the size of my passport. Her face as she sews is weighty, morose. Hanan produces a shiny, threaded scarf and takes to her bed, claiming stomach trouble. "It's a ritual," says my father. "I refuse to get caught up in this melancholy farewell ritual." And Sitti, dear Sitti, comes to me with three trinkets from her treasure trunk in hand. A fat yellow bead, a heart-shaped locket containing the image of the holy Mosque at Mecca, and a basketball medal. Two players are pitching the ball through the hoop. The incongruity of these items makes me laugh. "Where did you get these?"

She swears the basketball medal came from Mecca along with the locket.

"But do you know what this is?" my father points to the players. "Do you know what these men are doing?"

She says, "Reaching for God?"

She tells us the yellow bead will guarantee my happy marriage. It's very old, she says. I notice it has a seam, like plastic things have, but I don't mention it. My aunt brings a thread and attaches the trinkets to my prayer beads. When will I ever see these people again? I think, stricken with how far apart our lives have planted us. I think, maybe never. I think, I will always be seeing them.

A gang of kids from across the street chants at me whenever I pass on the upper landing, "HOWAREYOU?"-rolling the *r*, spoken as one word, like music. They learned it in school. Somehow they know I know what it means.

"I AM FINE!" I shout. "And how are YOU?"

Now they chirp, flutter, fly away from me. They are poor shy kids, dressed in dust and forty colors. They have this new red Arab hair, springing out in curls, and what do they play with? Stones! Sticks! The can that peas come in! And they are happy!

My favorite, a small girl named Hendia, wears a yellow headband that shines in the crowd.

"Hendia!" I will shout. "*Shu bidd ik?* What are you doing?" She leaps like a chicken being startled from behind. Yikes! I'm being spoken to! She runs and hides and never replies.

My uncle gets mad at the racket, he steps out and shoos the kids away.

On my last day I look for Hendia. I have gum for her, a packet of candies. She is gone, says her sister, to Ramallah to have her picture taken. "Tell her to find me when she gets back."

Later I hear her piping voice. "NAIMEH! HOWAREYOU?"

I run to the landing, drop her surprises down. She swoops upon them, looking at me curiously.

In Arabic I tell her, "Tomorrow-goodbye."

She says it in English. "GOODBYE."

She hides her face.

All the relatives file through the house to pay their respects. Sitti sits on the bed with her great-great grandson in her arms. I ask her if she knows the names of her hundred grandchildren. "Why should I?" she says. "I say, come here, little one—and they come."

I step out into the night, pulling on my sweater, to get one last sense of what we are leaving. One village, in a terribly troubled country far faraway from a world that discusses it. What do we really know? And a shadow leaps on me. startling. It is Hendia. She has been waiting in the shadow of the loquat tree for me to emerge. No telling how long she has been here; it is the first time she has entered the courtyard.

Into my hand she presses a package of peanuts. "GOODBYE!" she says again. And she runs away so fast I have nothing to thank but the moon.

◻ ◻ ◻ ◻ ◻

23

STEVEN SALAITA

Why I Was Fired

Devoted Husband.
Loving Father.
Soft-Spoken.
Deferential.
Civil.
Intemperate.
Inappropriate.
Angry.
Aggressive.
Uncivil.

In August 2014, I was fired from a tenured position at the University of Illinois at Urbana-Champaign. The firing made me a free-speech darling—or the world's most violent person since Stalin, depending on your perspective. It also sparked a debate about academic freedom, faculty governance, the Israel–Palestine conflict, and the role of social media in university life. That debate rages with no resolution in sight.

The story of my notoriety begins on July 21, 2014, when The Daily Caller ran an article about me titled "University of Illinois Professor Blames Jews for anti-Semitism." With the brio and wisdom for which right-wing websites are known, the piece begins, "The University of Illinois at Urbana-Champaign has continued its bizarre quest to employ as many disgusting scumbags as possible by acquiring the services of Steven Salaita, a leading light in the movement among similarly obscure academics to boycott Israel."

The article, and subsequent coverage, focused on several tweets I wrote in the summer of 2014. One tweet read: "At this point, if Netanyahu appeared on TV with a necklace made from the teeth of Palestinian children, would anybody be surprised?" In another, I wrote, "You may be too refined to say it, but I'm not: I wish all the fucking West Bank settlers would go missing."

It has since become popular to call me uncivil. Or intemperate. Or inappropriate. Or angry. Or aggressive. It's unseemly to describe myself, but because "unseemly" is an improvement over what many people now call me—why not? I am a devoted husband and a loving father. I never talk out of turn. I deliberate for long periods before making significant decisions. As is normal for somebody born and raised in southern Appalachia, I call everybody "sir" or "ma'am." I do not raise my voice at people. I am deeply shy and chronically deferential. That is to say, I am civil to a fault.

This exegesis on my disposition probably seems unnecessary, but it's important to distinguish between somebody's persona and his personhood, though in most cases one informs the other. This is the extent of my feelings on the matter: it is precisely because I am a loving person that I so adamantly deplore Israel's behavior.

My tweets might appear uncivil, but such a judgment can't be made in an ideological or rhetorical vacuum. Insofar as the concept of *civil* is profoundly racialized and has a long history of demanding conformity, I frequently choose incivility as a form of communication. This choice is both moral and rhetorical.

The piety and sanctimony of my critics is most evident in their hand-wringing about my use of curse words. While I am proud to have something in common with Richard Pryor, J. D. Salinger, George Carlin, S. E. Hinton, Maya Angelou, Judy Blume, and countless others who have offended the priggish, I confess to being confused as to why obscenity is such an issue to those who supposedly devote their lives to analyzing the endless nuances of public expression. Academics are usually eager to contest censorship and deconstruct vague charges of vulgarity. When it comes to defending Israel, though, anything goes. If there's no serious moral or political argument in response to criticism of Israel, then condemn the speaker for various failures of tone and appropriateness. Emphasis placed on the speaker and not on Israel. A word becomes more relevant than an array of war crimes.

Even by the tendentious standards of civility, my comments on Twitter (and elsewhere) are more defensible than the accusations used to defame me. The most deplorable acts of violence germinate in high society. Many genocides have been glorified (or planned) around dinner tables adorned with forks and knives made from actual silver, without a single inappropriate speech act having occurred.

In most conversations about my termination, Israel's war crimes go unmentioned, yet it is impossible to understand my tweets without that necessary context. My strong language—and I should point out that much of my language is also gentle—arises in response to demonstrable acts of brutality that in a better world would raise widespread rancor. You tell me which is worse: cussing in condemnation of the murder of children or using impeccable manners to justify their murder. I no more want to be respectable according to the epistemologies of colonial wisdom than I want to kill innocent people with my own hands. Both are articulations of the same moral rot.

In eleven years as a faculty member, I have fielded exactly zero complaints about my pedagogy. Every peer evaluation of my instruction—the gold standard for judging teaching effectiveness—has been stellar. Student evaluations ranked higher than the mean every time I collected them. Yet people affiliated with the University of Illinois at Urbana-Champaign have impugned my ability to teach.

Students are capable of serious discussion, of formulating responses, of thinking through discomfort. They like my teaching because I refuse to infantilize them; I treat them as thinking adults. I have never disrespected a student. I have never told a student what to think. Nor have I ever shut down an opinion. I encourage students to argue with me. They take me up on the offer. I sometimes change my viewpoint as a result. My philosophy is simple: teach them the modes and practices of critical thought and let them figure out things on their own.

The handwringing about students is pious, precious claptrap, a pretext to clean the stench from a rotten argument raised to validate an unjustifiable decision.

Troublesome assumptions underlie accusations about my fitness for the classroom. It is impossible to separate questions about my civility from broader narratives of inherent Arab violence. This sort of accusation has been used to discredit people of color (and other minorities) in academe for many decades. Administrators and the public monitor and scrutinize our actions in a manner to which our white colleagues are rarely subject. It is crucial to train us in the ways of civility lest our emotions dislodge the ethos our superiors hold so dear.

When it comes to opposing colonization, there is no need for dissimulation, which is the preferred vocabulary of the cocktail party and committee meeting. I could make a case that dissimulation is immoral. It is undoubtedly boring. When I say something, I have no desire to conceal meaning in oblique and wishy-washy diction. This is especially so when I respond to the various horrors of state violence and the depravity of those who justify it. On campus, such forthrightness is unconventional.

But no tenet of academic freedom considers failure to adhere to convention a fireable offense.

Professors are often punished for disrupting convention in informal ways, however. My case is interesting because administrators ignored the de facto standards that regulate our behavior and exercised their power directly. This should be worrisome to any scholar who isn't a sycophant.

People with doctorates who make claims unsupported by evidence and who uncritically repeat terms like *incivility* as if it describes anything other than their own dull prejudice are the ones most unfit to teach college.

Being called an anti-Semite is deeply unpleasant. Those who make the accusation should be responsible for providing evidence, yet it is I who has been saddled with the impossible task of disproving a negative. The rhetorical incoherence of my critics is evident in their ever-evolving justifications for my firing. First I was anti-Semitic. Then I was uncivil. Then I was a bad teacher. Then I was too charismatic. Then I was too angry. Then I was too profane. Then I was too radical. Then I was too unpatriotic. Then I wasn't really hired. Then I was unqualified in the field of American Indian studies. Then I benefited from nepotism. Then I was a poor scholar. Then my colleagues were incompetent. Then my colleagues were deceitful. Then my colleagues were ignorant. Then the American Indian-studies program required special guidance. Then the decision to hire me was based solely on politics. Then indigenous studies was illegitimate. Then the entire damn field needed to be shut down.

Part of our charge as educators is to encourage students to find the language that will help them translate instinct into concrete knowledge. It's the kind of preparation we all need to survive in the capitalist market-place. While antiauthoritarianism may start as an attitude, it has infinite capacity to develop into an ethic.

Distrusting the motivation of institutions and their managers often means demotion or recrimination. But there is reason to distrust authority on campus. Universities are lucrative spaces; nothing is lucrative without also being corrupt.

As Thomas Frank put it in an essay in The Baffler,

> The coming of "academic capitalism" has been anticipated and praised for years; today it is here. Colleges and universi-

ties clamor greedily these days for pharmaceutical patents and ownership chunks of high-tech startups; they boast of being "entrepreneurial"; they have rationalized and outsourced countless aspects of their operations in the search for cash; they fight their workers nearly as ferociously as a 19th-century railroad baron; and the richest among them have turned their endowments into in-house hedge funds.

Frank later pinpoints the reason for campus authoritarianism:

> Above all, what the masters of academia spend the loot on is themselves. In saying this, I am not referring merely to the increasing number of university presidents who take home annual "compensation" north of a million dollars. That is a waste, of course, an outrageous bit of money-burning borrowed from Wall Street in an age when we ought to be doing the opposite of borrowing from Wall Street. But what has really fueled the student's ever-growing indebtedness, as anyone with a connection to academia can tell you, is the insane proliferation of university administrators.

The numbers validate Frank's observation. Benjamin Ginsberg points out that in the past thirty years, the administrator-to-student ratio has increased while the instructor-to-student ratio has stagnated. The rise of untenured, or non-tenure-track, faculty exacerbates the problem; a significant demographic in academe lacks job security or the working conditions that allow them to maximize their pedagogical talent. Over a recent ten-year period, spending on administration outpaced spending on instruction. At American universities, there are now more administrators and their staffers than full-time faculty. In the past ten years, administrative salaries have steadily risen while custodians and groundskeepers suffer the inevitable budget cuts—as do the students whose tuition and fees supplement this largess.

When so much money is at stake, those who raid the budget have a deep interest in maintaining the reputation of the institution. Their privilege and the condition of the brand are causally related. The brand thus predominates. Its predominance often arrives at the expense of student well-being.

Take the matter of sexual assault. Reporting rates have recently risen, but all versions of sexual assault remain woefully underreported. There are numerous reasons that a victim chooses to keep silent. One reason is that she may expect a wholly inadequate, or even hostile, response from her own university. In 2014, Columbia University fielded twenty-eight federal complaints claiming the university had inadequately investigated reports of sexual assault. Florida State University, with the help of the Tallahassee Police Department, orchestrated a clumsy cover-up of a rape allegation to protect the star quarterback Jameis Winston. A different category of sexual assault infamously occurred at Pennsylvania State University, where the onetime defensive coordinator of the football team, Jerry Sandusky, was found to have molested numerous children, some of them on campus. The university's complicity is but an extreme instance of a common phenomenon.

In this era of neoliberal graft, universities barely pretend to care about the ideals upon which higher education was founded. Sure, administrators and PR flacks still prattle about dialogue and self-improvement and the life of the mind, but not even impressionable eighteen-year-olds believe that claptrap. They know just as well as their superiors that college is really about acquiring the mythical but measurable status conferred on them by a crisp sheet of cotton-bond paper.

As universities more and more resemble corporations in their governance, language, and outlook, students have become acutely brand-conscious. Guardianship of the brand thus predominates and overwhelms the primacy of thought and analysis to which the academy is nominally committed. Students no longer enter into places of learning. They pay exorbitant prices to gain access to the socioeconomic capital of affiliation with the most recognizable avatars, adorned magisterially with armor and pastoral creatures and Latin phrases.

Take that most sacred element of pedagogy, critical thinking. Many faculty don't know how to do it, never mind imparting instruction in the practice to those trying to learn it. (My conception of "critical thinking" includes acting in some way on the knowledge it produces, if only in the formulation of a dynamic ethical worldview.) One of the greatest skills that critical thinking provides is the ability to recognize and undermine bunk. In short, if critical thinking is to be useful, it must endow a reflexive desire to identify and understand the disguises of power.

This sort of focus is low on the list of what universities want from students, just as critical thinking is a terribly undesirable quality in the corporate world, much more damning than selfishness or sycophancy. Let us then be honest about critical thinking: on the tongues of cunning bureaucrats, it is little more than an additive to brand equity, the vainglorious pomp of smug, uptight automatons who like to use buzzwords in their PowerPoint presentations.

Critical thinking by faculty is even more undesirable. In research institutions, we are paid to generate prestige and to amass grant money; in teaching-centered colleges, we enjoy excess enrollments according to fine-tuned equations that maximize the student-teacher ratio; in elite liberal arts colleges, we pamper the kids with simulations of parental affection. Critical thinking is especially harmful to adjuncts, reliant as they are for income on the munificence of well-paid bosses who cultivate a distended assemblage of expendable employees.

Nowhere in our employment contracts does it say, "Challenge the unarticulated aspirations of the institution, especially when it acts as a conduit and expression of state violence; and please try your best to support justice for those on and off campus who are impoverished by neoliberalism." If we practice critical thinking, though, it is difficult to avoid these obligations.

Because of their high-minded rhetoric, it is tempting to believe that university managers care about ethics or maybe even about justice, but most managers care about neither. The exceptions, of course, deserve our praise—just don't poke around the highly ranked schools if you want to find them. The key to a successful managerial career isn't striving to be a good person, but developing enough instinct to cheat and charm at opportune moments.

Whatever independence can be acquired in academe requires a fundamental distrust of authority, be it abstract or explicit. There have never been pure epochs of uncorrupted democracy, but increasing corporate control disturbs greater sectors of American life, particularly on campus. There has to be a better way to conduct the practices of education.

What to do about injustice? I hear this question a lot since I was fired. I have no solid answer. My instinct, which I fully understand isn't actually instinctive, is simply to tell people to do what they feel comfortable doing. I'm not big on demands or injunctions. Yet I recognize that as somebody who now exists in a public position, I am summoned to analyze a set of dynamics in which I and the University of Illinois at Urbana-Champaign are embroiled. These dynamics are especially important to folks in academe who wish to pursue material commitments alongside theoretical and philosophical questions.

Graduate students and prospective graduate students are especially anxious these days. They are right to be. Decent humanities jobs are in decline. Grad-school slots have become more competitive. Any advantage is a great asset. Being deemed a troublemaker or a radical is no advantage.

Making trouble is precisely the function of the intellectual, though. And being radical is a solid antidote to boring work.

There have always been repression and recrimination in academe. Anybody with an eye toward a career as a scholar has to internalize this reality. Aspiring and established scholars should not abdicate intellectual commitments in order to please the comfortable. This would be careerism, not inquiry.

And that's the point. If we don't examine relationships of power and highlight the disjunctions of inequality, then we're not doing our jobs. (We're doing so according to the preferences of the managerial class, but pleasing its functionaries isn't generally the mark of an interesting thinker.) Upsetting arbiters of so-called common sense is an immanent feature of useful scholarship.

"What can/should we do?" is not a universal question. Consider that the labor of minority scholars is already politicized. We have to publish more. It's risky to be introverted, because so many white colleagues cannot tolerate a minority who doesn't pretend to like them. We have to act as diversity representative on all sorts of committees. We cannot be mediocre, because our tenure and upward mobility rely on senior colleagues who reward only their own mediocrity. It's hazardous for us to show emotion, because we're aware of the possibility of confirming to others our innate unreason. Adding *activist leader* to this list of tasks is a heavy undertaking. In many ways, simply deciding not to appease power is an active form of advocacy. It is the activism of survival.

Getting fired doesn't make me an expert on anything. I'm doing my best to make sure something productive comes of it, though. My having a job changes nothing if the system that orchestrated my ouster remains intact. I am merely a symbol of the stark imperatives of the wealthy and well connected. We all are, really. Unless the system changes at a basic level, everybody is merely buying shares in a corporation with the power to dissolve our interests the moment we become an inconvenience.

◻ ◻ ◻ ◻ ◻

24

MATTHEW SHENODA

Christopher Columbus
Was A Damn Blasted Liar

On the Narrative of Discovery in Global Literature

Some years ago I sat amongst a group of people influential in the contemporary literary scene in the United States. As I listened to one of the
individuals (who holds some significant decision-making power in the
literary world) speak about a writer that they discovered and whose career
they helped launch, I was struck by the way the narrative was unfolding.
I sat curiously listening to this hubris, this Columbusesque narrative,
trying to understand the fascination for the speaker to spin such a tale. It
so happened the writer at the center of this conversation was no stranger
to me, was someone I knew quite well. As the story went on and others
around the table congratulated this person for their stellar work in discovering this young writer, I couldn't shake the way this narrative negated
significant parts of this writer's life and lived experiences.

Too often have I heard editors, grant makers, and educators talk
about discovering this or that writer and too often has that writer been
a person of color, often from a country outside of the United States. Is
this act of discovery a real possibility or is it a holdover from a colonial
mentality that shapes the way in which writers of color in particular are
still molded and understood in the present literary landscape?

At the core of this telling was not an act of malice or even a conscious
sense of power and privilege. The individuals around the table clearly and
earnestly appreciated this writer's contributions to the world, or should I
say to *their* world. You see, as is often the case, this writer they spoke of,
as all writers serious about their craft, labored for many years and worked
intimately within various communities before they were discovered. And
where is the room for that reality? For even to say this person is *new*

to this landscape is quite different than to claim *discovery*, for newness implies a history, implies a trajectory, implies a mutual relationship as one who is new to a place is also new to the people of that place. But a narrative of discovery seems somehow to negate an individual's history and experiences. What's more is that this narrative is doubly damaging to so-called immigrant writers. Much like Columbus' narrative of discovery, this kind of telling negates a person's indigenaity and community.

In US literary narratives, the immigrant writer is somehow only fully birthed once their work arrives on US soil. There may be small recollections of their terrible pasts in their home country, but their real moment of virtue and dare I say freedom only happens once they are discovered in the United States. All this to say that the things they have written, taught, been taught, or cultivated in their home nations are largely negated. They are born anew in this land of plenty and as such are ripe for assimilation by those in power. Their contribution to the literary ethos of the United States seems ancillary to the fact that we have given them so much. There is in this power dynamic an uneasy sense of ownership and indebtedness. Rarely is it that those who control the literati of this nation recognize that *they* would in fact be lesser had it not been for those writers widening and helping reimagine the ways we understand literature, and frankly, life in this country.

My goal here is to roughly sketch just some of the issues that arise when we engage this topic, in hopes that a conversation can ensue amongst my fellow writers and readers of contemporary literature. By no means are my comments here meant to be comprehensive or exhaustive, but rather a primer to think about how we have an obligation to continue to engage literature in the twenty-first century.

To begin with, we must unpack what I will call the affliction of parochialism, a reality all too common in literary (especially poetry) circles. This affliction is defined foremost by an inability to see outside of one's self, one's own confines, geographies, institutions, regions, and nation. Because writers too often affiliate primarily with other writers, to be struck by this affliction is easier than one might think. If we read the same books, journals, and magazines, frequent the same virtual, cultural, and institutional spaces, we significantly hinder our ability to accept a world that is much wider in breadth, taste, and significance than the one we inhabit. We talk too commonly of a global age, or global literatures, but few embody such a reality. Instead, we occasionally allow those we other entry into this world and rarely venture outside of it ourselves, and this is the fundamental problem.

Not only is this an issue for the writer in question, but also for the reader, editor, grant-maker, educator, etc. This kind of narrative puts the responsibility of a global reality on those from othered places and rarely implicates, challenges, or educates the largely white members of the literary power structure in the US. Rarely is the editor challenged to engage in the home communities of these writers they claim to discover. Rarely are they held accountable to understand the roots and antecedents of these writers' aesthetics and literary traditions. Rarely are they called to rethink, realign or question their own tastes, interpretations, and aesthetic leanings. This reality creates a sorely uneven global literature where one group is indeed global and the other an apprehensive tourist given the power to shape their literary tourism as they see fit, never forced to face a rainy day on their perfectly curated literary vacation; always orchestrating how the world we all live in will be defined.

The Guyanese reggae band Arkaingelle sings in one of their tracks a simple summation of this predicament: "justice for all, not just those in the United States." Once we abandon our nationalistic sense of literature and begin to question our own assumptions about literature, notions of taste, craft, and aesthetics, only then will we begin to approach a true and equitable global literature.

◻ ◻ ◻ ◻ ◻

25

KAMELYA OMAYMA YOUSSEF

Frayed Towel Made Holy
Prayer [Rug] for This Nonbeliever

1.

Baba always insisted there was no god—that science, like him, was the chief engineer. Baba, who carried an empty infant-sized casket across Jabal Amel for a nephew stricken with typhoid. Baba, who escaped the warlords brandishing scriptured weapons to carve the bellies of pregnant women, umbilical cords pulsing with mothers' eldritch silence. Baba, for whom war was an unruly child born of God and ungodly obsessions. He believed not that he abandoned God but that he was abandoned by God. Instead, he instructed, we would live lives doing what God should have done: build a school in the village, repatriate the unjustly displaced, bring those wandering souls back to life.

2.

Every night, in the bed we shared, the oak tree peering into the window, I would lie with Jamila. She moved to Michigan from our village in Lebanon, all wheat fields and sun and donkey braying at dawn. She, my cousin, knew all the things I did not—she brought family secrets in her suitcase and together we'd hold them and wish them away like dandelions.

She taught me to pray my first and only prayer. I did not know the Qur'an.

She said it was OK that I did not know surat al nas. Not the one of the people. I didn't know surat al ikhlas. Not the one of salvation. Not the surah of the cow, nor the surah of the sinners, nor the surah of the elephant where the flock of martin sparrows amasses until sky blackens and they drop stones on armies, turn them to ash.

She said it was OK as long as I repeated that my fate rests in God. Itakalna 'aala Allah.

She dubbed me Muslim. I'd lay my towel beside Jamila's prayer rug. We would kneel, rest hands on our knees, stand up, close eyes, place our fingers at our temples.

Fearful and doubtless, I'd recite those words into the belly of each long, dark night.

3.

I was a buoy, resting with the atheism of my secular Arab parents in the ocean of a devout Arab Muslim community, with halal pizza served by the white lunch ladies, and looking cute to attend Ramadan lectures, and boys wearing black armbands stamped with white Arabic text and the sword of Zulficar, a band whose most effective function was accentuating the budding biceps newly born in the gyms of our community. My parents were unaware of the roiling social waters that I was navigating belieflessly. Islam kept us distant from whiteness, though then it was our neighbor. What lurked on the other side, if we were to cross, was erasure.

4.

I remember a woman named Zahra, whose house was three blocks north of mine, closer to the boundary delineating Dearborn from Detroit. My cousin would get on his bike and I would ride on the back pegs, and I would hold onto him for my life, and I would hold onto him for candy. Candy because Zahra's house was where we would go buy candy. I cannot remember how we entered her living room, whether we walked up concrete stairs to it, whether it was prefaced with a porch, whether she would sit on her porch to greet us—the limbs of this memory have faded. But I remember Zahra's white socks.

At Zahra's, all sorts of candy waited for us, neatly organized on the many small wooden tables dotting her living room, which we walked around as if a maze. I would go there with a dollar in my pocket, and I would buy seventy-five-cent small candy lipsticks, with brightly colored tops on white tubes. I always bought the pink ones because I was certain that the orange ones tasted like citrus, and that the purple ones tasted like grape, and my liking was always for strawberry and cherry or more succinctly, red, though it is most likely that all of these candies tasted the exact same. Our transactions were conducted mostly in quarters and entirely in Arabic. Specifically Lebanese.

I wonder how Zahra's candy shop prospered, how her life rolled along. If she has passed, I wonder if she is buried here in southeast Michigan or if she is buried back home. More truthfully, I wonder if Zahra ever existed because though my memory of her feels certain, there is no documentation of her, not in Facebook statuses or ethnographic texts, no mention of her in literature or any form of documenting collective memory. The kids we were may remember her but we are no longer them, and the porch we ate those candies on is gone. If someone conducts an archaeological dig in the playground pebbles at Oakman School, I wonder at how many bright pink candy lipstick tubes they will find. I wonder if they're mine.

5.

He walked shirtless through the endless stream of summer, like all pretty boys did. He, tall, a bronze sculpture released from its immortal stillness, walked the concrete pathway of Levagood Park, a green paradise the length of exactly six suburban blocks, along the edge of which we drove with the music turned up loud enough for it to be communal. Every day, we'd drive the perimeter of Levagood Park, thread the parking lots in search of familiar faces. And we always found them. Susu would pick me up at 11:15 a.m. and I had always just risen heavy from sleep, would always line the rims of my eyelids with ninety-nine-cent Wet 'N' Wild liner, put on my neon orange swimsuit and a dress, kiss my mother, and fly out the door to meet a white '01 Grand Prix, Susu my chariot. The goal was to arrive at Levagood right before what we were once told was solar noon, the time when the sun hung optimally in the sky, perpendicular enough to brown our skin to the particular shade of hot girl that suited our desires and those of the boys we'd love forever.

Every day at solar noon, he'd be playing basketball at the court beyond the parking lot, past the fence and the grass and the sidewalk.

"Guys, it's Mr. Levagood. He's here."

My girls all looked.

"He's so pretty. I want him in my pants."

I had held a beauty pageant in my mind for all the hot guys who walked that park, and by a unanimous vote, Mr. Levagood had won.

A few days later, we had finished a day of sunbathing and oscillating between the kiddie pool and the adult pool, always settling for the latter after one too many baby Hamoudies had taken a shit in the pool. This day, Moe pulled up in his new Infiniti coupe right as we were walking out. We vocalized our admiration for his new car and he told us to get in. If a boy had a new car, you wanted to be riding in it, and he wanted to take you around. The only fear was always that you'd see your cousin or neighbor or someone from your mother's village, someone who would tell your parents and everyone in their ancestral network that you indeed were riding in the car with a boy instead of rollerblading around Randa's house like you told your mother you would while she was preparing breakfast and watching the Arabic news.

I sat in the passenger seat of the Infiniti, Susu and Zeinab in the back and Moe drove slow. Across the parking lot, I spotted Mr. Levagood, a portrait in a car window frame, his bare chest illuminated by daylight and youth. I had been admiring him since the beginning of summer and I had never been less than four car-lengths and a fence away from him, still didn't know him by any other name.

Moe gently slowed his new car and waved in Mr. Levagood's direction. "Hass! What up?"

Hass. His name was Hassan. Mr. Levagood was Hassan. He neared the car and I felt my heart pound its summer song. He had a basketball in his hand and dropped it, let it roll to the meet the curb.

"Moooooooooe, what up cuz?" His voice had a rasp, and his golden laugh trailed and echoed in the wane of the aging day. He sounded as pretty as he looked. I felt the car fill with a certainty of God. He approached my window which framed my face, my lips, myself, and he propped his arm so near to the skin of my shoulder I could die.

"Ay bro, nothing, wallah, we're just chillin. Come by my garage later."

Later that summer, Mr. Levagood would become my boyfriend. He'd take me to Carrera's for dinner and talk about stand-up comedians and his niece and Lebanon and he'd hold up the butter knife to catch his own reflection. Even after our breakup, he'd gift me a watch lined with rhinestones from the department store at Fairlane Mall. He'd sneak into my room one night and hide in my closet when my mother knocked on the door. He'd hop out of my window when my mother forced the door open, her eyes wild with suspicion and a broom in her soft hand. He would message me poems some years later about beautiful eyes and Imam Ali and the need for justice in our sad world. He would be deported back to Lebanon, which he left for America as a child. He'd like my posts on Facebook and send me pictures of old times.

6.

In my Dearborn, because we were so far away from home, or what we believed to be home, home became the object of our gaze, the only pilgrimage we would take when we could finally afford it. It became the Beloved, our hearts seized by its absence, our souls in a tunnel somewhere, always en route to return. We found communion with each other, not as people who left a generation ago, but as people who are always still there. Nation for us was holy divine, paradise on this very earth. Nation had me searching for home in languages and airplanes and lovers and lonely apartments and nights spent in cars to catch a sunrise. Nation left me and is ever-leaving. It is my compass pointed toward an ever more northward star.

Burn the idols, a lover once told me. *No god, no nations,* he'd say. We were on a forest hike and I burned the idol for a moment in my mind— rendered the nation extinct and not mine, rendered myself rootless and from no particular place—and grieved. The sun sprayed its light through the trees and suddenly the aspen leaves looked like baklawa, the branches were Arabic script, and the trees all became olive and cedar, my mind performing its last-ditch protest. The white man that I loved and the Budweiser beer can on the ground implored me to exist here out of context but the wind speaks to me in Arabic and the rain on my forehead is the Mediterranean mist and I am so in love with the Beloved that I am sick.

7.

Rabi'a al-'Adawiyya believed her sickness to be a constant spiritual ailment, a longing to be with God, a soul in the torment of exile away from the beloved. She longed to be united with the divine, and awaited death, the bridge to join her with the beloved. Living was longing. Rabi'a was "a stranger in the Lord's country and lonely among the worshippers."

8.

Garden City was the kind of city we always lived on the edge of. We rolled up Swisher Sweets and cruised through its streets paved with bruised leaves in our smoky chariot, an '01 Ford Taurus with a dent on the front left bumper. Cracked white paint.

There, the perimeters of plazas were perpendicular with parking lots for the five-dollar shoe outlet where we got our shoes for prom and some Wednesdays, and the beauty supply where we got our fake eyelashes, those of us who had plucked them all out like some birds do when the cage is too small.

There, they had tanning salons named for their vacation destinations with their families: Palm Beach, Hawaiian, Back to the Beach, Tropic Sun, and Boca. There worked the white girls, their orange shoulders like bare branches where birds would otherwise perch. Our brown boys took them to prom instead of us.

Garden City was closer to us than the neighborhoods with the hair salons with Fadia, Fatima, Zeinab, Zee, and so many more of the boys first named Mohamed then knighted Moe in this newfound western tradition.

We were the ones who moved on up to neighborhoods without train tracks tracing them like a spine, nerve endings sprawling to abandoned homes and factories, automobile industrial complexes with floodlights constellating them despite the smoke and its thick stink familiar to the children in classrooms a quarter mile away.

There, in Garden City, anthropologists do not roam, nor do they graze the streets to feed on awnings written in liturgical languages. There, the FBI does not look through the suitcases people carry beneath their tongues.

My parents, here thirty years, are self-taxonomized homing pigeons. I heard them in the bathroom one day, clipping each other's wings. I heard no words. Only trilling and the crack of scissors on bone.

9.

When I was a young child, my paternal uncle, Amo Zein, had just immigrated from Lebanon to a makeshift bedroom in the basement of our house. He would ask me and my siblings if we understood what he meant when he described the landscape around our grandfather's house in Jibben: *jabal, wadi, can you see it, valley, bustan, hill, mountain, do you know it.* We didn't really but we laughed when he would carry us on his back and spin us hysterical, spin us dizzy.

Imagining a hilly landscape was beyond my perception—I lived on a flat street in a duplex corner house and we could look down our block and see the next city on the endless horizon. A Yemeni family lived in the upstairs unit. They had a son named Amir and we would skateboard together until our parents called us inside for dinner. After dinner, our families would sit on the porches drinking tea and this became a different kind of playtime, where immigrant Arab parents and their gender rules were present. In this part-two-playtime featuring parental supervision, we couldn't straddle the skateboard at the same time as if we were riding a snow sled and then fall over before we hit the end of the sidewalk, no watching the skateboard roll into the street as Ford coupes sped by with their amplified speaker systems and spinning silver rims.

My Amo Zein would coax me and Amir away from the skateboard onto the porch to talk to us about our respective homelands, mountainous Edens ravaged by war and American imperialism. One day, Amo Zein taught us how to sketch a mountain valley with a pencil and paper. I practiced this template for years after, drawing renditions of snow-peaked mountains with deep river valleys and silhouettes of trees on backdrop mountain ridges, during coloring time at Oakman Elementary School.

In that flatness, the only mountain valley I ever knew was the one I sketched between 1:05 and 2:05 p.m. in white-walled classrooms. I didn't see my first mountain valley until the waning of my adolescence. I didn't know that valleys could be wider than rivers, wider than interstate highways, wide and populated with houses and people who could look outside of their windows and see God's majesty instead of the serialized red-brick homes past gray paved sidewalks and brief grass-lined curbs on Orchard Avenue in Dearborn.

10.

I give tours at the Arab American National Museum. If I'm lucky, and I've been lucky a few times, I'll get people who are sent over by a government agency or a branch of the military to get a tour of Dearborn, home to the largest Arab population outside of the Arab world, and they'll ask me to take them to a restaurant in the area so they can practice speaking Arabic in the shop. *Why,* I ask foolishly. *Well,* they tell me, *it's cheaper to come to Dearborn than it is to go to the Middle East.* This is the story of how I quickly learned that my hometown is a training ground for the military.

Another Arab village lives in the Mojave Desert in Fort Irwin, where they have fake Iraqi and Afghani villages open for tourists and supporters of the troops (as FtIrwinITCBox@gmail.com told me in an email once). There, they conduct practice home invasions with actors paid to pose as Muslims, to have a dinner interrupted by doors swung open by young American soldiers, to scream and cry and surrender.

Here, homeland is simulacra, is Agrabah, is a copy of a copy, is an unseen object that does not resist.

11.

City,
it
has
been
too
long
since
i have heard a call to prayer the
one muffled you hear your head on a pillow
the sleep still in your hands and eyes both clutching
some realm   a dream   a voice   spills into your window
something like sunlight easy like water and god shrills you
awake. wherever there is land without god, we make god
or a bird perches on the point of a minaret and preens.

12.

Once I was having lunch with a coworker who served in the Marines in Iraq and Afghanistan. I asked him what it was like. Between bites, he told me that, in friendly villages, some of the hajjis would try to talk to them in English. *Oh, the older women would talk to you in English?* I asked. *No,* he said, *these hajjis were the children.*

13.

hajjis in detroit

i want to title a poem hajji poem because the word hajji exists in the
        english language
and has had many meanings and connotations before i had anything to
        do with it.

hajji (noun): the lady in the long navy abaya and paisley scarf, the frame
        to her portrait
the one with the grocery bags in each hand wondering if she could balance
        the jarra on her head like her mother used to back home.
hajjis are known to tell stories.
hajjis tuck treasures into their bras
    they, the masters of knowing
    what to carry when you have to leave
    everything behind.
hajjis tuck licorice under their tongues
        carried knives in past lives.

now hajji steals shopping carts from super greenland
    parks the cart afront her house
    for carting her purse down the street to market
    and for bags of groceries on the return home.
hajji cruises down the street in her 3arabaye.
    parks her ride on the verdurous bed
    next to the sidewalk
    before she cooks a mean meal
    to wash down this bitter life.

14.

Some time before she passed away, my grandmother had spent years in
and out of the hospital, stroke after surgery after an incident of falling,
her tired body bearing the weight of time and the dispersal of her children

across the continents. Her face appears in the video, and her silver braid peeks out from beneath her thin white veil. She is in a sea-foam green hospital gown in a bed covered with white sheets, the intravenous tubes hang next to her like vines. A voice behind the camera asks her: *What would you like to say to Kamelya?* She straightens her back and opens her mouth to speak: *Ya Kamelya. Ya binti. Ya dille ya habibti. Ya rouhi. Shta'tilik ya Kamelya. Allah yoHfozek w Allah yiHmeeki w Allah yijiblik waHad ibn halal. Bas, ya Kamelya, 'oo'a. 'oo'a takhdi waHad Amerkani.*

Oh girl, don't you dare take an American as your beloved. Do not make yourself home in a strange land. Do not stray far away. Stay close to us and stay close to God.

15.

I once dreamt that I met a man and that we fell in love. Within moments, our future together unfolded as a map of infinite space and oceans and alleyways. I loved him far into the dark expanse of the universe and then I asked him for his name. He disappeared right after he answered: The Deceit.

16.

Do not take a shower at night, my grandfather Abu Ali warned me. The jinn will be in there, splashing and dancing in the drops of water at your feet.

17.

It is told in hadith that the prophet himself was overtaken by jinn one day when he recounted events that did not occur, according to his wife 'A'isha. He had been afflicted by the jinn Labid ibn al-'awwam, who had bewitched him with a comb and a strand of hair and the outer shell of pollen from a date palm near the well of Dharwan. The prophet went to the well and found that the date palms nearby resembled the heads of devils. He insisted the well of Dharwan be filled with earth, never to be drawn from again.

18.

In a dream once, a prophet appeared to me in the form of Sahar Beydoun, the girl who sat behind me in third hour geometry. She warned me that on judgment day, God would ask us to write all the stories of our lives in Arabic. She then turned around and walked into a labyrinth of coffee shops and alleys that led to doorways that opened to couches and narrow walkbridges in parks that were packed, into a throng of shawarma vendors and children protesting with loudspeakers.

19.

I could not decide if I wanted to be her or to be in love with her, or if both had already occurred. We found the way to the unpaved overpass, over which the freight lines were laid, weaving through Detroit. No words between us, just a humming city. We each picked up wild ribbons of rusted scrap metal spawned from the lick of the now-cold steel. The sharp wind carved my thoughts onto the brick building walls around us. The cigarette we shared tasted of honey, ash honey, incinerator fumes honey, rusted train tracks honey, myrrh honey, America honey. Before she left the next morning, we painted a du'aa, a prayer, onto the steel ribbons and returned them back to their home.

Haribun minka ilayk, we wrote. I run away from you toward you.

20.

Three Arab Muslim girls from Dearborn walk into a warehouse party in Los Angeles. By 2:30 a.m., one is vomiting in the toilet, another is laughing with a blonde man named Space Wizard, and the third is the only woman in a circle of men making a coke deal. They sober up, go to a friend's recording studio, and freestyle rap with Armenian Angelenos, the third one using a credit card to arrange the cocaine in perfectly straight lines on the table. They watch for the sunrise over Echo Park Lake, and the third one exhales an Allahu Akbar as the sun pierces the twilight.

21.

In early Sufism, fire was chiefly associated with hell and evil. Rumi, who was a later Sufi, queered this singular notion of fire by contrasting it with light, relieving an image of meaning, by cleaving it ambivalent. Fire and light. Evil and good. The descent and the ascent. The punishment and the reward. The eternal dungeon and the eternal divine. Then 'Attar described Rabia al-'Adawiyya as "that woman on fire with love" for the divine. Struck with emotion for the luminous divine, for her, God was "the One God Who is the Fire of Pain and the Light of Joy to souls, according as they resist Him or will Him, either here or thereafter." She sought "an eternal union with an eternal flame." We are burning but we are not consumed, bodies in exile longing for home in the beloved divine.

CONTRIBUTORS

ELMAZ ABINADER's most recent poetry collection, *This House, My Bones,* was The Editor's Selection for 2014 from Willow Books/Aquarius. Her books include a memoir: *Children of the Roojme, A Family's Journey from Lebanon; In the Country of My Dreams . . .,* which won the Oakland PEN, Josephine Miles Award. Her plays include *Ramadan Moon, 32 Mohammeds,* and *Country of Origin.* She has been a fellow at residencies in Macedonia, Brazil, Spain, and Egypt, where she went as a senior Fulbright fellow. Elmaz is a cofounder of VONA/Voices, a writing workshop for writers of color. She teaches at Mills College and lives in Oakland. www.elmazabinader.com

GEORGE ABRAHAM is a Palestinian American poet, activist, and Bioengineering PhD candidate at Harvard University. They are the author of two chapbooks, *the specimen's apology* (Sibling Rivalry Press, 2019) and *al youm* (The Atlas Review, 2017). They are the recipient of fellowships from Kundiman, the Watering Hole, and Brooklyn Poets, as well as the honor of Best Poet from the 2017 College Union Poetry Slam International. Their work has appeared or is forthcoming in *Tin House, Boston Review, Beloit Poetry Journal, The Rumpus, LitHub,* and anthologies, such as *Nepantla, Bettering American Poetry,* and *The Ghassan Kanafani Palestinian Anthology.*

NABEEL ABRAHAM taught anthropology and directed the honors program at Henry Ford College for nearly thirty years. Among his published works are *Arab Detroit: From Margin to Mainstream* and *Arab Detroit 9/11* with Andrew Shryock and Sally Howell. He is currently working on a collaborative collection of new voices in creative nonfiction from Arab Detroit.

RABIH ALAMEDDINE is the author of the novels *Koolaids, I, the Divine, The Hakawati, An Unnecessary Woman,* the story collection, *The Perv,* and most recently, *The Angel of History.*

HAYAN CHARARA is the author of three poetry books, most recently *Something Sinister*, which won the Arab American Book Award. He edited *Inclined to Speak*, an anthology of contemporary Arab American poetry, and, with Fady Joudah, is series editor of the Etel Adnan Poetry Prize. His children's book about the July War between Israel and Lebanon, *The Three Lucys*, received the New Voices Award honor. He teaches in the Honors College and the creative writing program at the University of Houston.

SAFIA ELHILLO is the author of the poetry collection *The January Children* (University of Nebraska Press, 2017), and the novel in verse *Nima on the Other Side* (forthcoming 2021 from Make Me A World/Random House). She holds an MFA from The New School, a Cave Canem Fellowship, and a 2018 Ruth Lilly and Dorothy Sargent Rosenberg Fellowship from the Poetry Foundation. With Fatimah Asghar, Elhillo is coeditor of the anthology *Halal If You Hear Me* (Haymarket Books, 2019). She is a 2019–2021 Stegner Fellow at Stanford University.

JOSEPH GEHA is the author of *Through and Through: Toledo Stories* and the novel *Lebanese Blonde*. A professor emeritus of the creative writing program at Iowa State University, since retirement he has kept busy volunteering, painting in acrylics, and teaching cooking demos. Currently, he is finishing a memoir-cookbook, *Kitchen Arabic*, about his family's early years in America.

HADIL GHONEIM is a bilingual writer and author of several books for children and young adults. Her book, *Sana fi Qena*, (A Year in Qena) was on the 2016 IBBY honor list and was shortlisted for the 2014 Etisalat Award for Arabic Children's Literature. Hadil's essays, profiles, and interviews have appeared in numerous Egyptian media outlets. She is currently based in Michigan.

LAYLA AZMI GOUSHEY is a professor of English at St. Louis Community College in St. Louis, Missouri where she also teaches an interdisciplinary course on Arab and Arab-Diasporic cultures. Her dissertation research examines the teaching philosophies of eleventh century Islamic scholar Muhammad Al-Ghazali. She is also currently working on an oral history project focusing on Arab American activism in Texas after 1967. Her creative work has been published in journals such as *Yellow Medicine Review, Mizna: Journal of Prose, Poetry and Art Exploring*

Arab America, *Natural Bridge*, and *Sukoon Magazine*. Find her on Twitter @Lgoushey or at www.LaylaAzmiGoushey.com.

TARIQ AL HAYDAR's work has appeared or is forthcoming in *The Threepenny Review*, *DIAGRAM*, *North American Review*, and others. He is an assistant professor of English at the College of Arts at King Saud University in Riyadh, Saudi Arabia.

RANDA JARRAR is the author of two books, *A Map of Home* and *Him, Me, Muhammad Ali*.

FADY JOUDAH has published four collections of poems, *The Earth in the Attic*, *Alight*, *Textu*—a book-long sequence of short poems whose meter is based on cellphone character count—and, most recently, *Footnotes in the Order of Disappearance*. He has translated several collections of poetry from the Arabic and is the coeditor and cofounder of the Etel Adnan Poetry Prize. He was a winner of the Yale Series of Younger Poets competition in 2007 and has received a PEN award, a Banipal/Times Literary Supplement prize from the UK, the Griffin Poetry Prize, and a Guggenheim Fellowship. He lives with his wife and kids in Houston, where he practices internal medicine.

JOE KADI is a teacher and writer living in Calgary, Alberta, Canada. He's the editor of *Food for Our Grandmothers: Writings by Arab-American and Arab-Canadian Feminists*, and the author of *Thinking Class: Sketches from a Cultural Worker*, both published by South End Press.

MOHJA KAHF is the author of *The Girl in the Tangerine Scarf* (novel), and two books of poetry: *E-mails from Scheherazad* and *Hagar Poems*. A former slam poet (Nationals 1999) and winner of a Pushcart Prize (2010), Kahf is a professor of Comparative Literature and Middle Eastern Studies at the University of Arkansas, where she has been teaching since 1995.

PAULINE KALDAS is the author of *Looking Both Ways* (essays), *The Time Between Places* (stories), *Letters from Cairo* (travel memoir), and *Egyptian Compass* (poems). She was awarded a fellowship in fiction from the Virginia Commission for the Arts and has been a resident at the MacDowell Colony and the Virginia Center for the Arts. She is professor of English and creative writing at Hollins University in Roanoke, Virginia. www.paulinekaldas.com.

LAILA LALAMI was born in Rabat and educated in Morocco, Great Britain, and the United States. She is the author of the novels *Hope and Other Dangerous Pursuits*, which was a finalist for the Oregon Book Award; *Secret Son*, which was on the Orange Prize Longlist; and, most recently, *The Moor's Account*, which won the American Book Award, the Arab American Book Award, the Hurston/Wright Legacy Award, and was a finalist for the Pulitzer Prize. She is currently a columnist for *The Nation*, a critic-at-large for the *Los Angeles Times*, and a professor of creative writing at the University of California at Riverside.

LISA SUHAIR MAJAJ is a Palestinian American poet, writer, and scholar. She is the author of *Geographies of Light*, which won the 2008 Del Sol Press Poetry Prize, and coeditor of three collections of essays on international women writers: *Going Global: The Transnational Reception of Third World Women Writers*, *Etel Adnan: Critical Essays on the Arab-American Writer and Artist*, and *Intersections: Gender, Nation and Community in Arab Women's Novels*. Her poetry has been used in many venues, including the 2016 photography exhibit *Aftermath: The Fallout of War* at the Harn Museum of Art. She holds a PhD in Arab American literature from the University of Michigan, and has taught at a number of institutions.

KHALED MATTAWA currently teaches in the graduate creative writing program at the University of Michigan. He is the author of four books of poetry, and a critical study of the Palestinian poet Mahmoud Darwish. Mattawa has coedited two anthologies of Arab American literature and translated many volumes of contemporary Arabic poetry. His awards include the Academy of American Poets Fellowship prize, the PEN Award for Poetry in Translation, and a MacArthur Fellowship. He is the current Editor of *Michigan Quarterly Review*.

IMAN MERSAL is an Egyptian poet, essayist, translator, literary scholar, and professor of Arabic Language and Literature at the University of Alberta. She is the author of five books of Arabic poetry, selections from which have been translated into several languages. In English translation, her poems have appeared in *Paris Review*, *The Nation*, *American Poetry*

Review, and *Michigan Quarterly Review*. A selection of Mersal's poetry, entitled *These Are Not Oranges, My Love*, translated by the poet Khaled Mattawa, was published in 2008 (Sheep Meadow Press). Her most recent publications include an Arabic translation of Charles Simic's memoir, *A Fly in the Soup* (Al Kotob Khan), and a group of essays, *How to Mend: on Motherhood and its Ghosts* (Kayfa Ta and Mophradat).

PHILIP METRES is the author of ten books, including *Shrapnel Maps* (Copper Canyon, 2020), *The Sound of Listening* (2018), *Sand Opera* (2015), *I Burned at the Feast: Selected Poems of Arseny Tarkovsky* (2015), and others. His work has garnered a Lannan fellowship, two NEAs, six Ohio Arts Council Grants, the Hunt Prize, two Arab American Book Awards, the Watson Fellowship, the Creative Workforce Fellowship, and the Cleveland Arts Prize. He is professor of English and director of the Peace, Justice, and Human Rights program at John Carroll University.

SUSAN MUADDI DARRAJ's *A Curious Land: Stories from Home* won an American Book Award in 2016. It also won the AWP Grace Paley Prize and the Arab American Book Award. In 2018, she was named a Ford Fellow by United States Artists; her writing has also been recognized by the Maryland State Arts Council and the Greater Baltimore Cultural Alliance. She is a member of the One Maryland, One Book committee and the creator of the #TweetYourThobe movement. Susan's children's book series, Farah Rocks, starring Steven, a Palestinian American character, will debut from Capstone Books in January 2020.

NAOMI SHIHAB NYE's most recent books are *Voices in the Air—Poems for Listeners* and *The Turtle of Oman*, a novel for elementary readers, both from Greenwillow/HarperCollins and *The Tiny Journalist*, inspired by Janna Jihad Ayyad, from BOA Editions, 2019.

STEVEN SALAITA is author of nine books, most recently *We Could Be Free: Palestine in the Revolutionary Imagination*. He lives outside of Washington DC.

MATTHEW SHENODA is the author of the poetry collections *Somewhere Else* (winner of the American Book Award), *Seasons of Lotus, Seasons of Bone* and *Tahrir Suite* (winner of the Arab American Book Award) and along with Kwame Dawes he is editor of *Bearden's Odyssey:*

Poets Respond to the Art of Romare Bearden. He is currently Associate Provost for Social Equity & Inclusion and professor of literary arts and studies at Rhode Island School of Design (RISD) where he directs the Center for Social Equity and Inclusion. Shenoda is also a founding editor of the African Poetry Book Fund. For more information visit: www.matthewshenoda.com.

KAMELYA OMAYMA YOUSSEF is a writer from Dearborn, Michigan. Her works have been published in *Mizna, Agapé*, the *Michigan Quarterly Review*, and on the theater stage. She studied poetry and criticism at Wayne State University and is an MFA candidate in poetry at New York University.

ACKNOWLEDGMENTS

"On the Road with Bob: Peddling in the Early Sixties," by Nabeel Abraham, was originally published in *Arab Detroit: From Margin to Mainstream*, edited by Nabeel Abraham & Andrew Shryock (Wayne State University Press, Detroit, 2000).

"in which you do not ask the state of israel to commit suicide," by George Abraham, was originally published in *Apogee Journal* online (January 29, 2018).

"Comforting Myths: Notes from a Purveyor," by Rabih Alameddine, was originally published in *Harper's Magazine*, June 13, 2018.

"Going Places," by Hayan Charara, was originally published in *Witness* 24.3 (Fall 2011).

"At the Intersection," by Safia Elhillo, was originally published in *Elephant Media* (September 2016).

"Where I'm From—Originally," by Joe Geha, was originally published in *Townships* (University of Iowa Press, 1992).

"Machine Language," by Tariq al Haydar, was originally published in *Crab Orchard Review* 20.2 (Summer/Fall 2015).

"Biblioclast," by Randa Jarrar, was originally published by *The Sun* (March 2016).

"I Cannot Go to Syria," by Mohja Kahf, was originally published in *Apogee Journal* 10 (January 2018).

"Walking Home," "To Walk Cautiously in This World," and "A Sense of Direction," by Pauline Kaldas, were originally published in *Looking Both Ways* (Cune Press, 2017).

"So to Speak," by Laila Lalami, was originally published in *World Literature Today* (September/October 2009).

"Journeys to Jerusalem," by Lisa Suhair Majaj, was originally published in *The South Atlantic Quarterly* 102:4 (Fall 2003).

"Repatriation: A Libya Memoir," by Khaled Mattawa, was originally published in *The Massachusetts Review* 55.4 (Winter 2014)

"al-Sawt fi ghayri makanihi" (The Displaced Voice, translated by Lisa White). In: *The Middle Ear*, edited by Maha Maamoun and Haytham El-Wardany. Published by the Sharjah Art Foundation–SB 10–2011.

"The Paperless 'Palestinian' and the Russian P'liceman" by Philip Metres, was originally published in *The Margins* online (October 11, 2017).

"One Village," by Naomi Shihab Nye, was originally published in *Never in a Hurry—Essays on People and Places* by Naomi Shihab Nye (University of South Carolina Press, 1996).

"Why I Was Fired," by Steven Salaita, was originally published in *The Chronicle of Higher Education*, October 5, 2015.

"'Christopher Columbus Was A Damn Blasted Liar': On the Narrative of Discovery in Global Literature," by Mathew Shenoda, was originally published in *Guernica: A Magazine of Art & Politics* (June, 2014) and in *Others Will Enter the Gates: Immigrant Poets on Poetry, Influences, and Writing in America*, edited by Abayomi Animashaun (Black Lawrence Press, 2015).

"frayed towel made holy: prayer [rug] for this nonbeliever," by Kamelya Omayma Youssef, was originally published in the *Michigan Quarterly Review* 57.2 (Spring 2018). The text includes direct quotes from Du'a Abu Hamza Thumali, Amira El-Zein's *Islam, Arabs, and the Intelligent World of the Jinn*, and Margaret Smith's chapter on Rabi'a Aladawiya in *Middle Eastern Muslim Women Speak*, edited by Elizabeth Warnock Farnea and Bassima Qattan Bezirgan.